MW01278227

Printed by
Hobbs and Co.,
GLASGOW.

INVOCATION OF THE BLESSING OF
GOD ON THIS TREATISE.

"O Almighty God, who hast instructed Thy Church with heavenly doctrine, and hast caused the light of Thy glorious gospel to shine into the world; Give unto us Thy grace, that we may be no longer children tossed about with every blast of vain doctrine, but may be established in Thy most holy truth: through Jesus Christ our Lord. Amen."

"Blessed Lord, who hast caused all holy Scriptures to be written for our learning; Grant that we may in such wise hear them, read, mark, learn, and inwardly digest them, that by patience, and comfort of Thy holy Word, we may embrace and ever hold fast the blessed hope of everlasting life, which Thou hast given us in our Saviour Jesus Christ. Amen."

"Our Father, which art in heaven, Hallowed be Thy Name. Thy kingdom come. Thy will be done in earth, as it is in heaven. Give us this day our daily bread. And forgive us our trespasses, as we forgive them that trespass against us. And lead us not into temptation; but deliver us from evil: for Thine is the kingdom, the power, and the glory, for ever and ever. Amen."

INTRODUCTION.

(OR PREFACE TO THE FIRST EDITION.)

———

THE important subject of this treatise, viz.: the translation or rapture of the saints raised and changed, having been too much forgotten by the Church Catholic as a point of faith and hope, is brought before the minds of earnest seekers after truth, who, like Simeon, are "waiting for the consolation of Israel," and, like Anna, are looking "for redemption in Jerusalem."

The moment appears to be at hand when the first resurrection may begin, and when the living saints of the Lord, elected to this glory, may be changed into His likeness without tasting death; while both shall be caught up together to meet the Lord in the air, and so shall await the completion of the whole Church, the Bride of the Lamb.

Our thoughts in this treatise seem frequently limited to the firstfruits, to events in the immediate future and to the special hope for which the Church should be daily watching. But the translation of the risen and changed saints is not a disconnected act of God. It is a prelude to other mighty acts which must follow in due sequence. We speak of the gathering of a firstfruits, but we must not forget that the firstfruits are firstfruits of a harvest, and that the husbandman's heart, while thankful for his sheaf of firstfruits as an earnest of the coming harvest, is set upon the whole harvest which is to fill his garners. So we must not limit our thoughts only to a firstfruits, though we in this generation hope to have our part with them; but our prayers and thoughts must embrace the whole Catholic Church, the whole body of the Baptized living or departed.

The Lord Jesus Christ who is the Resurrection and the Life has come that every member of His mystical Body might have life and have it more abundantly. What thousands of volumes have been written on death! We have most of us heard from our youth up that there is only one thing certain, namely, *death;* for Christians have been forgetful of the words of the inspired Apostle—"We shall not all sleep [*i.e.*, die], but we shall all be changed" (1 Cor. xv. 51).

Alas! how little has been written on the other side, viz.: that it is not *necessary* that we should *all* die, nay that it is certain that *some will not die.* There is, therefore, scope for a humble attempt to recall the Church to her "blessed hope," especially *now* when, in the opinion of thousands of intelligent and godfearing Christians, we have arrived at the end of this dispensation, and should be expecting these great acts of God—the resurrection, the change and the translation of the saints at any moment— these acts being bound up with the glorious appearing and kingdom of our Lord and Saviour Jesus Christ.

Let us define the word "translation" and the fact which it embraces. "Translation" is derived from two Latin words, and means—*borne across, carried over*—as when thoughts expressed in one language are carried over into the word-symbols of another. It also means transference locally from one place to another. There is an inaccuracy in the popular use of the word "translation" in its theological sense, which it is often difficult to avoid. The Scriptures teach us (1 Cor. xv. 51, 52; 1 Thess. iv. 13-18) that some of the dead are to be raised before the rest, and some of the living are to be changed into immortality without death, and that both these companies are to be caught up as one body to meet the Lord in the air. Their removal is properly set forth by the word "translation"; though in current exposition it is often applied only to the change of the *living* and *their* rapture to meet the returning Lord. The word occurs three times in Heb. xi. 5 in connection with Enoch.

"Open Thou mine eyes, that I may behold wondrous things out of Thy law" (Psa. cxix. 18).

"Prosper Thou the work of our hands; O prosper Thou our handy-work" (Psa. xc. 17, Prayer Book Version).

LONDON,
January, 1902.

PREFACE TO THE SECOND EDITION.

To many the views advanced in this treatise may appear novel. That they are in some respects out of the beaten track is not to be denied; but that they are consistent with the views of the early Christian Church as well as with the statements of Holy Scripture, is confidently affirmed; while nothing has been advanced which can rightly be held to impugn directly or indirectly any recognized doctrine of the Catholic Faith, or the earliest traditions of the apostolic or post-apostolic times.

Some exception has been taken to Translation as being "The Church's Forgotten Hope," and a reviewer has suggested that "the Coming of the Lord" is the true hope of the Church. But St. Paul (1 Thess. iv. 15-17) links these two together; for the raising of the dead in Christ, the change of the living, and their joint rapture to meet the Lord in the air, are dependent on the first event—the return or second coming of the Lord, which depends absolutely on the will of the Father. The coming of the Lord is not only the hope of the Christian Church, but (if they knew it) of the Jews also; and not only of the Jews, but of the nations of the earth; and not only of the Gentiles or heathen, but of the whole groaning creation. But the element in it which is special to the Church, is the present hope of being changed into immortality without seeing death. This change is set before the whole Church as her hope; but who shall attain thereto? Scripture indicates that not all "the called," but only a "*few*," a remnant, "a firstfruits" shall in the first instance, attain to it; even, as in the case of Israel, of all those who had left Egypt over twenty years of age (see Numbers xxxii. 11), only Caleb and Joshua survived to enter the promised land. These may typify those who are alive, and remain unto the coming of the Lord, to whom shall be awarded the glory of the change without seeing death—a mere handful compared with the vast fields which are white unto the harvest.

November, 1902.

PREFACE TO THE THIRD EDITION.

THE greater part of this third Edition has been re-written for the better elucidation of the points under review; and in touching on points of difficulty, as yet unsolved, great pains have been taken to advance no theories or anticipations with reference to the events with which this dispensation may be expected to close, which may not be deduced from the Holy Scriptures, and is therefore in accordance with Apostolic doctrine. It is hoped that this work may continue to awaken interest in the hearts of seekers after truth, especially in its witness to the appearing of our God and Saviour Jesus Christ, as an instant hope, with which are bound up the first resurrection of the sleeping saints, the change of the living, and their *joint* translation in their several orders, to meet the Lord in the air (1 Thess. iv. 13-18). For the Lord—it would seem—will not in the first instance descend to the earth, nor will those who are Christ's (the raised and the changed) meet the Lord *on the earth*, but *in the air, in the clouds* (1 Thess. iv. 17; Acts i. 9-11), and, it may be, this fact helps to cause the neglected hope of the translation to be regarded as visionary.

God grant that through the study of these pages many may be led by His Holy Spirit to embrace this hope of the prize of their high calling, and by the grace of God to attain its realization, to the glory of God the Father, through our Lord and Saviour Jesus Christ.

LONDON,
   September, 1905.

CONTENTS.

PAGE

CHAPTER I.

THE SCRIPTURAL DOCTRINE OF THE TRANSLATION OF
THE SAINTS 1

CHAPTER II.

THE NECESSITY OF THE TRANSLATION 30

CHAPTER III.

TRANSLATION, GOD'S WAY OF ESCAPE FROM THE
COMING TRIBULATION 53

CHAPTER IV.

THE HOLY GHOST THE AGENT IN THE TRANSLATION
OF THE SAINTS 76

CHAPTER V.

SCRIPTURAL EXAMPLES OF THE TRANSLATION OF THE
LIVING; ENOCH AND ELIJAH 91

CHAPTER VI.

THE SEARCH FOR THE TRANSLATED 126

CHAPTER VII.

THE TRANSLATION OF THE SAINTS, NOT AS INDI-
VIDUALS, BUT AS ONE BODY 139

CHAPTER VIII.

TRANSLATION: THE SUBJECT OF THE TESTIMONY
OF THE "TWO WITNESSES" 170

CHAPTER IX.

TESTIMONIES TO THE HOPE OF TRANSLATION DURING
THE CHRISTIAN DISPENSATION 196

CHAPTER X.

THE REVIVAL OF THE HOPE OF TRANSLATION IN
THESE LAST DAYS 235

CHAPTER XI.

THE MIMICRY OF SATAN 272

CHAPTER XII.

THE DUTY OF WATCHING AND PRAYING FOR THE
ATTAINMENT OF THIS HOPE 302

APPENDICES.

No.   PAGE

1. The Case of Mr. John Asgill, A.D. 1703; extracts from his writings - - - - - 321

2. Extracts from *The Coming of Messiah in Glory and Majesty*, by Ben Ezra, A.D. 1812 - - - 328

3. On the Book of Enoch - - - - - 330

4. Remarks on the "Man-child," by the Rev. G. S. Faber, B.D. - - - - - - 331

5. On the "Didaché, or Teaching of the Twelve Apostles" - - - - - - 333

6. The Mosaic over Bishop Alexander's grave at Tipasa, near Algiers, about A.D. 390 - - 335

7. Extracts from Sermons by Martin Luther - - 337

8. The Prophetic Anticipations of Jane Lead in A.D. 1697; quotations from her writings - - - 341

9. A short notice of Count N. L. von Zinzendorf - 346

10. On the Biblical use of the word "Apostle" - - 349

11. The Sect of the Luciferians and their Work - - 352

12. Ancient Collects and Prayers from "The Liturgy and other Divine Offices of the Church" - 354

INDEX OF CONTENTS.

Scriptural Preface ; or Prolegomena.

CHAPTER I.

PAGE

THE SCRIPTURAL DOCTRINE OF THE TRANSLATION - 1

Special Revelations given to St. Paul - - - 3
His Epistles—to the Church in Thessalonica - - 5
And to the Church in Corinth - - - - 7
The Second Coming of the Lord - - - 10
Proved from Holy Scripture - - - - 11
Also the First Resurrection - - - - 11
Jesus Christ—the Resurrection and the Life - - 12
References to the Old Testament - - - - 14
The Mysteries, or secrets revealed to the Church - 17
The Book of the Revelation: does it apply exclusively
    to the Christian Church? - - - - 20
The Sealing of 144,000: does it refer to the literal Israel? 22
The Israel of God - - - - - - 24
The Sealing, the opening of the Sixth Seal, and the
    great French Revolution - - - - 27
Bishop Ellicott's Commentary on Rev. vii. 1-8 - - 29

CHAPTER II.

THE NECESSITY OF TRANSLATION , - - 30

Resurrection and Translation necessary for a Twofold
    Witness to Christ - - - - - 30
Christ having died, no necessity exists for *all* to die 33

PAGE

CHAPTER II.—*Continued.*

False popular opinions concerning death -   ·   ·   35

The change of the Saints, who are *alive* at the Coming
of the Lord, necessary   ·   ·   ·   ·   37

The Types of the Law: Firstfruits of the Barley Harvest   39

The application thereof to Christ -   ·   ·   ·   40

Also to His Church -   ·   ·   ·   ·   ·   42

Ascension, a corollary from Resurrection   ·   ·   45

The Firstfruits of the Wheat Harvest   ·   ·   ·   46

Its spiritual application to the Christian Church   ·   47

The Feast of Tabernacles -   ·   ·   ·   ·   49

Translation—the fulfilment of historical and prophetic
types in Holy Scripture   ·   ·   ·   ·   50

Summary of Reasons for the Necessity of Translation   52

CHAPTER III.

TRANSLATION, GOD'S WAY OF ESCAPE FROM THE
COMING TRIBULATION   ·   ·   ·   ·   53

Luke xxi. quoted   ·   ·   ·   ·   ·   ·   53

The precursory Signs of coming Troubles foretold   ·   55

The Figure of the Man-child   ·   ·   ·   ·   57

Internal dangers   ·   ·   ·   ·   ·   ·   60

External dangers: the Red Dragon: Translation necessary   61

The Pavilion of the LORD -   ·   ·   ·   ·   65

The Necessity and Mercy of the Great Tribulation   ·   71

On our Lord's discourse, recorded in Luke xvii. 20-37   73

Each Dispensation has ended in Judgment, yet with
the Escape of a Remnant   ·   ·   ·   ·   74

CHAPTER IV.

THE HOLY GHOST, THE AGENT IN THE TRANSLATION   76

The general Law of the action of the Holy Spirit   ·   76

Scriptural Testimonies to the action of the Spirit of
God: Examples   ·   ·   ·   ·   ·   77

PAGE

CHAPTER IV.—*Continued.*

The Superiority of the Mind or Spirit over Matter - 79

The Doctrine of Materialism, false and unscriptural - 80

The Holy Spirit's action in effecting the bodily change
of the living Saints - - - - - 81

The Resurrection, Change and Translation are the
consummation of the work of the Holy Spirit
in them - - - - - - 83

The Power of Attraction *upwards* contrasted with the
action of Gravitation *earth-wards* - - - 84

The truth of the Holy Ghost *dwelling in the Baptized*
is not sufficiently realized - - - - 88

CHAPTER V.

SCRIPTURAL EXAMPLES OF TRANSLATION: ENOCH
AND ELIJAH - - - - - - 91

The Character of Enoch - - - - - 91

His Prophecy quoted by St. Jude - - - - 95

He announced the Second Coming of the Lord - 96

Elijah - - - - - - - - 98

His previous history - - - - - 99

His last journey with Elisha - - - 100

Elisha, the Eye-witness of Elijah's Translation - - 104

The two Symbols of the Holy Spirit: Wind and Fire   106

The Reasons for the Translation of Enoch and Elijah
without death - - - - - - 107

Moses and Elijah on the Mount of Transfiguration - 111

Life and Immortality first seen in the case of our Lord   114

Wherein our Lord's Ascension differs from Translation   116

The Nature of the Change imparted to the Translated   119

The Work which may be assigned to the Firstfruits - 121

Translation of Enoch and Elijah: typical of the future
Translation of other Saints - - - - 122

A practical Lesson from the Characters of these men   124

PAGE

CHAPTER VI.

THE SEARCH FOR THE TRANSLATED   -   -   -   126

For Enoch   -   -   -   -   -   -   -   126
For Elijah by the Sons of the Prophets -   -   -   127
The same spirit of Unbelief manifested at the Resur-
    rection of our Lord   -   -   -   -   -   130
How will the Tidings of the Translation of the First-
    fruits of the Church be received by the world ?   133
Translation not desired by the Church in general   -   136
Quotation from a Sermon by the Rev. W. Dow, 1853   138

CHAPTER VII.

THE TRANSLATION OF THE SAINTS, NOT AS INDI-
    VIDUALS, BUT AS ONE BODY   -   -   -   139

The definite Teaching by St. Paul concerning the
    Church as being *One Body* in Christ   -   -   14
The Relation of Christ to the Church, His mystical Body   143
"All the Elect form one single family" (Père Lambert)   144
The different Gifts and Graces in the Church   -   -   147
The Church can only *as one body* reach the Fulness
    of Perfection   -   -   -   -   -   -   148
The Figure of the Man-child considered : Rev. xii.   -   150
The Gathering of the Firstfruits—144,000—only an initial
    step in the perfecting of the Church   -   -   154
Reasons for believing that the Resurrection, Change
    and Translation will be *progressive* -   -   -   155
The Typical aspect of the Feasts of the Jews   -   -   156
The three Periods of the Jews' Return from Captivity   159
The three Companies outlined in the Book of the
    Revelation   -   -   -   -   -   -   159
The second Company and the Two Witnesses   -   -   160
The Perfecting of the Church as One glorious Body   -   162
The whole Church is to be the Bride of the Lamb   -   167
Extract from a book by Père Lambert   -   -   -   168

PAGE

CHAPTER VIII.

TRANSLATION: THE SUBJECT OF THE TESTIMONY OF
    THE TWO WITNESSES   -   -   -   - 170

On the Duality or Plurality of Testimony   -   - 171
Examples of this in Holy Scripture   -   -   - 173
The Testimony of the Two Witnesses   -   -   - 174
Who will be the Two Witnesses? -   -   -   - 176
The Subject of their Testimony, Resurrection, and
    Translation   -   -   -   -   -   - 178
The special Witness at the End, as at the Beginning
    of this Dispenation to *Resurrection*   -   - 180
What the clothing in Sackcloth indicates   -   - 181
The Substance of a true and special Witness for God - 183
The Results of the Testimony of the Two Witnesses - 184
Their Rejection and Martyrdom   -   -   -   - 187
Their Relation to the Feasts of the Law -   -   - 188
Daniels' Prophetic Seventy Weeks   -   -   - 193
The same Prophetic period in Rev. xi., xii., xiii.   - 194

CHAPTER IX.

TESTIMONIES TO THE HOPE OF TRANSLATION DURING
    THE CHRISTIAN DISPENSATION   -   -   - 196

First Century of the Christian Era   -   -   - 196
Second Century   -   -   -   -   -   - 197
Third and Fourth Centuries; the gradual Decline of
    the Heavenly Hope   -   -   -   -   - 198
The causes to which this decline was due   -   - 201
The influence of Origen and Augustine -   -   - 202
Quotation from Dean Alford   -   -   -   - 203
Augustine's View revived by Bishop Wordsworth   - 204
Lack of Testimony in the Eastern or Greek Church   - 205
Likewise in the Western or Roman Church   -   - 205
Hildegardis von Bingen   -   -   -   -   - 207
Simeon Levita -   -   -   -   -   - -. 207.

b

CHAPTER IX.—*Continued.*

PAGE

Melanchthon and Luther   -   -   -   -   -   209
Johann Arndt   -   -   -   -   -   -   -   210
John Robinson, one of the Pilgrim Fathers   -   -   211
Extract from Calvin's "Institutes"   -   -   -   212
Quotations from "The Second Book of Discipline"
    and from Milton's "Areopagitica"   -   -   213
George Lorentz Seidenbecher   -   -   -   -   214
Jacob Tauben   -   -   -   -   -   -   -   215
Extracts from Mrs. Jane Lead's Writings -   -   -   217
John Asgill   -   -   -   -   -   -   -   219
Count N. L. von Zinzendorf   -   -   -   -   220
Phil. Matthew Hahn -   -   -   -   -   -   220
Emanuel Lacunza—"Ben Ezra"   -   -   -   -   222
The French Revolution   -   -   -   -   -   223
Remarks by De Maistre on the Bible Society   -   -   225
Rev. J. M. Campbell of Row -   -   -   -   -   226
Rev. Haldane Stewart's Prayer for Outpouring of the Spirit   226
Meetings at Albury for studying the Prophetic Scriptures   226
A Spiritual Movement in Bavaria -   -   -   -   227
A widespread feeling of some coming change   -   -   231
Mahdism—the Messianic belief of the Mohammedans -   232
The Archbishop of Canterbury's invitation for Prayer
    for the Outpouring of the Holy Spirit   -   -   234

CHAPTER X.

THE REVIVAL OF THE HOPE OF TRANSLATION IN
    THESE LAST DAYS   -   -   -   -   -   235

The Prophecy in Joel ii. 28-32   -   -   -   -   236
The meaning of the "Latter Rain"   -   -   -   237
How will the Outpouring of the Holy Spirit be effected
    in the Church?   -   -   -   -   -   238
The Lord's answer to the Cry of the Church   -   -   240
Apostles in the Church from A.D. 1832-1901   -   -   242

PAGE

CHAPTER X.—*Continued.*

Note on Halley's Comet   -   -   -   -   -   242
Apostles are distinguished from all other Ministers of
    Christ   -   -   -   -   -   -   -   244
The name "Apostle"   -   -   -   -   -   245
The special Mode of Mission of Apostles   -   -   246
The Plenary Grace conferred through Apostles   -   247
The Universal Jurisdiction of Apostles   -   -   -   247
Apostles sent forth directly by the Lord Himself   -   249
The Truths proclaimed by them   -   -   -   -   250
Miracles not now necessary in the Church   -   -   252
The Difference between the Primitive Church and the
    Church as she is now   -   -   -   -   254
The Offices of Prophet, Evangelist, and Pastor under
    Apostles -   -   -   -   -   -   -   257
The Gathering of Congregations under Apostles   -   259
The Particulars wherein they are distinguished from
    other bodies of Christians   -   -   -   -   260
They hold the Common Faith of the Church   -   -   263
The Apostles' Testimony to the Crowned Heads of
    Europe   -   -   -   -   -   -   -   265
A Question often asked   -   -   -   -   -   266
Hymn : "Lord of the bounteous harvest,"   -   -   269
Extract from a letter to the *Hartford Times*, U.S.A.,
    by the late Rev. W. W. Andrews   -   -   -   270

CHAPTER XI.

THE MIMICRY OF SATAN   -   -   -   -   -   272

The two different Greek words *Demons* and *the
    Devil*   -   -   -   -   -   -   -   273
Satan's Antagonism to God and the Church   -   -   275
Concerning Miracles -   -   -   -   -   -   278
Antichrist—the Incarnation of Satan ; False Messiahs   279
The Devil seeks to oppose or imitate the work of the
    Holy Ghost in the case of individual men   -   280

CHAPTER XI.—*Continued.*

PAGE

Satan's Opposition to and Mimicry of the Gospel   -   282

The New or False Gospel -   -   ·   -   - 283

Anabaptists in Munster (Germany) in the Sixteenth
     Century—a prefiguring of the Reign of Satan   - 284

False Apostles -   ·   -   -   -   -   - 284

False Prophets -   ·   -   -   -   -   - 285

Simulation, or Imitation of the Resurrection, Rev. xiii. 286

Antichrist—a Counterfeit of Jesus Christ   -   - 287

Mormonism -   -   -   -   -   -   - 289

Mormonism contrasted with the Lord's Work -   - 291

The Signs of the Times -   -   -   -   - 293

Materialism, Socialism, Spiritism—"the three Articles
     of Godlessness"   -   -   -   -   - 294

Analysis of Phenomena recorded in the Gospels, which
     are or may be simulated by Satan -   ·   - 295

Two sects of Devil-worshippers in Paris -   ·   - 298

St. Paul's Warning -   -   -   -   -   - 298

Devil-worship in the Middle Ages -   ·   -   - 299

Extract from a Pastoral Letter by Cardinal Richard,
     Archbishop of Paris, A.D. 1904   -   ·   - 300

CHAPTER XII.

THE DUTY OF WATCHING AND WAITING FOR THE
    ATTAINMENT OF SALVATION   -   -   - 302

The incorrect popular belief and teaching on the
     Condition of the Saints after Death   -   - 303

Unscriptural Views as to the Conversion of the World 304

The Lord's admonition to "Watch and Pray": His first
     command; "Watch" -   -   -   -   - 306

Because of the suddenness of Translation   -   - 307

The Lord's second command; "Pray always" -   - 309

That we may be "*accounted worthy* to escape" -   - 313

The *Character* of the Firstfruits -   -   - 313

The *Prize* of the high calling of God in Christ Jesus 314

What our practical Duty is -   ·   -   - 317

SCRIPTURAL PREFACE;

OR,

PROLEGOMENA.

St. Paul, the great apostle of the Gentiles, writes these inspired words to the primitive Churches:

I.

"Unto the Church of the Thessalonians:"

"But I would not have you to be ignorant, brethren, concerning them which are asleep, that ye sorrow not, even as others which have no hope.

"For if we believe that Jesus died and rose again, even so them also which sleep in Jesus will God bring with Him.

"For this we say unto you by the word of the Lord, that we which are alive and remain unto the coming of the Lord shall not prevent them which are asleep.

"For the Lord Himself shall descend from heaven with a shout, with the voice of the archangel, and with the trump of God: and the dead in Christ shall rise first:

"Then we which are alive and remain shall be caught up together with them in the clouds, to meet the Lord in the air: and so shall we ever be with the Lord.

"Wherefore comfort one another with these words" (1 Thess. iv. 13-18).

II.

"UNTO the Church of God which is at Corinth:"

"Behold, I shew you a mystery; We shall not all sleep, but we shall all be changed,

"In a moment, in the twinkling of an eye, at the last trump: for the trumpet shall sound, and the dead shall be raised incorruptible, and we shall be changed.

"For this corruptible must put on incorruption, and this mortal must put on immortality.

"So when this corruptible shall have put on incorruption, and this mortal shall have put on immortality, then shall be brought to pass the saying that is written, Death is swallowed up in victory.

"O death, where is thy sting? O grave, where is thy victory?

"The sting of death is sin; and the strength of sin is the law.

"But thanks be to God, which giveth us the victory through our Lord Jesus Christ" (1 Cor. xv. 51-57).

III.

"UNTO the Church of God which is at Corinth" (second epistle):

"For we know that, if our earthly house of this tabernacle were dissolved, we have a building of God, an house not made with hands, eternal in the heavens.

"For in this we groan, earnestly desiring to be clothed upon with our house which is from heaven:

"If so be that being clothed we shall not be found naked:

"For we that are in this tabernacle do groan, being burdened: not for that we would be unclothed, but clothed upon, that mortality might be swallowed up of life.

"Now He that hath wrought us for the self-same thing is God, who also hath given unto us the earnest of His Spirit" (2 Cor. v. 1-5).

The Church's Forgotten Hope.

CHAPTER I.

The Scriptural Doctrine of the Translation.

HOLY SCRIPTURE—God's prophetic chart—is the only sound basis of Christian doctrine, and to it the final appeal must ever be made. In it the future, as well as the great hopes for our present acceptance and consolation, connected therewith, are revealed. Trustworthy knowledge of the future can be derived only from revelation. It is God only who can lift the veil, and woe be unto us if we seek to lift it by unlawful means. If then God in His grace and foreknowledge has unveiled certain future events, it becomes man's duty to study the revelation vouchsafed, otherwise he must come under condemnation for neglect of what the Lord has been pleased to make known.

The second coming of the Lord, the first resurrection, the change of the living without death, the translation of the saints, the judgment to come, the kingdom of God, the deliverance of the groaning creation, the final victory of good, are all

B

matters of pure revelation; and if we, as Christians, *believe* this revelation, it will affect our lives, and we shall walk by faith in the light and power of the same, rejoicing in hope of the glory of God. These divine and glorious secrets were revealed to the members of the early Church for their conso- lation under the trials, sorrows, and persecutions which they were called upon to endure. As they are clearly set forth throughout the accepted canon of the Holy Scriptures, and professedly received by the five hundred millions who form the multitude of the baptized, it is a matter of no slight wonder that, practically, they have been forgotten by the Christian Church for centuries. It is clearly our duty to acknowledge these truths, to which re- newed attention is invited; for, being enshrined in Holy Scripture, they cannot be fanciful or heretical; and to ignore them must be a spiritual sin of no small magnitude, entailing serious consequences to ourselves and others.

These truths are nowhere so directly stated as by St. Paul, the apostle to the Gentiles; for, with explicit clearness, he reveals the mystery of the resurrection of the dead in Christ, the change of the living without death, and their joint rapture to meet the Lord in the air; and there can be no doubt that what he taught the church in Thessa- lonica, he would also teach all the churches which he planted in Asia Minor, Greece, or Illyria. St. Paul was the recipient of many and special revela- 2 Cor. xii. 1-5. tions, and it seems probable that, when he was caught up to the third heaven, he heard and saw not only much which it was not possible to utter, but also much which he was permitted to reveal.

His rapture to the third heaven and to paradise gave him a prevision and foretaste of what the translation will be both to the living and to the departed, whether "in the body or out of the body" he could not tell. Thus translation will come as an equally blessed experience to both classes — to the living and to those who are raised from the dead. This glorious truth may have come to the great apostle as a direct revelation from the Lord, or by words of prophecy through the medium of prophets. The apostle Paul had undoubtedly received special revelations from the Lord; for example, respecting the Holy Eucharist, in regard to the Church as the Body of Christ, and to the Gentiles being one with the Jews in the Church; and thrice in his epistle to the Romans does St. Paul use the expression "my Gospel," on which he throws light by saying that he received it not of man, but by the revelation of Jesus Christ. Hence, the full doctrine of the first resurrection, the change of the living, and their joint translation, may have been one of these revelations which do not appear to have been vouchsafed in such fulness to any other of the apostles, save to St. John, when he received that wonderful apocalypse in the isle of Patmos. St. Paul also speaks of the "abundance of the revelations" which were given to him, on account of which he received the thorn in the flesh that he might not be exalted above measure. There is one point of interest about the passage in his epistle to the Corinthians which

2 Cor. xii. 3.

See 1 Thess. iv. 15.

2 Cor. xii. 1-7.

deserves attention.   St. Paul mentions the time as
having been "above fourteen years ago" when he
had these spiritual experiences; and, as he wrote the
second epistle to the Corinthians about the year
A.D. 60, this would fix the date of his visions
at about A.D. 46; while the first epistle to the
Thessalonians was written A.D. 54, or about eight
years later than these revelations, in which epistle
he so prominently refers to the resurrection of the
dead in Christ, to the change of the living saints,
and to their joint translation to meet the Lord in
the air.   Moreover, as the apostle Paul had not

Acts i. 21.   companied with our Lord on earth like the other

Luke xxiv. 27,   apostles, whose minds He had opened that they

44, 45.   might understand the Scriptures, including all
things which were written in the law of Moses,
and in the prophets, and in the Psalms, concerning
Himself, and as he was the Lord's chosen apostle
to the Gentiles, he needed to receive a special
revelation as to the faith and hope, the doctrine
and ordinances of the Church, these having to be set
in order according to the mind of Christ.   Further-
more, for the instruction and guidance of the Gentile
Church, it was necessary that his teaching should
be *written* as well as *spoken* to the churches, and
that certain of his epistles should be handed down
to posterity.   It is only in his epistles to the
Corinthians and to the Thessalonians that St. Paul
writes in detail concerning these hitherto unrevealed
truths and glorious catholic hopes.

These epistles were not written to individuals—

1 Cor. i. 2.   to "the *saints*"—but to "the *Church of God* which

"is at Corinth" and "unto the *church* of the Thessa-
"lonians"; and it may be noted, further, that in
both these churches there appears to have been an
abundant manifestation of the supernatural gifts
of the Holy Ghost.   Though to the church in
Corinth St. Paul wrote, "Ye are enriched by him
"[the Lord] in all utterance, and in all knowledge;
". . . . so that ye come behind in no gift;
"waiting for the coming of our Lord Jesus
"Christ," yet he perceived that plain teaching on
resurrection, on immortality, on the change without
death, and on the translation, was required to
enable the wavering members of that church to
confute those who doubted or denied the resurrection of the dead.   He wrote to impress on
the Church for all time the absolute necessity
of the resurrection of the dead, and of *faith in the
resurrection*, and in that immortality which would
be manifested at the Lord's coming.

To the church at Thessalonica St. Paul wrote as
to those who, having "turned to God from idols
"to serve the living and true God; and to wait for
"his Son from heaven," had laid hold of the hope
of His coming again.   He placed before them the
prior resurrection of their departed brethren, the
change of the living, and their joint translation at
the coming of the Lord, in order to *comfort* them
in their persecutions and tribulations; and meanwhile he exhorted them not to quench the Spirit
nor to despise prophesyings.

In St. Paul's writings there are three grand
passages bearing on this subject: the first is the

1 Thess. i. 1.

1 Cor. i. 5-7

1 Cor. xv.

1 Thess. i. 9-10,

1 Thess. v. 11.
19, 20.

sublime Christian classic passage in the earliest epistle written to any Christian church, viz. that to the church of the Thessalonians A.D. 54. He alludes to the same subject in his epistle to the Corinthians about the year A.D. 59, and subsequently in his second epistle to the same church, A.D. 60. As these passages have been quoted in the Scriptural preface, they need not be repeated here *in extenso*.

The first epistle to the Thessalonians is full of the hope of the second coming of the Lord, to which reference is made six times, and it contains that — to them — new and clear statement of the doctrine of the resurrection of the dead in Christ, previous to the change of the living and of the joint translation of the raised and changed saints. St. Paul prefaces this revelation with a peculiar formula which indicates its importance, and which he uses on three other occasions when uttering special revelations—"But *I would not have* "*you to be ignorant*, brethren, concerning them " which are asleep." The apostle would comfort the Church concerning those of her faithful members who, having died, had been disappointed of their hope of entering into the kingdom by translation without death, and for whom the survivors mourned. He says that they will come back with the Lord when He returns to the earth, and then claims special inspiration for the revelation he is about to make; this being that the living shall have no pre-eminence over the sleepers; that the Lord " shall descend from heaven"; that "the dead

1 Thess. iv. 13-18.

in Christ (not all the dead) shall rise first"; and that the living faithful believers shall then, together with the raised saints, be caught up in the clouds to meet the Lord in the air.   But to enable them to do this, their bodies must have undergone a change—which he expounds later to the Corinthian church.   The two united companies (the two armies of Canticles vi. 13) shall then be for ever with the Lord, which is to be their culminating joy and privilege.   These four sublime points of revelation were for the comfort of the mourning Church. And he adds "Wherefore comfort one another " with these words." In the next chapter he writes in the same strain, when he says—"God hath not " appointed us to wrath, but to obtain salvation by " our Lord Jesus Christ, who died for us, that, " whether we *wake* or *sleep*, we should live together " with him. Wherefore comfort yourselves together, " and edify one another, even as also ye do." This was the apostolic comfort ministered as the result of revelation from the Lord Himself.

   In the first epistle to the Corinthians the same subject is pursued as follows—"Behold, I shew " you a mystery; we shall not all sleep [*i.e.* die], " but we shall all be changed, in a moment, in the " twinkling of an eye, at the last trump: for the " trumpet shall sound, and the dead shall be raised " incorruptible, and we shall be changed. For this " corruptible must put on incorruption, and this " mortal must put on immortality." Here, there is the same distinction between the dead, who are raised, and the living, who are changed, which is

Margin notes:

1 Cor. xv. 51, 52.

1 Thess. v. 9-11.

1 Cor. xv. 51-53.

John xi. 25, 26.

discernible in our Lord's words, when He says—" I
" am the resurrection, and the life: he that
" believeth in me, though he were dead, yet shall
" he live: and whosoever liveth and believeth in
" me shall never die," to which reference will

1 Cor. xv. 51,
52.

again be made. The contrast between the dead and
the living is further brought out thus—" We shall
" *not all sleep*, but (whether dead or living) we shall
" *all be changed*," and again—" The *dead* shall be
" raised incorruptible, and *we* shall be changed."
The first allusion here is to those who have fallen

1 Thess. iv.
16, 17.

asleep, and who, as dead in Christ, shall rise first;
hence the pronoun "we" clearly must refer to the
living, its use being equivalent to the expression—
" then we which are alive and remain." Thus
the same truths that had been imparted to the
Thessalonian church are brought before the Corinthian church, in a more summarized manner, but
in the same sequence. There is the same distinction
between the first resurrection and the change with-

1 Cor. xv. 53,
54.

out seeing death. The words are: " For this cor-
" ruptible must put on incorruption, and this mortal
must put on immortality "—*i.e.*, the bodies of the
departed saints must be raised incorruptible, while
the mortal bodies of the living saints must be
clothed with immortality. " So when this corrupt-
" ible shall have put on incorruption *(i.e.*, in the first
" resurrection), and this mortal shall have put on
" immortality *(i.e.*, in the change without death),
" *then*," and only then, " shall be brought to pass
" the saying that is written, Death is swallowed up
" in victory." Then the apostle utters the holy

challenge, "O death, where is thy sting?" Not in the living saints who have escaped death. "O " grave, where is thy victory?" Not over the raised saints, who have been set free from death with the life that dies no more. Well might he exultantly cry out—"Thanks be to God, which giveth us the 1 Cor. xv. 57 " victory through our Lord Jesus Christ."

There is a third passage in St. Paul's writings in which he distinctly refers to this change. "We 2 Cor. v. 1-3. " know that if our earthly house of this tabernacle " were dissolved, we have a building of God, an " house not made with hands, eternal in the " heavens. For in this we groan, earnestly desiring " to be clothed upon with our house which is from " heaven: if so be that being clothed we shall not " be found naked." In this passage, after comparing our present body to a tabernacle or tent, and, by inference, the resurrection body to a heavenly temple, he goes on to say, "For we that are in this taber- " nacle do groan, being burdened: not for that we " would be unclothed, but clothed upon, that mortality " might be swallowed up of life." Here he distinctly expresses the wish not to be *unclothed,* or in other words to die; not to become a mere spirit or ghost; nay, he would be *clothed upon,* receiving the immortal body with such change of the body as is expressed in the words, "that mortality might be " swallowed up of life." Nothing can be stronger than this assurance that the mortal can really put on the immortal, through such a change as is set forth by the expression "swallowed up of life." The expression "swallowed up" is a very expressive Isa. xxv. 8

1 Cor. xv. 54.
2 Cor. v. 4.
one, and suggests an overwhelming victory, not merely over death by emerging therefrom, but from not having been overcome by death in any shape whatever. Thus the figure of being "unclothed" brings before us the idea of death; while that of being "clothed upon" inspires us with the hope, not of resurrection out of death, but of *change into immortality without passing through death*, followed by removal into the presence of the Lord, to be effected by means of translation.

In the epistle to the Philippians, St. Paul gives another beautiful example of this twofold hope. He lays a sort of double emphasis on the first Phil. iii. 10, 11 resurrection — the resurrection "*out from among the dead*" * [τὴν 'εξανάστασιν (τὴν ἐκ) τῶν νεκρῶν]—as a special prize worthy of ardent pursuit; and he Phil. iii. 20, 21., R.V. also says "our citizenship is in heaven; from " whence also we wait for a Saviour, the Lord " Jesus Christ; who shall fashion anew the body " of our humiliation, that it may be conformed " to the body of His glory." Here the first resurrection, the change without death, the Lord's coming and our eternal union with Him are clearly revealed for our encouragement in faith and in the patience of hope.

As regards the coming of the Lord, from which

* The original Greek implies this truth more clearly than the English text, for literally it runs—"If by any means I " might attain unto the out-resurrection of the dead " (A.V. Greek, *Textus receptus*), or " the out-resurrection, that from "the dead " (R.V. Greek). See Scrivner's Greek Text A.V. and R.V. This is the most emphatic form possible, even in the Greek language which lends itself freely to emphasis.

the truths of the first resurrection and the change of the living radiate, it is a promise which may briefly be proved from Holy Scripture. First, there is the testimony which fell from our Lord's own lips, when He distinctly said : " I will come again, John xiv. 3. " and receive you unto myself; that where I am, " there ye may be also." Here is a direct statement from Him who is the Truth and the Life ; and one word from Him must be more authoritative than volumes of human arguments. Again He says, " When the Son of man cometh, shall he find Luke xviii. 8. " faith on the earth?" " Blessed are those servants, Luke xii. 37- " whom the lord when he cometh shall find watch- 40. " ing;" . . . . " Be ye therefore ready also, for the " Son of man cometh at an hour when ye think " not." To apply these passages to death, as is so often done, is to pervert their obvious meaning.

Neither need the first resurrection, as distinguished from the general resurrection, be dwelt upon save to state its truth in the language of Holy Scripture. It was revealed to Daniel that many (*i.e.* some, not Dan. xii. 2. all) " that sleep in the dust of the earth shall awake " at a particular epoch.* Moreover the Lord Jesus promises a special recompense which shall be given at the " resurrection of the just." The same truth Luke xiv. 14. is hinted at in His words—" The hour is coming, John v. 25. " and now is, when the dead shall hear the voice

* The Hebrew here reads " many *from among* the sleepers . . . . *these* shall be unto everlasting life ; but *those* (the rest of the sleepers who do not awake at this time), shall be with shame" (Tregelles). The Jewish commentators support Tregelles. This is the only passage in the Old Testament in which everlasting life is mentioned.

" of the Son of God: and *they that hear* shall live."

Heb. xi. 35. In the epistle to the Hebrews we read of " a better " resurrection "; and the truth is stated plainly in the Rev. xx. 5, 6. Book of the Revelation, where the first resurrection is twice mentioned as a special reward. St. Paul 1 Cor xv. 23, 24. also alludes to it when he says—" But every man " in his own order: Christ the firstfruits; afterward " they that are Christ's at his coming. Then " cometh the end." And lastly he uses the expres- Phil. iii. 11. sion " the resurrection out from among the dead " (Greek), to which reference has already been made.

Very emphatic also are the words which fell from the lips of the Lord Himself with reference to the change of the living saints at His coming, when He John xi. 25, 26. says—" I am the resurrection, *and the life:* he " that believeth in me, though he were dead, yet " shall he live : and whosoever *liveth* and believeth " in me shall never die." The Lord here declares Himself to be *the Resurrection*, as concerning those who have fallen asleep *(i.e.,* the dead); and He also declares Himself to be *the Life*, as concerning those who are alive and remain unto His coming, and who should not therefore taste death. The whole passage must be read to see its full significance; and we may be sure that in describing Himself as (1) the Resurrection, and (2) the Life, Jesus is not employing mere synonyms. Each word has a separate significance. He is the Resurrection, as the first begotten from the dead; and by virtue of His resurrection, His dead saints shall be raised incorruptible, receiving spiritual and immortal bodies, like unto their Lord's glorious body; this is the first

resurrection. But the risen Lord is also emphatically
the LIFE, not merely as the divine embodiment of
eternal life out of death, so that, though His saints
be dead, yet shall they live; but as having power to
quicken them without their seeing death; so that
when He shall appear—if they be then living and
believing in Him, and be looking for Him—they
shall never die. This certainly seems to be the full
force of His words; for, as the last Adam, He is
made "a quickening Spirit." Thus hath the Father   1 Cor. xv. 45.
given to the Son to have life in Himself; and   John v. 26
Jesus Christ came that His saints " might have   John x. 10.
" life, and that they might have it *more abundantly.*"
The Lord through His death has destroyed him
that had the power of death, and would deliver   Heb. ii. 14, 15.
those " who through fear of death were all their
" lifetime subject to bondage." It should be observed that the Lord's order is exactly that followed
by St. Paul in giving his new revelation to the
Thessalonian church. " The dead in Christ shall   1 Thess. iv
" rise first: then [Greek ἔπειτα, *i.e.*, *hereafter*] we   16, 17.
" which are alive and remain shall be caught up
" together with them in the clouds, to meet the
" Lord in the air." It is after giving utterance to
this grand spiritual axiom of His being the Resurrection and the Life, that the Lord goes on to say:
" He that believeth in me, though he were dead,   John xi. 25, 26.
" yet shall he live : and whosoever liveth and believeth
" in me shall never die." The Lord Himself seems
to hint at the rapture of the living saints when He
says—" I tell you, in that night there shall be two   Luke xvii. 34-
" men in one bed ; . . . . Two women shall be   36.

" grinding together ; . . . . Two men shall be
" in the field ; the one shall be taken and the other
" left."

The Church then should be looking and *longing*
for the Lord's return ; for it is written : "unto
" them *that look for him* shall he appear the second
" time without sin unto salvation." Again, "When
" he shall appear, we shall be like him ; for we
" shall *see* him as he is."

In the Old Testament there are also rays of light
upon this glorious revelation given to us in the New
Testament, though in the former "we see through
" a glass darkly." Still, we may thank God for
two recorded cases of translation without tasting
death, viz.: those of Enoch and Elijah, which will
be considered in detail in a subsequent chapter.
There are, moreover, two historical types bearing
on this subject. The passage of the children of
Israel dryshod over the river Jordan at the close of
their wilderness wanderings has often been considered
as a type of translation or victory over death, of
which the river Jordan has been an universally
acknowledged figure. Their passage over the Red
Sea might typify resurrection begun, in the renewal
of the Holy Ghost, which type was perfected in the
crossing of the river Jordan *dryshod*. Elijah and Elisha
crossed the same river through its divided waters
just before the literal translation of the former, so
that this passage of the river has been recognized as
a familiar type of the translation of the living saints
who shall not taste of death. "What ailed thee,
" O thou sea, that thou fleddest? thou Jordan, that

Marginal references:

Heb ix. 28.

1 John iii. 2.

1 Cor. xiii. 12.

Psa. cxiv. 5, 7.

" thou wast driven back? . . . . Tremble, thou
" earth, at the presence of the Lord."   Hannah, in
her glorious song of triumph, hints at the resurrection, and even at the change of the living, when
she sings, " The LORD killeth, and maketh alive: 1 Sam. ii. 1-10.
" He bringeth down to the grave [death], and
" bringeth up [resurrection]. . . . . He raiseth
" up the poor out of the dust, and lifteth up the
" beggar from the dunghill, to set them among
" princes, and to make them inherit the throne of
" glory."   In this passage the change of the
living, and the rapture and glorification of both the
raised and the changed are implied.

In the writings of David, allusions to the same
truth may be discerned, though in a veiled manner.
" O LORD, thou hast brought up my soul from the   Psa. xxx. 3.
" grave:" here, resurrection is announced; " Thou
" hast kept me alive that I should not go down to
" the pit:" here, the change of the living is implied,
and the sequel is their joint translation.   " I cried   Psa. xxx. 8, 9,
to thee, O LORD; . . . . What profit is there   11.
" in my blood, when I go down to the pit? Shall
" the dust praise thee; shall it declare thy truth?
" . . . . Thou hast turned for me my mourning
" into dancing: thou hast put off my sackcloth,*
" and girded me with gladness."—" I shall not die,   Psa. cxviii. 17.
" but live, and declare the works of the LORD."   In
another Psalm the question is put: " What man is   Psa. lxxxix. 48.

---

* Sackcloth is typical of the humiliation of a repentant
sinner, for, as it was made of goat's hair, it points to the
goat as a sin-offering.   It may also be typical of our
present body of humiliation.

" he that liveth, and shall not see death? Shall he
" deliver his soul from the hand of the grave?"
Let the apostle answer: "We shall not all sleep,
" . . . . the dead shall be raised incorruptible,
" and we [the living] shall be changed:" and again,
" We shall be caught up *together with them* in the
" clouds, to meet the Lord in the air." In another
Psalm a hint of the change without death may be
Psa. xlviii. 14. discerned. "For this God . . . . will be our
" guide even unto death"—literally, upon (or above)
death, as rendered by the Syriac version. " He will
" guide us to the point whereat death shall not
" overcome us, but we shall *overcome it;* "—*Cocceius.*
" He will guide us *over death;* "—*Pusey.* The context is not concerning guidance *up to death,* but
concerning deliverance *from it,* even from destruction when imminent.

In several passages of Scripture there are hints,
not precisely of the change and translation, but
respecting those who shall be alive when the Lord
returns. St. Peter in preaching to Cornelius speaks
Acts. x. 42. of the Lord as "ordained of God to be the Judge
" of quick and dead;" and also in his first epistle,
1 Peter iv. 5. of His being "ready to judge the quick and the
" dead."   St. Paul alludes to the same truth in
Rom. xiv. 9. writing to the Romans, and also in his epistle to
2 Tim. iv. 1. Timothy; and it is embodied in the three great
creeds of the Catholic Church—the Apostles' Creed,
the Nicene Creed, and the Creed of St. Athanasius,—
that the Lord shall judge the quick and the dead;
in which connection it may be remarked that to
judge does not necessarily mean to *condemn,* but

embraces praise as well as blame, reward as well as punishment.*

Sufficient Scriptural evidence has been adduced to establish these three points, viz.: that some of the departed saints shall be raised before the rest; that the living saints who are ready shall be changed into the Lord's likeness without death; and that both shall be caught up together to meet the Lord in the air, when He " shall appear the second time " without sin (or sin-offering) unto salvation." Heb. ix. 28.

There is another interesting aspect in which these truths may be considered. Not only are they matters of pure revelation, but they are chief among the glories of revelation; for they are pre-eminently mysteries or secrets which, until revealed unto the Church, had been kept hidden from the beginning of the world. There is always a romance and mystery in a great secret; but what shall we say of the secrets of God? Surely they must embody many wonderful things which human imagination could never have anticipated or conceived.

Thus in our Lord's teachings He uttered things which had been kept secret since the foundation of the world, things which many prophets and righteous men had desired to see and hear, but had neither seen nor heard; things, however, which the first apostles were privileged to see in the works of Christ, and to hear from the lips of their divine Master. Mat. xiii. 16, 17, 34, 35.

---

* The Greek word in the above passage denotes "living," while "quick" is an old English word from the Anglo-Saxon " cwic," which means "alive."

St. Paul uses the word " mystery " several times in his epistles, and some Greek scholars consider it to be the equivalent of " secret," such as the secret revealed to the initiated in the case of the Eleusinian mysteries.* The great secret, next to the purpose of God in the mystery of the Incarnation, was that the Church should be the Body of Christ— a secret which the Lord in due time made known
Col. i. 24-27. through His apostles, but which no angelic or human mind could possibly have discovered or imagined. St. Paul in his epistle to the Romans speaks of
Rom. xvi. 25. "the revelation of the mystery, which was kept " secret since the world began," as being connected with his gospel and the preaching of Jesus Christ.

From the central and fundamental mystery of the Incarnation other and subordinate secrets radiate, each in its place inestimable. Of these may be cited the first resurrection, of which in the Old Testament only hints are given by the prophets
Isa. xxvi. 19. Isaiah and Daniel, and which hints doubtless they
Dan. xii. 2. themselves did not understand. It was a profound secret that some of the dead should rise before the rest; that some of the living should be changed into the Lord's likeness without seeing death ; and that the two companies *as one* should be translated from the earth to meet the Lord in the air.

The point here is that these wonderful truths with which the Church should be familiar, but of which she has been forgetful, were once absolute secrets, beyond the imagination of men or of angels. For

* The initiated were called μύσται (mystics).

—at least so far as is known—from the beginning of
the creation, even among the unfallen angelic armies,
there could be no whisper of the unrevealed secrets
of God. The Incarnation of the Son of God was
of course originally a divine secret, but some intimation of it may have been given when, at the creation,
the sons of God shouted for joy, foreseeing, as
they probably did, the final victory of good; but
even if this great mystery was outlined, there were
other truths which were kept secret, as St. Paul
wrote to the Roman and Corinthian churches. There
were foreshadowings of God's great salvation in the
Patriarchal and Mosaic dispensations, but there still
remained many secrets to be partially disclosed by
the Lord Jesus, and to be more fully unfolded later on
by His apostles, which were not so much as hinted at
before. Among these were the mystery of the Christ
of God, the Head and the members; the organization
of the Body of Christ; the union of Jew and Gentile
in one Body; the first resurrection and the change
and translation of the living saints without death,
as completing the firstfruits of the new creation.

But alas! this secret of the change of the living
is now almost as great a secret as of old; for the
Church Catholic, to whom it was entrusted, practically ignores it; very few believe in it save as a
remote contingency; still fewer lay hold of it as a
purifying hope. There are many so-called open
secrets, which were once secrets but have been
revealed; and yet, by their having been forgotten,
they are practically secrets still, so far as most of
those interested in them are concerned. But "the

Job xxxviii. 3-7.

Rom. xvi. 25, 26.
1 Cor. ii. 7, 8.

Psa. xxv. 14.

" secret of the LORD is with them that fear him ;
" and he will show them his covenant." Oh, that
by the power of the Holy Ghost the veil may be
removed from our blind and unbelieving hearts !

In our consideration of these truths, let us, as
members of the Church Catholic, take a wide
horizon and not limit ourselves to a narrow circle ;
for this grand hope of the first resurrection, and of
the change without death, is set primarily before
the whole Catholic Church, and not merely before
any small community of Christians representing
the firstfruits. It is set before the Baptized now as
their immediate hope, and as being the next step
onward in the evolution of God's grand purpose of
redemption ; thus it belongs to the Church as a
whole ; but if, through unbelief, the visible Church
will not lay hold of the hope set before her, and
will not press into the kingdom of God, the Lord
will, nevertheless, have those who, like a sheaf of
firstfruits, shall be an earnest of the coming harvest.
These are they who cry unto Him with heart and
Psa. lxxxv. 7.   soul, " Show us thy mercy, O LORD, and grant us
" THY SALVATION."

As there will be frequent references in this treatise
to the Book of the Revelation, it may be well to
consider a point which is sometimes taken for
granted, and which involves a crucial question, viz.:
whether this sacred book applies exclusively to the
Christian Church, or whether any reference to the
literal Israel is contained therein. It seems to be a
reasonable inference, *primâ facie*, that the Apocalypse
of Jesus Christ, which He signified to the Seven

Churches by the hand of His Apostle John, primarily concerns the Church of Christ, which is an election from both Jews and Gentiles. The book containing this revelation was written after the incarnation, death, resurrection, and ascension of our Lord; after the founding of the Christian Church; after the Jews had rejected the heavenly calling of the Gospel; after God had turned to the Gentiles "to "take out of them a people for his name"; and after the destruction of Jerusalem, and the national casting away of Israel "until the fulness of the "Gentiles be come in." It was the revelation which God gave to Jesus Christ after He had been raised from the dead, and when He was seated at the right hand of the Father; and that it primarily concerns the new creation—that new spiritual Body of which the Lord is the Head—admits of no reasonable doubt. It could not then, for these reasons, belong primarily to the literal Israel, whose history and destiny had been fully disclosed in the Old Testament. The Jew being still under the old covenant, this revelation must primarily pertain to the election under the new covenant, that of the Spirit in Christ Jesus; nevertheless the Apocalypse, according to the germinating power of Holy Scripture, might embrace a *secondary* reference to the literal Israel.

The book opens with a vision of the Lord in glory, walking among seven golden candlesticks, which are declared to represent the Seven Churches in Asia, headed by their united angels or bishops. These Seven Churches are acknowledged to be a symbol of the Universal Church; and the epistles addressed

Acts xv. 14.

Rom. xi. 25.

Rev. i. 11-20.

to them to be prophetic, *inter alia*, of the consecutive
history of the Church. Each of these special addresses
ends with the command to "hear what the Spirit
"saith *unto the churches*." After this the apostle is
shown glorious visions of the unseen world, the
imagery of which gives a glimpse of the good things
to come, of which the Law—the Jewish economy—
was only the shadow. Then he sees visions apparently covering the times of the Gentiles, a period
during which the literal Israel is cut off, while the
divine purpose is being worked out in the baptized
election. In the fourth chapter we read of a door
being opened in heaven, with the vision of the four
living creatures (similar to that of the cherubim seen
by the prophet Ezekiel), and detailed revelations are
given of the things which must be hereafter; then
comes the episode of the sealed book, followed by
the opening of the seven seals successively.

In Rev. vii. the sealing of the 144,000 out of
the tribes of Israel is described. The expression,
"sealed . . . . of all the tribes of the children
"of Israel," followed by the names of the literal tribes
(Dan excepted) has perplexed some commentators,
and has led them to apply this vision to the
literal Israel. But such an application would
introduce confusion into the book, by giving it an
earthly, after it had first received a heavenly,
meaning; while, looking at the position of the
sealing in the prophecy at large, and the historical
or chronological application of the seven seals to
the Church, its application to Israel after the flesh
would appear to be incongruous. For why should

Rev. ii. 7.

Heb. x. 1.

Rev. iv. 1.

Ezek. i.

Rev. vii. 1-8.

the vision concerning the Church suddenly break off at this point under the sixth seal and go back to the literal Israel, of whose sealing, with "the "seal of the living God," Holy Scripture is elsewhere silent; whilst on the other hand the early Christians after believing the Gospel are said to have been sealed with the Holy Spirit of promise, *Eph. i. 13.* which is a spiritual act towards the spiritual Israel, or "Israel of God," for their preservation ere the *Gal. vi. 16.* winds of judgment are suffered to blow upon the earth? Moreover, St. Paul makes use of this word "sealed" to denote the anointing of the Holy Ghost, *2 Cor. i. 21, 22.* which in the primitive Church was ministered to *Eph. i. 13; iv. 30.* the saints by the laying-on of the hands of the apostles.

But if the sealed from among the tribes be indeed the firstfruits of the spiritual Israel, who are the great multitude of the succeeding vision? They *Rev. vii.* must be that glorious harvest of which the firstfruits are the earnest, including the fulness (πλήρωμα) of the Gentiles, and especially those who have been ripened in the fires of judgment—those who have come out of the great tribulation, who have not attained to be of the firstfruits, but who are now safe in the garner of God.

The Jews were the first to receive the offer of the Gospel, but nationally they rejected it; therefore God turned to the Gentiles to "take out of them a people *Acts xv. 14.* "for his name." In due time God will turn again to His ancient people, whom He has not cast away; but their glory will then be that of the terrestrial, *Rom. xi. 2.* since nationally they have lost that of the celestial.

Whether their lower position will remain unchanged throughout eternity has not been revealed.

There are two parallel truths which run throughout Holy Scripture, involving two applications of God's written word, that in *the letter* and that in *the spirit*. There is a Christ personal and a Christ mystical; there is a literal Israel and a spiritual Israel; and, although the expression "spiritual Israel" does not occur in Scripture, yet its equivalent is found when St. Paul writes to the Galatians of *the Israel of God* (Gal. vi. 16; *cf.* Gal. iv. 22-28, Heb. xii. 22, 23), having previously told them that in Christ "there is neither Jew nor Greek . . . . "for ye are all one in Christ Jesus." Further, the apostle writes to the Romans: "He is not a Jew, "which is one outwardly, ... But he is a "Jew, which is one inwardly; and circumcision is "that of the heart, in the spirit, and not in the "letter." Again, he tells them that "they are not "all Israel, which are of Israel;" and to the Philippians he writes: "For we are the circumcision, "which worship God in the spirit, and rejoice in "Christ Jesus, and have no confidence in the flesh."

It is remarkable in this connexion that the expression "Israel of God" should be used in an epistle addressed to the Gentile converts in Galatia, in the centre of Asia Minor; in which epistle, moreover, the apostle rebukes the advocates of circumcision, or what was known as the Judaizing party in the Church. In the same epistle he furnishes a clue to the true prophetical interpretation of certain localities and persons mentioned in the Old Testa-

Gal. iii. 25-29.

Rom. ii. 28, 29.

Rom. ix. 6-8.

Phil. iii. 3.

ment; for, referring to Sinai, Jerusalem, Abraham,
Sarah, Hagar, Isaac, and by implication, Ishmael,
he indicates their spiritual application.   In like
manner he argues in his epistle to the Romans that   Rom. iv. 13-17.
through faith we become related to Abraham as our
spiritual father, and that we inherit through Christ—
the promised Seed—the promises made to Abraham.
In writing to the Corinthians, St. Paul applies the
history of Israel, with all that befell it, to the Christian Church, stating that the Jews were examples
(*figures*, *types*, margin), of which he gives four
defined illustrations; adding that these had been
"written for our admonition, upon whom the ends   1 Cor. x. 1-11.
"of the world [or age] are come."   In writing to   Eph. ii. 11, 12.
the Ephesians the apostle proves that the Gentiles
had been admitted to the privileges of the Gospel
equally with the believing Jews, and that in Christ
there is no difference between them.   For, before
telling them that Christ had broken down the
middle wall of partition between Jew and Gentile
(making in Himself of twain one new man), he says:
"At that time ye were without Christ, being aliens
"from the commonwealth of Israel."   The same
principle of spiritual and symbolic application can
be discerned in the Book of the Revelation, where
allusion is made to the great city, "which spiritually   Rev. xi. 8.
"is called Sodom and Egypt, where also our Lord
"was crucified."   Here the reference is to Christendom, not to the literal Jerusalem.

We learn from Scripture that the earthly Jerusalem
prefigured the heavenly Jerusalem—the one being
the divinely-chosen capital of the literal Israel, and

the other a spiritual and heavenly city of "the
"Israel of God," even as St. Paul describes it:
Gal. iv. 26. "Jerusalem which is above is free, which is the
"mother of us all." To the Hebrew Christians
Heb. xii. 22. the apostle writes: "Ye are come unto . . . .
"the heavenly Jerusalem," on which further light
is obtained from the Book of the Revelation, where
Rev. xxi. 2, 10. the same heavenly city is called "the holy city,
"new Jerusalem,"—"the holy Jerusalem, descending
"out of heaven from God." Hence, if Jerusalem
may be spiritual and heavenly, why, by parity
of reasoning, may not the same be affirmed of
Mount Sion (Zion) also, in Rev. xiv.? But there
is the direct authority of Scripture for this sug-
Heb. xii. 18,
22, 23. gestion; for in Heb. xii. the apostle says: "Ye
"are not come unto the mount that might be
"touched, . . . but ye are come unto Mount Sion,
"and unto the city of the living God, the heavenly
"Jerusalem." As no one could suppose that the
literal or earthly Zion is here meant, the reference
must be to a spiritual or heavenly Zion; and, if this
reasoning applies to the *place* where the company
of the 144,000 is found, why should it not apply to
the sealed company from all the tribes of Israel
(Dan excepted), and justify the inference that they
Heb. iii. 1. are not literal Jews, but Christians, the "partakers
"of the heavenly calling?" Since the Apocalypse is
throughout emphatically "the Revelation of Jesus
"Christ, which God gave unto him," it obviously
concerns the whole mystery of Christ (of the Christ
τοῦ Χριστοῦ Col. ii. 2) *i.e.* of Christ and His body the
Church; and this consideration suggests a complete

and final answer to those who would contend
that those out of the tribes of Israel, who are
the subjects of the sealing, are literal Jews,
more especially as the omission of the tribe of Dan
marks an intentional departure from the complete list
of the tribes of the literal Israel.   Besides, "the
revelation of Jesus Christ" can certainly have no
present application to the Jews inasmuch as *they
still refuse to acknowledge Him as their Messiah.*
Will those who object to apply Rev. vii. and
xiv. to Christians point out in what way, beyond
the enumeration of the tribes in chapter vii., this
company of 144,000 sealed saints can be identified
with the tribes of the LITERAL Israel, and also explain
the omission of the tribe of Dan?   If not, on what
authority do they draw a distinction between these
two chapters and the rest of the book?   Again: have
these two chapters during nearly two thousand years
been without application to those who, as Christians,
have received them as the word of GOD?

Moreover, this sealing takes place after the opening
of the sixth seal: and some biblical scholars and
students of prophecy* have applied the imagery of
this seal to the French Revolution of the eighteenth
century (1789-1795), so that the sealing would apply
to the Church rather than to the Jew, viewed in the
light of its chronological position, if the visions
admit of an application to this present dispensation.

It may then be safely affirmed that in the Apo-
calypse the references to "the tribes of the children   Rev vii. 4.

* We may instance the names of Cuninghame and Frere.

" of Israel" require to be strained to give them any
application to God's ancient people, whose destinies
may be found in Ezekiel's concluding visions.   In
Rev. ii. and iii. the condemnation of those who "say
"they are Jews and are not, but do lie," rather proves
this point; for, if the churches of Pergamos and
Philadelphia suffered from Jewish persecution, the
Lord disowns the persecutors as being really "Jews"
in the sense of the election. The context, however,
in the application of these seven epistles to the
spiritual history of Christendom, from the Apostolic age down to the last days of Laodicean
lukewarmness, points to assaults directed against
the faithful by false brethren, withstanding the
Divine purpose in the Church.   Of those who
constituted the synagogue of Satan—the accuser of
the brethren—it is written: "Behold, I will make
"them to come and worship before thy feet,
"and to know that I have loved thee."   These
words are addressed to the church in Philadelphia,
whose faithfulness, love, and patience represent
spiritual graces that are precious to the Lord. Yet,
as God's revelation admits of varied fulfilments it
may have a *secondary* application to the literal Jew
during the troubles of the last days of this dispensation.   Something analogous to the sealing mentioned in Rev. vii. may have taken place before
the destruction of Jerusalem under Nebuchadnezzar,
as would appear from the ninth chapter of Ezekiel,
when the man clothed in linen, with the writer's
inkhorn, was bidden to set a mark upon the foreheads
of those who sighed and cried for the abominations

Marginal references:
Rev. ii. 9.
Rev. iii. 9.
Rev. iii. 9.
Ezek. ix. 2-4.

done in Jerusalem, in order that they might be preserved from the impending judgment.   Christians however, as members of the mystical Body of Christ and partakers of the heavenly calling, have their inheritance laid up for them in heaven with the Lord, and their heartfelt cry should be : "Oh that Thou wouldest rend the heavens, that Thou wouldest come down." Col. i. 5. Isa. lxiv. 1

The following is Bishop Ellicott's Commentary on Rev. vii. 1-8 :—

" Some have thought that the sealed ones must be Jewish
" Christians; they are disposed to take the twelve tribes
" literally.   The scope of the previous verses seem decisive
" against this view.   The time of judgment and trial is
" drawing near; we have seen the tokens of the coming
" storm in the opening of the sixth seal; our wish is to
" know the lot of the saints of God; this chapter answers
" this wish; they are safe, having the seal of God.
" The Christian Church absorbs the Jewish, inherits her
" privileges, and adopts, with wider and nobler meaning,
" her phraseology.   She has her Jerusalem, but it is a
" heavenly Jerusalem (Heb. xii. 22); a Jerusalem from
" above (Gal. iv. 26); a new Jerusalem (Rev. xxi. 2; cf.
" chap. iii. 12); and to that Jerusalem of God, the true
" Israel of God, the chosen generation and royal priest-
" hood of every age, turns the eye of faith."—*Ellicott's*
Commentary, page 565.

The following is from the Speaker's Commentary, page 588 :—

" That Israel, and more especially the Jews, are taken
" in this book in the highest and best sense is clear from
" chap. ii. 9; iii. 9; and thus the language here indicates
" the blessed company of faithful people, the Israel of
" God."

CHAPTER II.

The Necessity of the Translation.

————

THERE is an important, yet unfamiliar view of translation which needs to be considered, and that is its *necessity*. The change of the firstfruits from among the living, and their translation together with the firstfruits of the raised dead, is a mighty and (we may add) a necessary act of God. God is not prodigal in the exhibition of miracles, and only works them when they are required by the necessity of the case.

1 Thess. iv. 15-17.

John xi. 25.

(1.) The change of the living is necessary, for it is bound up with the resurrection of "the dead "in Christ," that there may be a twofold witness for Christ as the RESURRECTION and the LIFE, according to His word: "I am the resurrection, "and the life."

1 Cor. xv. 21, 22.

John v. 28, 29.

That resurrection is a necessary step in the evolution of God's purpose of redemption is evident. Speaking generally, the sentence of death has passed upon all men; so that, if men are to inherit the kingdom of God, it must be under new conditions, and of those conditions *resurrection-life* must be one. Resurrection was a necessity in the case of our Lord Himself. He was made man, and bore the sins of the whole world, as the one, true, and perfect sin-offering, this involving the sacrifice of Himself, even unto death. "But it was not possible," said St. Peter, "that he should be *holden of death*": for if this sinless Man had remained dead it would have been a blot on the equitable and righteous government of God, and a stupendous loss to the whole creation. Hence the resurrection of Jesus was a *necessity*, in proof of the Divine acceptance of His spotless sacrifice; and for the carrying out of His Father's promise, that His flesh should not see corruption, but should be speedily raised from the dead. It was also a necessary prelude to His ascension and reception of the gift of the Holy Ghost, on behalf of His brethren, and for the fulfilment of His work of intercession as High Priest, and of everlasting rule as King. Wherefore, since resurrection was a necessity in the case of our Lord and Head, it must also be a necessity for the members of His mystical Body—the Church,—and for the deliverance of the whole groaning creation for which Christ died. "For as in Adam all die, even so in "Christ shall all be made alive." All men therefore shall rise again; but the first resurrection is the special hope set before the Church Catholic that thereby her members, being delivered from the bondage of corruption, may be advanced as *sons* into the glorious liberty of the children of God, being manifested as "the children of the resurrection."

The point under consideration is not the general resurrection *but the first resurrection, the change of some of the living saints, and the translation of both.* The raising of some of the dead, and not of all the

Acts ii. 24.

1 Cor. xv. 14-19.

Psa. xvi. 10.
Acts ii. 25-27.

1 Cor. xv. 22.

Luke xx. 36.

dead at once, is an act of the sovereign will of God; it has its relation to the change of the living and to their joint translation to meet the Lord in the air. The risen saints will form the great majority of the firstfruits, the living who are changed being comparatively a small minority. If then some must be *raised* to attain to the glory of the kingdom, so must some be *changed* without *dying*, that both may be translated to meet the Lord in the air and to come with Him at His second advent. Thus Christ will be seen as "the resurrection," when by the word of His power, He raises them who sleep in Him, vindicating His word and title, "I am the "resurrection." This is the first step in the manifestation of His great salvation; but He also added, I am "the Life;" "I am come that they might "have life, and that they might have it *more abun-* "*dantly;*" and how can the superabundance of the eternal life, which is inherent in Him, be more plainly manifested than by His changing the saints who are alive and remain unto His coming, without their having to pass through the terrible dissolution of DEATH? By these mighty acts, a *double* witness is borne to Christ—as the Resurrection, and also as the Life. The Lord said of Himself that He was "the way, the truth, and the life," and to this, abundant testimony shall be afforded in the changing of the living saints into immortality without seeing death. Hence the change of the living and their translation are necessary as a witness to Christ as the *Life*, as the One to whom the Father has given to have life in Himself.

1 Thess. iv. 17.

John xi. 25.

John x. 10.

John xiv. 6.

(2.) Another reason for the necessity of translation is that, while the sentence of death has passed upon all men, for that all have sinned, yet, inasmuch as Christ exhausted the sentence in Himself and thus abolished death, there was thenceforth, strictly speaking, no need for any Christian to die,* save in obedience to the will of Christ and for the glory of God.   But, owing to the unbelief of the Baptized, death has continued to reign ever since the resurrection of Christ unto the present day; so that we are not yet set wholly free from its power. Still, inasmuch as we, the Baptized, are united to Christ the risen Man, we should know by experience the power of His immortal life within us, and should be yearning for that change in which mortality shall be swallowed up of life.   The expression that Christ has "brought life and immortality to light," implies some great advance on all that had gone before.   The Lord would surely rather see His redeemed people changed into His image without death, than that they should descend into the pit under the grasp of the enemy; and as He must desire to put forth His great power to effect these cognate wonders—the raising of the dead and the changing of the living—the question arises, Why

Rom. v. 12

John xxi 19.

2 Tim. 1, 10.

---

* See Appendix I. This is the drift of Mr. Asgill's argument, viz. that death is our enemy, but that it is a vanquished enemy, and that we should not fear it, nor yield to its terrors; because Christ through death has destroyed him that had the power of death, that is, the devil; and has delivered them, who through fear of death were all their lifetime subject to bondage.

Heb. ii. 14, 15

D

has He not done so? What has hindered Him? Surely the obstacle must be in ourselves, in the Baptized, through our indifference and lack of faith. Alas! the Lord is straitened now, as He was of old, when He could not do many mighty works in Nazareth because of their unbelief. And we, as members of His Church, shall continue to hinder Him until we come to look upon death not only as a curse and a penalty, but as a dishonour to God, a thing abominable in His sight.

Matt. xiii. 54-58.

In the law of Moses, which we must remember was a shadow of heavenly things, the Lord typified His abhorrence not only of sin, but of the *result* of sin, which is DEATH. Any contact with death was abomination in the sight of God, and a cause of defilement to man. It entailed moral and ceremonial uncleanness, and exclusion from all the ordinances of the sanctuary for seven days. "He that toucheth the "dead body of any man shall be unclean seven days." "Whosoever toucheth one that is slain with a "sword . . . . or a dead body, or a bone of a "man, or a grave, shall be unclean seven days."

Num. xix. 11, 16.

For this defilement, the water of separation, a sort of sacrificial water, with its complex rites was provided, the lustration by which lasted for seven days. These ordinances had not been observed by Israel, for the holy temple of God at Jerusalem had been defiled by the adjacent burial of the kings of Judah, which profanation was severely forbidden in the restored temple of Ezekiel: "My holy name shall "the house of Israel no more defile . . . . by "the carcases of their kings"; "Let them put away

Num. xix. 1-22.

Ezek. xliii. 7, 9.

". . . . the carcases of their kings far from me."
In chapter ix. of the Book of Numbers we have an
interesting account of some who, having been defiled   Num. ix. 6-8.
by the dead body of a man, were disqualified from
eating the passover, and for whom special legislation
was required. Again, the high priest, upon whose
head the holy anointing oil had been poured, was
not permitted to rend his garments in grief for the
death even of his nearest kin; and at the death of
Nadab and Abihu, Moses warned their father Aaron,   Lev. x. 6, 7.
the high priest, not to exhibit any external signs of
mourning lest wrath should come upon all Israel.
Thus was the divine abhorrence of death testified in
the law of Moses; and, if men form a different
estimate of death, making it a friend and not an
enemy ("death, the last enemy"), they must have   1 Cor. xv. 26.
departed from the standard of the sanctuary, and   (Greek.)
followed their own carnal imaginations.

The following rhapsodies from one of our leading
English poets* will shew the false estimation in which
death is popularly held :—

" Death ! the great counsellor, who man inspires
   With every nobler thought and fairer deed !
Death ! the deliverer, who rescues man !
Death ! the rewarder, who the rescued crowns !
Death ! that absolves my birth—a curse without it—
Death gives us more than was in Eden lost ;
This king of terrors is the prince of peace."

---

* Rev. Edward Young, author of *Night Thoughts*. See also
Shakespeare's *Henry VI.*, Part I., Act ii., Scene 5 :—
     " The arbitrator of despair,
  Just Death, kind umpire of men's miseries,
  With sweet enlargement doth dismiss me hence."

" A few among the poets may with poetic license speak kindly of the dread foe of our race, the ruthless invader of happy homes and slayer of our loved ones, but to the mass of mankind he is the king of terrors. Death, then, must be overcome; he yields, but it is to force, and not to love. If he is indeed 'the gate to endless joy,' he opes because he *must*; not that he would have the saints pass through his portals to glory. Milton's terrible personification of death *(Paradise Lost*, Book II.) is a more appropriate picture than that presented by Young and others."*

Whence, then, arises this great divergence from the teachings of the Scriptures, where death is regarded as an enemy, a pollution, a degradation, a penalty, a curse? Is it not because the end of salvation, the resurrection, as set before us in the Gospel of Jesus Christ as a living practical hope, has been forgotten; or, if it has not been wholly ignored, it has been looked upon not as a cardinal but as a subsidiary factor in the promised salvation, making future glory to be attained through death, instead of through resurrection? How then must the Lord have sorrowed, since His ascension, over the ravages of the enemy in His inheritance for more than eighteen hundred years because His people, instead of pressing on to the first resurrection and to the change without death, have sinned, as did Israel of old, in making a covenant with death, in remaining among the graves and lodging in the monuments.

Isa. xxviii. 15.
Isa. lxv. 4.

* From *Endless Life* (pp. 53, 54), by J. L. Barlow; Pickering & Inglis, Glasgow.

The sanctuaries of the Lord of life and glory—the Christian churches—are used as burial places (an adopted Pagan practice), and defiled with the remains of the dead, who are eulogised in fulsome epitaphs.

Death, as an almost invincible conqueror, has for ages worked desolation on the earth, although in the former dispensations there were instances of his defeat; in the cases of Enoch and Elijah through translation, and in those persons whom Elijah and Elisha, respectively, raised from the dead; but these cases were few and far between, and only pointed onwards to the time when death should receive his death-blow in the resurrection of Jesus, the power of which shall be made manifest in the first resurrection as an earnest that it will be extended to all men in the general resurrection.

Resurrection is the manifestation of the victory over death; but in the change of the living and their translation, victory is manifested under more transcendent circumstances, when, to use the Scriptural figure, death will be literally "swallowed up" "in victory," of which a promise was given by the LORD, through the prophet Isaiah. For the accomplishment of this triumph, the change without death and the translation are necessary. *1 Cor. xv. 54. Isa. xxv. 8.*

(3.) In the case of those faithful saints who shall be alive at the coming of the Lord, a necessity exists for their direct change into immortality, and for their translation, for these living ones will be in an exceptional position. How are they to be dealt with? They are alive and remain; and it is opposed to St. Paul's express teaching to imagine *1 Thess. iv. 15.* *1 Cor. xv.*

that they will go through the disintegrating process called "death," and that, after tasting of death, they shall be instantaneously raised again.* Being in an exceptional position, may it not rightly be expected that their mortal bodies shall be changed in an abnormal manner, and that thus they will share the blessedness of the risen ones? There can be no doubt about their translation, since this truth has been distinctly revealed in Scripture. To be caught up into the clouds to meet the Lord must involve a sudden previous change in the case of those who are the subject of this rapture. The apostle was referring to their case when he wrote that those who are alive and remain (on the earth) at the appearing

1 Thess. iv. 17. of the Lord, shall be caught up, together with the risen dead, to meet the Lord in the air; so that these privileged ones shall pass into immortality without seeing death, receiving in their sudden change all that is involved in resurrection. They shall not be raised from the dead, for they will not have died; but without death, their natural body shall be changed into a spiritual body, for flesh

1 Cor. xv. 50. and blood cannot inherit the kingdom of God, and without a transition from mortality to immortality it would be impossible to be for ever with the Lord. The change of the living is bound up with the raising of the dead in Christ, and both

* Such an idea contradicts that article of the creed, according to which Christ is to be the Judge of the *quick* as well as of the dead. On this particular point see an extract from the work of Ben-Ezra on *The Coming of Messiah in Glory and Majesty*, in Appendix II.

are necessary in order that the saints may be translated to meet the Lord in the air.

(4.) Further, the change and the translation of the living are necessary, because the departed without the living cannot be made perfect, even as the living cannot obtain their change and translation into life eternal independently of the resurrection of the departed. After recording the names and actions of some of the grand heroes of faith, the writer of the epistle to the Hebrews adds: " These " all, having obtained a good report through faith, " received not the promise: God having provided " [*foreseen*, margin] some better thing for us, that " they without us should not be made perfect."

Heb. xi. 39, 40.

(5.) Translation is a necessity for the living saints as a way of escape from the storm of that great tribulation which shall overtake mankind, and more especially the Baptized in the last days; but this point will be considered in detail in the next chapter.

(6.) The rapture or translation of the saints is a necessity in order that the types of the feasts of the Law may be fulfilled. That these have their application to Christ and His Church is expressly stated by the Lord and His apostles; and, although these types have been antitypically fulfilled in Christ Himself, nevertheless they have their secondary application to the Church as His BODY.

(*a.*) The first recorded feast is that of the first-fruits of the barley harvest. " The Lord spake unto " Moses, saying, Speak unto the children of Israel, " and say unto them, When ye be come into the

Lev. xxiii. 9-11.

" land which I give unto you, and shall reap the
" harvest thereof, then ye shall bring a sheaf [*omer*
" or *handful*, margin] of the firstfruits of your
" harvest unto the priest: and he shall wave the
" sheaf before the LORD, to be accepted for you:
" on the morrow after the sabbath the priest shall
" wave it."

Before the harvest could be reaped, this omer had
to be solemnly waved before the LORD, as the pledge
of the ultimate ingathering of the whole, and as an
acknowledgment that "the earth is the LORD'S, and
the fulness thereof."

This sheaf or omer of the first ripe ears of barley
(which might fill the bosom of him that bound the
sheaves) taken from the harvest field, was "the first
" of the firstfruits," and was associated with "an he-
" lamb without blemish . . . . for a burnt offering
unto the LORD." It was gathered just after sunset
on the fifteenth day of the month Nisan, and brought
to the priest, who had laid it up until the following day; and on the sixteenth, which was "the
" morrow after the sabbath " (the paschal sabbatic
feast day) it was waved before the LORD, to be
accepted by Him. The omer was waved always on
the sixteenth of Nisan, on whatever day of the
week it might fall. This type points first to Christ
Himself as the antitypical sheaf, and burnt offering
—"as of a lamb without blemish and without spot "
—who, perfected through suffering, and sacrificed as
our Passover, rose from the dead on the morrow
after the weekly sabbath, early on the first day of
the week, and was, as it were, waved before the

Psa. xxiv. 1.

Psa. cxxix. 7.

Ex. xxxiv. 26.
Lev. xxiii. 12.

1 Pet. i. 19.

LORD* in His resurrection. He was "the first of the
"firstfruits;" as it is written: "Christ the first-
"fruits; afterward they that are Christ's at his
"coming." Thus, St. Paul applies this type of
the firstfruits (as well as that of the passover) to
Christ Himself. He is the true Firstfruits of
humanity, the first risen man presented and accepted by the Father on behalf of all men; for in
all things it behoved Him to have the pre-eminence.
But it is a generally accepted principle that what
is true of Christ *Himself* in His experiences, and as

Ex. xxxiv. 26.

1 Cor xv. 23.

1 Cor. v. 7.

Col. i. 18.

* "We cannot but observe that the sacrifice of the passover,
on the fourteenth of the month Nisan, and the feast consequent thereupon (including the waving of the firstfruit sheaf
of barley on the morrow of the sabbath, that is, upon the
sixteenth of Nisan), typically refer to the crucifixion of the
Lord, and His resurrection from the dead. . . . . The firstfruit sheaf of barley is the type of the resurrection, as the
foundation of the Gospel preached for remission of sins.
. . . . The several events, [viz.] the crucifixion of our
Lord, His resurrection, and the descent of the Holy Ghost,
actually took place at the respective seasons, if not on the
precise days, on which the passover, the waving of the
firstfruit sheaf, and the feast of firstfruits, were respectively
observed. . . . . There is something very significant in
the Lord observing the legal type before He fulfilled it
antitypically. Dying on the fifteenth, He rose again on the
seventeenth of the month, as the passover had been slain on
the fourteenth at even, and the firstfruit omer or sheaf had
been waved on the sixteenth, the like interval of one day
occurring both in the type and in the antitype."—*Readings
on the Liturgy*, Vol. I., pp. 289, 290. (See also the *Worship
of the Old Covenant*, by Rev. E. F. Willis, M.A., p. 196.)
Thus our Lord's resurrection marked a new epoch, the
bringing of life and immortality into light *(cf.* Greek)—the
antitype being more glorious than the type, and indicating
a new departure, viz.: the abolition of the old dispensation,
and the introduction of the new, which is spiritual, heavenly,
and everlasting.

the firstfruits of the human race, shall in measure be true and reproduced in His Body, Christ *mystical.* When St. James writes of the Father as having begotten James 1. 18. us with the word of truth, "that we should be a " kind of firstfruits of his creatures," it is evident that he alludes to the whole Church, in relation to the rest of God's creation, as the firstfruits thereof. But it is also set forth in the Scriptures that within the Church herself there shall be the antitypical fulfilment of the various legal types, and that there shall be some among the Baptized who will stand to the rest of their brethren in the relation of first-fruits, even as the first sheaf of the harvest. If the Pentecostal and other feasts of the Tabernacle may be applied to the Church (as is usually done), then the first feast connected with the passover—that of waving the sheaf of firstfruits before the LORD— may not be ignored, but must admit of a like typical application. These feasts are not now being considered in their exhaustive application to the Church of Christ as a whole, but as bearing upon the dawn of the first resurrection, and the change without death, culminating in the joint translation of the firstfruits of the Church.

The following remarks with reference to the actual meaning of the "sheaf," written by the Rev. John Gill, D.D. (1697-1771), in his "Com-mentary on Leviticus," xxiii. 10, 11, will be apposite to the subject :—

"*Sheaf:* This in the text is called an *omer*, which was the tenth part of an ephah, Ex. xvi. 36, and so Jarchi (A.D. 1104-1180) interprets it here.

" According to the Jewish writers, when the sheaf was reaped, the corn was beaten out and winnowed and dried by the fire, and then ground in a mill; and an omer, or a tenth part of an ephah, of the flour of it was taken, and oil and frankincense put upon it, a handful being then put upon the altar, the rest being the priest's. But the omer, before the handful was taken from it, was waved by the priest in the Tabernacle or Temple, where was the presence of God. Gersom says the waving was towards the east. The waving was an acknowledgment to the Lord of heaven and earth, that the fruits of the earth and the plentiful harvest were of Him, and to give Him the praise and glory of it."

The type of the firstfruits of the barley harvest being waved before the Lord, ere the rest of the harvest was reaped, may thus set forth the resurrection of some of the saints, perfected through suffering, and of their being waved or presented by the Lord " without fault before the throne of God." They are doubtless represented by the 144,000 sealed ones who stand with the Lamb on Mount Zion, who follow Him whithersoever He goeth; and who are described as " being the firstfruits unto God and to the Lamb." This redeemed company being expressly called " first-"fruits," it is not unreasonable to infer that it bears an antitypical relationship to this feast of firstfruits, and that it may embrace and perhaps partially form a secondary fulfilment of this particular type.

The waving of the sheaf of barley before the LORD was the definite act of presenting it to Him for His acceptance. Under the Law, the waving

Rev. xiv. 5.

Rev. xiv. 1-4.

of an offering to the Lord was exhibited in a twofold
manner: first, as in the presentation of living men
for the service of the Lord, such as the initiation
of the Levites to their office, which consisted in
their being led up and down before the Lord, as it
Num. viii. 11.   is written: "And Aaron shall offer [*wave*, margin]
" the Levites before the LORD for an offering [*wave*
" *offering*, margin] of the children of Israel": and
in certain parts of sacrificial animals, after they had
Exod. xxix. 22-   been slain and their blood poured out, being waved
27, 35.   before the Lord at the consecration of the high
priest and of the priests; whilst of the people's
Lev. vii. 30.   peace offerings, the breast was "waved for a wave
" offering before the LORD." Our Lord's going up
and down among His disciples for forty days
previous to His ascension, answers to the waving
of the firstfruits of the barley harvest; and it was
at the expiration of this period that He was called
of God His Father to ascend and to receive consecration as High Priest, when at the same time He
Rev. v. 6.   presented Himself as the "Lamb as it had been slain."

The fundamental difference between the Lord's
ascension and the translation of the saints must not
be lost sight of, for the ascension was the personal act
of the Lord Jesus, the action of His own will in
union with that of His Father; as He said to Mary
John xx. 17.   Magdalene, " I ascend unto my Father, and your
" Father; and to my God, and your God." But
translation is the act of God upon His saints in trans-
ferring or exalting them from earth to heaven by His
holy will. It is not their personal act, nor is it by
their own volition that it is or can be accomplished,

though it is not effected without their concurrence, as it is written, "Thy people shall be *willing* in the " day of thy power"; yet as our Lord's ascension into heaven was the natural sequence to His resurrection, so likewise will the translation of the saints be consequent on the resurrection of the dead in Christ, and on the change of the living without death. Thus ascension into heaven is a corollary to resurrection; and these ideas of resurrection and ascension may involve the intermediate ones of the change of some of the living and of their translation. Psa. cx. 3.

Resurrection and the change without death give fitness and ability for ascension. But ascension need not follow immediately upon resurrection, even as our Lord did not ascend to the Father for forty days after His resurrection. The humble aspirant for such exaltation requires a divine call, and it may be also a period of probation in which he is being fitted to answer that call, after which consecration to higher service may be expected to follow.

Ascension has its affinity with translation, for it may be said that translation involves ascension, and that ascension involves translation. Translation is thus connected with resurrection and, moreover, with the change of the living; but bearing in mind the one fundamental idea of translation — a removal from place to place, from earth to heaven— the radical agreement of ascension and translation is easily discerned, and transformation or change of condition is implied in both.

(*b.*) The next feast of firstfruits which God commanded the Israelites to keep was "the feast of Ex. xxxiv. 22

"weeks, of the firstfruits of wheat harvest." The
wheat ripened later than the barley; therefore
fifty days after "the sheaf of the wave offering"
they were bidden to "offer a new meat offering unto
"the LORD," which was also called "firstfruits,"
and consisted of two wave loaves of fine flour. These
loaves, which were also designated "the firstfruits
"unto the LORD," were made of two omers of
wheat (one omer to each loaf) and were baked with
leaven. Great care was taken in the gathering of
the ears of wheat. They are said to have been
the first ripe ears dotted about the fields, and
plucked up singly with their whole stalks by
authorised men who cut away their roots. They
were treated in a special manner; for, after their
grain was threshed or beaten out, winnowed, and
ground into flour, it was passed through *twelve
sieves*, and then baked with leaven, and made into
two loaves. It is remarkable that this was the only
instance in which leaven was commanded to be
associated with the offerings of God; its use being
distinctly prohibited in all other offerings. The
prominent idea here is not the offering of grain
in its natural condition, and its being presented to
the Lord as a gathered sheaf, but that of grain
worked up through various processes into two loaves,
baked with leaven, to form "the bread of the first-
"fruits" for a wave offering before the Lord.

A few points taken from the description that
Josephus has given of the ceremonies connected with
the presentation of this offering may be quoted:—
When the loaves were prepared, a company of

Lev. xxiii. 15-17.

Lev. xxiii. 20.

twenty-four elders called "standing men" (or men
of standing) carried the offering to Jerusalem.
Arriving in the evening they remained in the open
air singing the psalms of David. Just before midnight the priests' trumpets were blown, and as the
new day dawned the temple gates were thrown open.
As they approached the temple, the Levites came down
to them, and then Psalm xxx. was sung antiphonally,
the third verse being taken as a refrain until the
cake was handed in: "Thou hast brought up my Psa. xxx. 3.
"soul from the grave"—(a resurrection host): "thou
"hast kept me alive, that I should not go down to
"the pit," or Hades—(a translation host). Here
is set forth the twofold company of the firstfruits.

What is the spiritual application of this type to
the Christian Church? It would appear, judging
from the intimations of Holy Scripture, that the
presentation of the firstfruits is the harbinger of a
greater ingathering. Of what are the two loaves
firstfruits? Surely of a coming and plentiful harvest.
This offering of the two wave loaves at the feast of
Pentecost, fifty days after the presentation of the
sheaf of firstfruits of the barley harvest on the morrow
after the sabbath, points to a further work for the
perfecting of the Christian Church at the end of
this dispensation, though it is not due to any fresh work
of *gathering* under new or restored institutions. It
points to a twofold company, not compacted together as a wave sheaf or omer, but so united in its
corporate character that, while maintaining its duality,
it forms one meat offering, one "bread of firstfruits."
This type, therefore, may have an application to a

second company of firstfruits from the Church, for the
Lord has revealed through His apostle John, that a
mighty work will be done by those whom He desig-
nates His "two witnesses." These shall give a testimony
for a stated period, and shall gather from among
the Baptized the remainder of the saints who shall
be fitted for presentation before the general harvest
and who shall escape the great tribulation.

Rev. xi.

A word here may be desirable on the relation of
these two figures of firstfruits.

The first is of the barley harvest; the second is
of the wheat harvest. The first was connected with
the feast of the Passover; the second with that of
Pentecost. The first was a sheaf, or rather omer,
which was waved before the Lord, the second was
embodied in two loaves, baken with leaven, which
were also waved before the Lord.

The first was called " the first of the firstfruits," the
latter "the firstfruits unto the Lord"—hence the name
firstfruits belonged to both of them, and it did not belong to the harvest. The practical question connected
with these two types of firstfruits, regarding them in
an antitypical and spiritual light, is whether they
may *together* compose the band of firstfruits who are
represented by the 144,000 on Mount Zion with the
Lamb.* It may be accepted as an axiom that

Ex. xxxiii. 19.
Lev. xxiii. 17.

---

* Elisha's connection with "the bread of the firstfruits,"
the twenty loaves of barley and full ears of corn in the
husk (2 Kings iv. 42), seems to point in this direction, for
the prophet Elisha, who followed Elijah and was endowed
with a *double* portion of the Spirit, is recognized as a type of
the Two Witnesses. It may also be suggested that the
144,000 sealed firstfruits mentioned in Rev. vii. 4, xiv. 1, may
represent a symbolic or typical, and possibly not an exact or
literal number.

what are not firstfruits are harvest, and that the Rev. vii. harvest is distinct from the firstfruits. We have Rev. xiv. only *two* companies brought before us in Rev. vii., the sealed company, which appears to be identical with the 144,000 who stand on Mount Zion with the Lamb, and the great multitude. The barley sheaf or omer must form part of the firstfruits. Will the firstfruits of the wheat harvest—the two loaves of Pentecost, be reckoned among them also? It may be so. We cannot say definitely. The two loaves, as well as the omer of barley, are waved before the Lord. These may have a double relation, an aspect towards the first of the firstfruits in one direction, and to the great multitude in the other, and may thus form a connecting link between the first and third companies.

The act of waving in both these types points to a definite act of presentation, as the result or climax of translation. The two bands of firstfruits have not been reaped *en masse* with the sickle, nor stored in the barn; but, having both escaped the great tribulation, they have been brought into the Temple of God and presented as wave offerings before the Lord.

It may be that those who have been first gathered shall await the perfecting of their brethren, and that then the first two companies (elected out of all generations) may together form one complete temple consisting of the Holiest and Holy Place, distinct from the outer court, which will be formed by the great multitude. Rev. vii.

(*c.*) The third great feast ordained by God was "The Feast of Tabernacles," or the ingathering of the Lev. xxiii. 34- fruit of the land, which was the conclusion of the 39. whole harvest, when all the sheaves were brought in from the field, and stored in the garner of the husbandman, not having been waved before the Lord.

These sheaves obviously include those who are last gathered in, and who form the completion of the great multitude which St. John saw standing before the throne of God, these having washed their robes and made them white in the blood of the Lamb. Not being of the firstfruits they form the general harvest; of which harvest the sealed company are in a special sense described as "firstfruits unto God and to the Lamb."

(7.) Another reason for the necessity of the translation of the firstfruits is to fulfil certain *historical* and prophetic types of Holy Scripture. Thus, our Lord refers to the historical types of Noah and his family, and of Lot and his wife in reference to the escape from the coming troubles, and likewise to the case of Jonah as a type of His own resurrection. The translation of Enoch and of Elijah may be cited as historical types of the coming rapture of the saints before the conclusion of this dispensation. There are also many definite prophecies in the Scriptures concerning translation which await fulfilment, some of which were quoted in the first chapter.

(8.) Another reason for apprehending the necessity of this act of resurrection, change and translation, is the condition into which Christendom has lapsed, calling for a Divine supernatural intervention, wherein God will give an explicit testimony to His existence and power. The Lord, when on earth, declared that His advent should come as a snare upon all them that dwell on the face of the whole earth, at a period when Christendom will have fallen into a

Rev. vii. 9.

Luke xxi. 35.

state of indifference and widespread infidelity, not
to say of antagonism to God and to His Christ.
Men will be, as the Lord said, occupied in building,
in planting, in marrying; in other words, in worldly
pursuits, in social duties and pleasures; so that the
thought of the Lord's return will be alien to their
minds, and will, too often, be received with scorn
and unbelief; "Where is the promise of his coming?   2 Peter iii. 4.
" for since the fathers fell asleep, all things continue
" as they were from the beginning of the creation."
But it is not the normal procedure of the Lord to
take even His forgetful people unawares. He always
gives them some sign, some warning, that they
may be without excuse.   No doubt, according
to our Lord's predictions, physical and natural
signs will not be wanting; but there shall also
be supernatural signs, signs in the spiritual heavens.
If any one were asked what would be the most
startling sign to a slumbering Church of the
near coming of the Bridegroom, what could he
possibly forecast? Surely nothing more wonderful
or illustrative of God's power, wisdom, and goodness,
than the raising of some of the dead, accompanied
by the changing of a number of the living saints,
and the translation of them both to a place of safety,
while the storm clouds of tribulation are waxing
darker and darker, ready to burst upon a careless
and unbelieving Christendom.   When, therefore,
men have forgotten the existence of God, or, at any
rate, when thousands have come to regard Him as
an abstraction, instead of believing in Him as *the
living God*, then this Divine intervention will take

place, and men will suddenly confront the fact that the Lord God Almighty, whose providence extends to the affairs of men in a marvellous manner, has intervened by bringing about the translation, in which the raised and changed saints have been caught away from earth to heaven.

The reasons given above for the necessity of that great act of intervention on the part of God in the rapture of the raised and living saints, as revealed in Holy Scripture, may be summarized as follows:—

(1.) A witness is needed to Christ as the *Life*, as well as to Christ as the *Resurrection*.

(2.) Since Christ has died there is now no *necessity* for the death of *all* men.

(3.) Translation without death seems to be the only way of meeting the case of the elect saints who are alive and remain upon the earth unto the coming of the Lord.

(4.) Further, without the change of the living, the departed saints cannot be made perfect.

(5.) It affords an exceptional and miraculous way of escape from the tribulation which shall overwhelm the whole earth.

(6.) It is necessary in order that the types of the Law may receive their fulfilment;

(7.) And also that the historical types and prophecies of Holy Scripture may be fulfilled.

(8.) It will be a startling sign and testimony, to a careless and apostatizing Christendom, of the existence, power, and grace of the living God.

CHAPTER III.

Translation, God's Way of Escape from the Coming Tribulation.

———

" WATCH ye therefore, and pray always, that ye may Luke xxi. 36.
" be accounted worthy to escape all these things
" that shall come to pass, and to stand before the
" Son of man."

These are our Lord's words, and the prominent
ideas contained in them are the escape promised
from coming judgments, the preparation of watchfulness and prayer required for it, and the prize to be
attained, viz.:—to stand before the Son of man.
And, as our Lord speaks of coming dangers, this
verse should be read in connexion with the preceding
context.

When the Lord warned His disciples to take heed
that they were not deceived by false Christs, He
further said: " When ye shall hear of wars and Luke xxi. 9.
" commotions, be not terrified: for *these things (i.e.,* the
" throwing down of the temple and its goodly stones),
" *must first come to pass.*" Then He predicted the Luke xxi. 10, 11.
uprisings of nation against nation, great earthquakes,
famines, pestilences, fearful sights, and great signs
from heaven, and added—" *But before all these,* they Luke xxi. 12-24.
" shall lay their hands on you, and persecute you;

" . . . . And when ye shall see Jerusalem com-
" passed with armies, then know that the desolation
" thereof is nigh. . . . . and Jerusalem shall be
" trodden down of the Gentiles, until the times of
" the Gentiles be fulfilled. And there shall be signs
" in the sun, and in the moon, and in the stars; and
" upon the earth distress of nations, with perplexity;
" the sea and the waves roaring; men's hearts failing
" them for fear, and for looking after those things
" [the things detailed in verses 9, 10, 11] which are
" coming on the earth: for the powers of heaven
" shall be shaken . . . . And when *these things*
" [*i.e.*, these signs in the heavenly bodies, etc.] begin
" to come to pass, then look up, and lift up your
" heads; for your redemption draweth nigh . . . .
" And take heed to yourselves, lest at any time
" [during all the centuries that would elapse] your
" hearts be overcharged . . . . and so that day
" come upon you unawares. . . . . Watch ye
" therefore, and pray always, that ye may be accounted
" worthy to escape all these things that shall come
" to pass, and to stand before the Son of man."

Luke xxi.
25-36.

In this passage our Lord gives only the outline
of future events, leaving it to be filled in with further
details by His apostles, as the Holy Spirit should
give them light on things to come. Nevertheless, by
the revelation which He accorded to His apostle
John, the Lord made known many things that should
come to pass, which were before unknown. This
is true as regards the details of the troubles and
judgments coming upon the world, and of the escape
of those who shall stand in the place of safety with

John xvi. 13.

the Lamb, on which subjects special light is vouchsafed in the Book of the Revelation.

It should be observed that in Luke xxi., verse 11,
our Lord foretells fearful sights and great signs
from heaven, while in verse 25 He predicts signs *in*
the sun, the moon, and the stars. Now, as these
heavenly luminaries symbolize the Church of God
in various aspects, the signs therein point to an eclipse
of light, in consequence of which they are darkened.
This, therefore, would refer emblematically to the
denial of the divinity of the Lord Jesus Christ who
is called "the Sun of righteousness," to the general　Mal. iv. 2.
apostasy of the visible Church, of which the moon
is a symbol, and to the falling away of bishops,
rulers (or stars) in the Church. And as St. John　Rev. i. 20.
was told that "the waters" which he saw "are　Rev. xvii. 15.
" peoples, and multitudes, and nations, and tongues,"
there can be no doubt that the roaring of the sea
and of the waves is figurative of democratic, re-
volutionary, and anarchical outbreaks among the
nations. These signs are the precursors of the
coming storm of judgment, issuing in ultimate deliverance in the kingdom of God.

St. Matthew records a similar catalogue in which　Matt. xxiv.
the Lord narrates the signs of the end of the age,
with the addition of betrayal by friends, of the
arising of false prophets, of spiritual evil, abounding
iniquity, and great deceptive signs and wonders;
whilst He urges the same lesson of watchfulness,
and warns His hearers against being overtaken in
sensual pursuits, worldliness, and pleasure: "For then　Matt. xxiv. 21.
" shall be great tribulation, such as was not since

" the beginning of the world to this time, no, nor
" ever shall be."

St. Mark also gives an outline of coming troubles;
the Lord's recorded words being—" For in those days
" shall be affliction, such as was not from the be-
" ginning of the creation which God created unto
" this time, neither shall be. And except that the
" Lord had shortened those days, no flesh should
" be saved : but for the elect's sake, whom he hath
" chosen, he hath shortened the days." Thus the
three synoptic Gospels agree in their testimony as
to the sorrows coming on the earth, and to their
unparalleled character in variety and intensity. It
will be a time of unprecedented trouble and suffering, of apostasy and wickedness, of physical and
spiritual anguish.

If then these signs in the Church and in the
world are beginning to come to pass; if they are
observable in the spiritual heavens, looking at the
present worldly condition of the Church who has
forgotten that her true citizenship is in heaven;
if the unrest of the nations increases from day to
day, baffling the understanding of statesmen ; if
there is perplexity among the most far-seeing in
Church and State, owing to apparently ineradicable
moral evils seething beneath the surface of the
Christian civilization,—then let the faithful be watchful, for it is evident that a spiritual crisis in the
history of the world is approaching. It is nothing
less than the last great conflict for supremacy between
good and evil,—in a word, whether God or the
Devil shall have the mastery. This contest was

Mark xiii. 19,
20.

foretold by God in Eden, when He said to the
serpent—"I will put enmity between thee and the   Gen. iii. 15.
" woman, and between thy seed and her seed; it
" shall bruise thy head, and thou shalt bruise his
" heel."

In the beautiful prophetic song of Hannah, at the
birth of her child Samuel, the same strain is audible,
when she sings: "The adversaries of the Lord shall   1 Sam. ii. 10.
" be broken to pieces; . . . . and he shall
" . . . . exalt the horn of his anointed." The
last words of king David concerning the sons of
Belial are to the same effect, when he says that they
shall be as thorns thrust away, and shall be utterly   2 Sam. xxiii. 6, 7.
burned with fire. The Psalms are full of the same
theme; as, for instance, the second Psalm; and the
prophets Isaiah, Jeremiah, Ezekiel, Joel, and especially Daniel, witness to the same final struggle   Dan. xi. xii.
between Messiah and His enemies, for everlasting
supremacy.

St. Paul and St. Peter write in like manner; but
this contest, this time of tribulation, is more enlarged
upon in the Book of the Revelation than in any of
the apostolic epistles. These conflicts and sorrows
are likened to birth pains, and the tribulation mentioned in the Apocalypse is emphatically designated
in the Greek, "The tribulation, the great." All these   Rev. vii. 14.
things appear to be implied in the figure of the
woman labouring to be delivered of the man child
as "the beginning of the sorrows," and in the
subsequent events mentioned in the twelfth chapter.   Rev. xii.

There are many phases in which this figure of
the man child may be studied, but the aspect now

under consideration is that of threatened *danger*, and the *escape therefrom*. It may be well to quote the

Rev. xii. 1-5.

passage:—"And there appeared a great wonder in "heaven; a woman clothed with the sun, and the "moon under her feet, and upon her head a crown "of twelve stars: and she being with child cried, "travailing in birth, and pained to be delivered. "And there appeared another wonder in heaven; "and behold a great red dragon, having seven heads "and ten horns, and seven crowns upon his heads. "And his tail drew the third part of the stars of "heaven, and did cast them to the earth: and the "dragon stood before the woman which was ready "to be delivered, for to devour her child as soon "as it was born. And she brought forth a man "child, who was to rule all nations with a rod of "iron: and her child was caught up* unto God, "and to his throne."

The first point to notice in this passage is that the woman suffers, and is in pain to be delivered. Her birth-pains are called in the Greek ὠδῖναι, a word applied to women in travail, and used by

Matt. xxiv. 8.
Rom. viii. 22.

our Lord of the coming world-wide tribulation, and by the apostle Paul of the present condition of the groaning creation. This figure of a woman

---

* See 1 Thess. iv. 17. The idea of being "caught up" as rendered in the Greek is more literally that of being "snatched away," "seized hastily," as by the swoop of an eagle (from ἁρπάζω). "Rapture" conveys a similar idea. It is from the Latin verb *rapio*, I snatch; while the idea of "translation" (from the Latin *transfero*, past part. *translatus*) implies simple transference from one place to another.

in travail is frequently used by the prophets to denote great anguish, as may be seen in the books
of Jeremiah and Micah: "For I have heard a   Jer. iv. 31.
" voice as of a woman in travail, and the anguish
" as of her that bringeth forth her first child, the
" voice of the daughter of Zion, that bewaileth
" herself, that spreadeth her hands, saying, Woe is
" me now!"—"Be in pain, and labour to bring forth,   Micah iv. 10.
" O daughter of Zion, like a woman in travail."

The next point for consideration is the *birth* of
the man child. There is always an interest attaching
to the birth of a firstborn, especially if it be the
son of a king. The birth of a child has, on different
occasions, played an important part in God's plan
of redemption; as, for instance, the births of Isaac,
Moses, Samson, Samuel, Josiah, John the Baptist,
and, lastly, the birth of our Lord Himself.

Some commentators apply this type of the man
child to our Lord Jesus Christ Himself; but the
whole context connects this vision with the order
of future events, and not with the antecedent birth,
resurrection, and ascension of our Lord Jesus Christ.
There can be no reasonable doubt, from the details
given, that the Church Catholic, headed up by
apostles, is depicted. Here then is the woman, the
Church, about to bring forth her firstborn, an event
that must greatly affect her subsequent history, that
of the world, and, it may be said, that of the whole
creation also. Surely the birth of the Church's
firstborn cannot fail to be a cosmic event. As
a virgin with child was the sign of the first
advent of our Lord on earth, so also is the figure

of a woman with child a sign connected with His
second advent; this woman representing the Church
of Christ, wearing as her crown the Lord's chief
ordinance of a twelvefold apostleship.

On all sides danger threatens the woman and her
offspring. Doubtless internal dangers, spiritual conflicts within the Church herself, perils from false
brethren, tribulation from dire persecution, predicted
by the Lord and by His apostle Paul, are set forth
by the travailing pains of the woman in her labour
to bring forth the man child. But in this time of
trouble, that which has taken place in previous
generations will no doubt occur again, when it shall
be seen that the advancing civilization of nineteen
centuries has not changed either the bigotry or the
malice of the human heart when it is instigated to
wickedness by the devil, and shall not prevent the fires
of persecution from being lighted once more, after
all the boasted toleration of modern Christendom.

Some of the persecutions which have taken place,
at once so fearful and so hideous, can only be cursorily
mentioned. Of these the chief were the ten persecutions under the Roman emperors; afterwards those
of the middle and following ages, which occurred
more or less throughout Europe, but especially in
France against the Albigenses, Huguenots, and Cam-
isards; those in Italy against the Waldenses; in Spain
against all who were denounced as heretics, through
the fury of the Inquisition; in the Netherlands against
the Reformed; and lately in Russia against the Jews.
Alas! that so many of these persecutions should have
been carried out by Christians against Christians,

John xvi. 21.
1 Thess. v. 3.

Rev. ii. 10.

by fellow countrymen against their compatriots, by brothers against brothers, even as the Lord had predicted! Judging from the Apocalypse and other books of Holy Scripture, it seems probable that these horrors will be re-enacted with every possible aggravation in the time of the end, according to the terrible announcement that the beast shall make war with Rev. xiii. 7. the saints and shall overcome them—though, God be thanked, only for a little while—for the man of the earth, when inspired by Satan, is still as deceitful, selfish, and violent as he has ever been throughout the history of the world.

The *external* dangers seem to be the most prominent in the apocalyptic picture, and these are typified by another remarkable figure. A great red dragon stands before the woman, waiting to devour her child as soon as it is born. There is significance in the colour *red*, and in its being here specially mentioned, for it is always connected with bloodshed. At the time of the French Revolution, and later on in that of the French Commune, red was the colour chosen by the anarchists as their badge, and it was emblematic of their deeds of vindictive cruelty. Now, the great red dragon, who has seven heads and ten horns, and seven crowns upon his heads, seems to set forth Satan putting forth his diabolic power in the last and most oppressive form of what is known as the fourth or Roman Empire, when it shall be divided into the ten predicted kingdoms. His active personal agent, the Antichrist, shall consolidate his power over the ten kings of apostate Christendom, aided by the false prophet, who is represented by

Isa. ix. 15. the tail of the dragon. And as the dragon's tail
draws down the third part of the stars of heaven,
and casts them to the earth, so the false prophet is
represented as enticing from their heavenly calling
a certain number of Christian bishops, or angels,
Rev. i. 20. who are typified by "the stars." Thus will the dragon
persecute the Church, but he will first seek to frustrate the translation of the firstfruits, of whom the
man child in this vision is the symbol.

In the apocalyptic figures there are many interesting
points which might arrest attention, but in this chapter
the subject under consideration is *the translation as a
means of escape;* and therefore the most prominent
thought, in connection with the man child, is its
extreme danger from external sources, and its miraculous escape, through the intervention of God, by its
being caught away or translated. The child of the
woman is symbolic; and for the moment it may
be assumed that this figure represents a company or
body within the Church Catholic. [This hypothesis
will be considered in detail in the seventh chapter.]

The danger to the child is so imminent that there
appears to be no way of deliverance. It is truly
a case for what the ancients called a *deus ex machinâ,*
by which they meant the intervention of the gods
in some unexpected manner—the phrase being taken
from dramatic representations on the stage. Man's
extremity, however, is God's opportunity. The man
Rev. xii. 5. child is caught up to God and His throne by a sudden
rapture; not by an ignominious flight from a victori-
ous enemy, but by an escape through a Divine act
of interposition, "with a high hand," like the Exodus

of Israel from Egypt, the Lord going before them, and being also their rereward. The actual destination of the man child is elsewhere described as Mount Zion, for when the apostle John saw the company of 144,000 there with the Lamb, they were declared to be "before the throne of God." This deliverance at the eleventh hour, or, as it were, *in extremis*, is effectual, even as in the case of Lot's miraculous escape out of Sodom; for in all generations "the "Lord knoweth how to deliver the godly out of "temptations." Rev. xiv. 5.

2 Peter ii. 9.

This subject may be illustrated by another figure, viz., that of a besieged city, surrounded by the enemy and desolated by famine, like Jerusalem when assaulted by Nebuchadnezzar, or when, some seven centuries later, it was encompassed by the Romans. At the siege of Jerusalem under Titus there appeared to be no possibility of deliverance from the beleaguered city; yet the faithful few reached their place of refuge at Pella. *

Wherefore, looking at the warnings of our Lord and of the prophets of old as to a time of tribulation with which this dispensation shall end, should not we, His people, His Baptized, take to heart His admonition to pray for an escape from the things which shall come to pass? And is it not a just

* The ecclesiastical historian Eusebius, who wrote early in the fourth century, states that the Christians during an unexpected lull in the siege of Jerusalem withdrew, in obedience to our Lord's prophetic warnings (Matt. xxiv. 15, 16; Mark xiii. 14) to Pella, at the northern extremity of Perea, and thus escaped the calamities by which the doomed city and the nation were eventually overwhelmed.

conclusion to infer the necessity of translation as
the means whereby this escape shall be effected,
through a special act of God in transporting His
firstfruits into a place of safety from the calamities
which are about to desolate the earth and ravage
Christendom, and which shall threaten to extinguish
the name of Christ among men? Further, does
not the passage about the firstfruits in Rev. xiv. 1-5
warrant the presumption that the escaped remnant
shall be taken up into the immediate presence of
God and of the Lamb? Shall not the saints who
Luke xxi. 36. have been redeemed from among men then " stand
before* the Son of man"? Are not the change
and translation implied in this expression of our
Lord? When He bade His apostles, and through
them all believers, and the Church herself as a
corporate body, to watch and pray that they might
be accounted worthy of a special escape, He also
held out as a prize this subsequent privilege of
standing before the Son of man. In Eastern countries it has from ancient times been regarded as a
mark of the highest honour to be permitted to stand
Gen. xli. 46. before the king; as when, for example, Joseph stood
before Pharaoh, king of Egypt, and king Saul sent
1 Sam. xvi. 22. to Jesse, saying, "Let David stand before me; for
" he hath found favour in my sight." It is to this
honour, and not only to the escape from danger,

---

* In Luke xxi. 36 the preposition is ἔμπροσθεν, *in front of,*
but in Rev. xii. 5 it is πρὸς, *a motion towards,* the distinct
shades of meaning indicating the difference between an
act completed and an act begun.

that the Lord would encourage His saints to attain; even as it is written, "This honour have all his " saints."   Psa. cxlix. 9.

The present point is: How shall this position be reached? Those who are endangered must be rescued from the scene of danger: but this is the earth, not to say the whole earth (at any rate the οἰκουμένη, the habitable or civilized world, "the " whole world"), from which these persecuted saints must be delivered and transported to a place of safety—the secret hiding-place of the Lord—be it the air, or the heavens. Hence rapture from the earth in some form or other seems to be an implied necessity. There is a beautiful thought in the Psalms connected with the safety and hiding away of the firstfruits, namely *the pavilion of the LORD.* "For in the time of trouble he shall hide me in his " pavilion: in the secret of his tabernacle shall he " hide me; he shall set me up upon a rock" (Mount Zion, Rev. xiv. 1; 2 Sam. v. 7): and again, "Thou " shalt hide them in the secret of thy presence from " the pride of man: thou shalt keep them secretly in a " pavilion from the strife of tongues."* Both of these passages are full of exquisite suggestions. In both the common feature of a time of trouble, an outbreak of the pride of man, and a strife of tongues, is present; in both there is a clear reference to a place of refuge,   Luke ii. 1.

Psa. xxvii. 5.

Psa. xxxi. 20.

---

* The prophet Habakkuk uses the remarkable expression, " there was the hiding of his power," or, as the Hebrew may be literally rendered, "the hiding-place of his power"— conveying the idea of the power of God shewn in safe-guarding His people by translating them to a secret place.   Hab iii. 4.

F

to which the idea of secrecy is attached: this being symbolized by the most holy place in the Taber-

Psa. xci. 1, 4. nacle. "He that dwelleth in the secret place of " the most High shall abide under the shadow of " the Almighty;" "He shall cover thee with his " feathers, and under his wings shalt thou trust." There is here an allusion to the cherubim in the most holy place overshadowing the sacred ark, from between which the LORD, who dwelt in the bright shechinah, the visible symbol of His presence, shining on the wings of the cherubim, would cast His shadow of protection and blessing. Thus the conception of resurrection, change, and translation is not an afterthought for deliverance on the part of God, but is part of His foreordained purpose; a means whereby He will put the enemy to shame, and shew Himself to be the God whose love and power and wisdom are unsearchable, and whose ways are past finding out. Our Lord's words of

Luke xxi. 36. admonition, quoted at the beginning of this chapter, contain a veiled reference to the change and transla- tion; for they imply an unbroken continuity between the escaping of those things that are coming on the earth and the standing before the Son of man, as of events following in direct sequence. But if death were first to occur, and then resurrection, there would be a break in the continuity, which the little word "and" (connecting the "escape" with the "standing") does not warrant. We gather that the

Rev. xii. man child is transported to a place of safety, being caught up to the throne of God; we learn that

Rev. xiv. the 144,000, who correspond to the figure of the

man child, are before the throne, and that they are on Mount Zion; so we can have little difficulty in identifying the place of safety to which the translated are removed. It is remarkable how often Mount Zion is in Scripture associated with the Lord's throne and rule, with safety and escape, and with deliverance: " For out of Jerusalem shall go " forth a remnant, and they that escape out of " Mount Zion" (2 Kings xix. 31); "Upon Mount " Zion shall be those that escape" (Obad. 17, margin). See also Rev. xix. 1, Isa. ii. 3, Joel ii. 32.

It was on Mount Zion that David erected a tent for the ark of the Lord before it was received into the Temple of Solomon, which was destined to be its abiding resting-place, and some have suggested that it was identical with Mount Moriah, and was the site of the Temple. However that may be, it is the place of safety for the firstfruits; and the secret of God's Tabernacle may be situated there also, though whether it be there in a literal or in a spiritual sense we are unable to say in our present state of knowledge. On the other hand, the pavilion of the LORD may be in the clouds, where we are to meet the Lord in the air. What a joyful meeting that will be between the Lord and the living and changed saints, and the departed and risen saints; and between both companies, before they are transported as one glorious phalanx, "the firstfruits unto God " and to the Lamb," to Mount Zion, to stand with the Lamb before the throne of God ! Rev. xiv. 4, 5.

Although it does not appertain to this part of our subject to examine the symbolism of the vision in

Rev. xii. in detail, beyond the narrative of the birth and catching away of the man child, which have been dwelt upon in their figurative bearing on the rapture of the saints, still the subsequent experiences of the Woman—the Church—must not be overlooked, for they indicate repeated perils and escapes, and point instructively to the divine care exercised by God on behalf of all His children, and not only of the firstfruits; but the troubles to which the Woman will be exposed will come under review in greater detail, in the chapter on "The Two Witnesses."

An important question, both doctrinal and practical, meets us here, and that is: Shall the whole Church attain to the rapture and the escape from the coming judgments; or, the firstfruits only being exempted, shall the bulk of the Church go through the great tribulation? It is essentially a matter of revelation, and therefore the answer to this question must be sought for in Holy Scripture.

Rev. vii.   In the seventh chapter of the Apocalypse only *two* companies are described — the sealed, whom the winds of judgment are not permitted to hurt; and the great multitude which no man can number, who pass through the great tribulation. The number of the sealed is small as contrasted with the vast multitude of those who come out of the great tribulation.

If, as some suppose, the sealed constitute the whole Church, it would seem, judging from the figure, as if the Church were a very small body; and, if this be so, what position will the great multitude hold? They are not Jews, therefore they must belong to the Church; and we ask, In what position are they? Their natural place, as members of the body of Christ, is to form part of the Church, and no other position can be assigned to them.

In Revelation xii. the figure of the man child represents a comparatively small company who are translated; for after this the persecuted woman, who is symbolical of the Church at large, takes two flights into the wilderness, after which she, with the remnant of her seed (who also suffer persecution at the hands of the dragon), will attain ultimate deliverance. But her experiences during her two flights were different. During the first she appears to have been completely sheltered from Satanic persecution, the war in heaven resulting in the defeat of the dragon and his angels, and this is the period of the successful testimony of the Two Witnesses; whereas during the latter period she is exposed to the full fury of the dragon, the beast, and the false prophet, the Witnesses being warred against and eventually slain, although (under the figure of the two wings of a great eagle) they have been instrumental in assisting the woman in her second flight. It would thus appear that the second company of the Church has decided affinities with the firstfruits on the one hand, and possibly with the harvest on the other, and yet even if united with the body of the firstfruits as a whole, they may constitute a distinct company forming the holy place in the Temple of God, while the other two companies respectively form the most holy place and the outer court.

In Rev. xiv. the company of 144,000 (previously sealed) is seen standing with the Lamb on Mount

Zion, in a place of security and free from the subsequent troubles which surge around. The identity of these three figures may be assumed, viz.: the sealed (Rev. vii.), twelve thousand from each of the twelve tribes of Israel (Dan excepted, but Levi included); the 144,000 standing with the Lamb on Mount Zion (Rev. xiv.); and the man child (Rev. xii.). They each apparently set forth the same small and elect company representing antitypically the firstfruits of the barley harvest, and possibly the two wave loaves or firstfruits of the wheat harvest. This company will be small compared with the innumerable sheaves of the great ingathering. The sequence and typology of the Feast of Ingathering (which followed very closely upon the Day of Atonement) seem to indicate that the majority of the Baptized who will be saved, after repentance and subsequent humiliation, will have to undergo the discipline of the great tribulation for their purification and for their preparation for the kingdom of God, owing to the condition into which Christendom—the professing visible Church—has now lapsed. Very few Christians —a very small number, like those typified by the omer of barley and by the two wave loaves of wheat—cherish the hope or desire for the Lord's appearing, while to the millions of the Baptized it is a forgotten hope, for the attainment of which they are utterly unprepared, and upon whom the day of the Lord must come as a thief in the night. But it is a necessity that they should be prepared for His coming, and if they will not yield themselves to the gentle pleading of the Holy Spirit and respond to

the love of God, then, perforce, they must pass
through the purifying fire of the outpoured judgments of God and the storm of His indignation
during the reign of Antichrist.

Hence the great tribulation will be a matter of
NECESSITY. The Baptized have come into an evil
condition; they have forgotten their hope; they have
become schismatic, worldly, impure, and they are in
danger of quenching the Holy Ghost; therefore as
it was necessary to bring the Jews under the rod to
teach them the ways of God, which they would not
otherwise learn, it will also become necessary to
subject the professing Church on earth, not to the
fire of the Lord in Zion, but to His furnace in   Isa. xxxi. 9.
Jerusalem, in order to purge her from her worldliness and all filthiness of the flesh and of the spirit.

A promise is given to Philadelphia of immunity   Rev. iii. 10.
from the hour of temptation or the great tribulation,
and the Lord Himself held out this hope when He
bade His apostles, and His Church through them,
to watch and pray that they might escape the things
which should come to pass; but the majority of the
Baptized, having lapsed into the Laodicean condition,
need the Lord's rebuke and chastisement. Yet it
must be acknowledged that the needed discipline is
really an act of MERCY on the part of God, to which
those will gratefully testify who are saved with an
everlasting salvation, even though it be through
this ordeal of suffering. They might have been
ripened by God's love, but they heeded not the
voice of the Spirit speaking in the great congregation; they were careless and neglectful; but yet

God in His mercy instead of destroying them by His fiery judgments, will purify them thereby, and pluck them as brands out of the burning. Thus ripened by the fire of His jealousy, they will render praise and glory to Him who has redeemed them from all evil.

Many pious people, who think that it is a reflection on the mercy of God that the Church should have to go through the great tribulation, ignore the transcendent holiness of God, and that without holiness, no man shall see the Lord: therefore, if the Church is to be presented "faultless before the presence of "his glory with exceeding joy," and if she will not be wooed by His love, she must be chastened by the rod of judgment to cleanse her from all defilement of worldliness, self-will, and superstition. These brethren appear to limit their ideas to the small section of what they term the true and spiritual Church of Christ, and they ignore the multitude of the Baptized, whom they consider to have fallen away from their hope and to be out of the pale of the Church; but we thank God that His mercy is infinitely greater than man's, and that He will, notwithstanding even the failure of the Baptized taken as a whole, shew forth His glory on a colossal scale in the salvation of a great multitude which no man can number. God's mercy is great unto the heavens, and His truth unto the clouds; and His ways and thoughts are higher than ours, as the heavens are higher than the earth, for

Jude 24.

Psa. lvii. 10.

Psa. ciii. 11.

> " The love of God is broader
> Than the measure of man's mind,
> And the heart of the Eternal
> Is most wonderfully kind."

The great tribulation will be as much an act of *mercy* as of *necessity*, for thereby an innumerable multitude shall be saved, to stand before the throne of God and of the Lamb, these constituting the bulk of the Baptized, the harvest of the Church.

Our Lord, after His solemn discourse on the coming of the kingdom of God, speaks of the troubles with which this dispensation will end, and the destruction that the sudden coming of the Son of man will inflict; and He concludes by giving three illustrations of what is generally known as the rapture of the living. He prefaces it with the solemn words, "I tell you." "I tell you, in that "night there shall be two in one bed; the one "shall be taken, and the other shall be left. Two "shall be grinding together; the one shall be taken, "and the other left. Two shall be in the field; "the one shall be taken, and the other left." *

To give the above passage its spiritual application, the expression "two in one bed" may include those who at the Lord's coming are in their graves, of whom some shall be raised at the first resurrection, while the others are left sleeping in their graves. The two women grinding corn may refer to the ordinary pastoral work proceeding in the churches, resulting in the one case in readiness to be caught away, and in the other in being left behind to contend with the coming troubles. Likewise the two men in the field, with their varying experiences, suggest missionary effort in the world at large, for

Luke xvii. 20-37.

Matt. xiii. 38.

* The words which are in italics in the A.V. are not in the original Greek, and are omitted in this quotation.

our Lord tells us that " the field is the world." Some labourers in the vineyard may be looking for the Lord's appearing; whilst others, godly men though they be, may be forgetful of the hope.   When the disciples asked, "Where, Lord ?" He answered them in a proverb:—"Wheresoever the body is, thither " will the eagles be gathered together."

Luke xvii. 37

As in the above figures the thought is prominent of the sudden taking away or rapture of the saints, the idea of translation may be lawfully applied to St. Paul's expression in which " by the coming of " our Lord Jesus Christ, and by our *gathering together* " *unto him*," he beseeches the Thessalonians to be steadfast.   In this connection the promise of the LORD through the prophet Isaiah may be quoted:— " They that wait upon the LORD shall renew their " strength; they shall mount up with wings as " eagles."   And this last expression is suggestive of St. Paul's words: " Then we which are alive " and remain shall be caught up . . . . to meet " the Lord in the air." [See note, p. 58 *supra*.]

2 Thess. ii. 1.

Isa. xl. 31.

1 Thess. iv. 17.

Each dispensation has ended in failure and in judgment, yet with the escape of a remnant.   The antediluvian era closed with the judgment of the Flood and the escape of a very small remnant. When Sodom was overthrown by fire, only Lot and his daughters were rescued ; and when the destruction of Jerusalem closed the dispensation of the Law, comparatively few escaped to enter upon the next epoch.   Thus will it be again; but as this, the dispensation of the Spirit, exceeds the previous ones in grace and privilege, and consequently in responsibility, so will the judgments which close it exceed the former judgments in severity, and be in a direct ratio to the riches of God's grace which have been despised.

The character of these judgments having been so plainly foretold, we should watch and pray that we may attain to the promised escape, and be privileged to stand among the earliest band of first-fruits, before the Son of man, when He comes in His kingdom.

Looking at the importance of flight into a place of safety, the prophet Jeremiah says, "Give wings "unto Moab, that it may flee and get away." The Church in her time of sorrow, and doubtless even many of her faithful members also in these present days, in view of the things that are coming on the earth, may be inclined to cry out in the language of David: "Oh that I had wings like a dove! for then "would I fly away, and be at rest. I would hasten "my escape from the windy storm and tempest." *Jer. xlviii. 9.* *Psa. lv. 6, 8.*

But there is a brighter promise in connection with this figure; for in another psalm the sweet singer of Israel speaks not only of humiliation, or perhaps of death, but of resurrection, of the change, of translation, when he utters the prophecy: "Though "ye have lien among the pots, yet shall ye be as "the wings of a dove covered with silver, and her "feathers with yellow gold;" full of love and truth in the glory of the risen Christ, through the transforming power of the Holy Ghost. May this be our speedy, corporate, and individual experience! Amen. *Psa. lxviii. 13.*

CHAPTER IV.

The Holy Ghost the Agent in the Translation.

THE fourth point for consideration in the doctrine of the translation of the saints is one of vital importance, namely, Who is the *Divine Agent* in effecting the translation? The translation is a supernatural and, in the sight of man, a miraculous act, which is not to be effected by any angelic agency; and it is certain that it could not be accomplished by man himself, any more than any other of the great acts of God in the redemption of the human race. Man can neither regenerate nor sanctify himself; man cannot raise himself from the dead, nor can he change himself into a condition of immortality; man cannot transport himself into the air nor can he glorify himself. But as the Holy Ghost is the acknowledged Author of several of these great acts in the work of our salvation,— admittedly of the first three—why should He not be the Author of them all? As sanctification is due to the indwelling of the Holy Spirit, so must the change of the saints into immortality, their translation to meet the Lord in the air, and their appearance with Him in glory be due to the action of the same Spirit, when He shall have perfectly conformed the saints to the image of the Son of God.

(1.) There are Scriptural testimonies to the action of the Spirit of God, from which the reasonable inference may be drawn that it is *He* who will be the Agent in the resurrection, change, and translation of the saints. The first example of such spiritual action is seen in the translation of Enoch, for it is written, "He was not; for God took him." Gen. v. 24. The result is here ascribed to God, and, judging from the analogy of Holy Scripture, it must have been due to the action of God the Holy Ghost.

Again, in the case of Elijah, it should be observed that Obadiah attributes the wonderful disappearance of the prophet to the Spirit of God, when he says: " And it shall come to pass, as soon as I am gone " from thee, that the Spirit of the LORD shall carry " thee whither I know not; and so when I come and " tell Ahab, and he cannot find thee, he shall slay " me." Hence it cannot be doubted that the prophet's subsequent translation was effected by the selfsame Spirit. Moreover, those who desired to search for Elijah spoke to Elisha in the same strain—" Behold " now, there be with thy servants fifty strong men; " let them go, we pray thee, and seek thy master: " lest peradventure the Spirit of the LORD hath " taken him up, and cast him upon some mountain, " or into some valley."

1 Kings xviii. 12.

2 Kings ii. 16.

The supernatural action of the Spirit is seen also in the visions and movements of other prophets of Israel, especially in the case of Ezekiel, who writes thus: "The spirit lifted me up, and took me away, " and I went in bitterness, ...   but the hand " of the LORD was strong upon me." Again, " He

Ezek. iii. 14.

Ezek. viii. 3.

" put forth the form of an hand, and took me by a
" lock of mine head; and the spirit lifted me up
" between the earth and the heaven, and brought
" me in the visions of God to Jerusalem, to the door
" of the inner gate that looketh toward the north."

A similar transporting action of the Spirit is
narrated in the New Testament in the case of
Philip the evangelist, after he had baptized the
Ethopian eunuch: "And when they were come up
" out of the water, the Spirit of the Lord caught
" away Philip, that the eunuch saw him no more:
" and he went on his way rejoicing. But Philip
" was found at Azotus."

St. Paul alludes to his wonderful spiritual experience and to his rapture into heaven as follows:—
" I knew a man in Christ above fourteen years ago,
" (whether in the body, I cannot tell; or whether
" out of the body, I cannot tell: God knoweth;)
" such an one caught up to the third heaven.
" . . . . how that he was caught up into para-
" dise, and heard unspeakable words, which it is
" not lawful for a man to utter." This rapture may
also, no doubt, have been effected by the same Holy
Spirit. Thus, as Holy Scripture records several cases
of an actual removal of persons whilst in the body,
into heaven or to other parts of the earth, and attributes this phenomenon to the Spirit of God, it cannot
be contrary to Scripture to ascribe the rapture or
translation of the firstfruits of the saints to the action
of the same Holy Spirit. What power in heaven
or earth could catch the saints up to God and to
His throne but the very Spirit of the living God?

Acts viii. 39, 40.

2 Cor. xii. 2-4.

Rev. xii. 5.

That the Holy Ghost is the Agent in the resurrection and in the change may be inferred from St. Paul's words, "If the Spirit of him that raised up Jesus "from the dead dwell in you, he that raised up "Christ from the dead shall also quicken your "mortal bodies by his Spirit that dwelleth in you" —quicken them into resurrection life, if dead; quicken them into the immortal life, if they have not tasted death. | Rom. viii. 11.

(2.) If in subordinate earthly things there is a great truth in the acknowledged axiom of the superiority of mind (including spirit) over matter, how much more must it be true of the power of the Holy Ghost over the material bodies, as well as over the spirits, of created men. "God is a "Spirit," and the Almighty has so marvellously formed the spirit in man, that it is reckoned among the chief acts and wonders of creative power; as it is written, "The LORD . . . . stretcheth "forth the heavens, and layeth the foundation of "the earth, and formeth the spirit of man within "him." The nature of man is threefold, consisting of body, soul, and spirit; and if the work of God is now principally carried on in his spirit, it is only an earnest of what will be manifested in his whole being in the resurrection. Among all the creatures of God, man alone has been given a spirit which is designed to be the dwelling place of his Almighty Creator; this distinguishing characteristic resembling the shrine, the most holy place of the Tabernacle, in which was manifested the Shechinah, the visible token of God's presence and indwelling. It is in his | John iv. 24.

Zech. xii. 1.

1 Thess. v. 23.

spirit that man, even now, by faith lays hold of and apprehends the deep things of God.

That the doctrine of materialism is false and un-scriptural must be admitted, since man cannot evolve mind — and much less spirit — out of matter. To this effect the Scripture testifies: "There is a spirit "in man: and the inspiration of the Almighty "giveth them understanding." It is in the *spirit* that the mighty forces of intelligence and volition are primarily discerned, and from which action emanates. The power of God, who is a Spirit, is seen in the creation of matter, which is a great mystery; for matter is not inherently eternal, seeing that it was created, and therefore had a beginning. GOD only is uncreated and eternal. But, in forming man, God gave the pre-eminence to spirit and mind in their relation to matter, and also power over it, although the spirit in man acts through an inter-mediate instrumentality. What is the power by which we move or speak? Is it not by our spirit, the autocrat, who keeps his court in the innermost shrine? On every side are seen the triumphs of spirit and of mind over matter. The stupendous edifice of a Gothic cathedral affords practical proof that the hand of man is the efficient instrument in its construction, that matter is a secondary though necessary element, and that the conceptive genius of mind and the action of spirit direct the workmen by whom the temple is built, and each stone laid in its allotted position.

Unless the spiritual exercise of the divine volition is believed and accepted, neither a right apprehension

Job xxxii. 8.

nor an exalted view of the power of God can be obtained.   And if by His will God can create matter, He can likewise modify or destroy it without the intervention of any instrumentality.   Can the mind of man conceive the will of God, in its terrible energy, crushing a planet or reducing a globe to ashes?   David said, "Twice have I heard **Psa. lxii. 11.** "this; that power belongeth unto God."

As God, and God only, can *create*, so God only can raise the dead, and this marvel must be wrought by the power of the Holy Ghost.   Wherefore, if the Spirit of God can raise the dead, He can also change the living into the Lord's likeness, and remove both from the earth to meet the Lord in the air. No other power in heaven or on earth can effect this; so that resurrection, change, and translation are three salient acts in which the power of the Holy Spirit over matter is about to be exemplified in the case of the Church of God.

(3.) We next proceed to consider the *mode* of the Holy Spirit's action in effecting the change of the bodies of the living saints into the image of the heavenly and their translation, together with the risen saints, to meet the Lord in the air.   And it will be found that the divine act in bringing to pass this marvel of divine power may be expected to be in strict analogy with the previous work of the Holy Ghost in quickening the spirits of those who are in Christ, that work being then extended to their bodies also.   What is the general law of the action of the Holy Ghost in reference to His working in the change and translation of the saints?

G

Is it not a just and reverent conclusion that the
Holy Ghost will quicken the bodies of the saints
not as an external influence but as an *internal power ?*

Acts x. 44-46.   Although, as is seen in the case of Cornelius, the
actings of God the Holy Ghost are not limited to
the ordinances which God Himself has instituted,
nevertheless it is the truth that, as a general rule,
our first reception of the Holy Ghost is by the grace
of God in holy baptism, when, through the omnipotent action of the divine Spirit, our spirits are
regenerated with the resurrection life of Christ.
This is the seed, the germ of eternal life, which,
having been implanted in our spirits, should develop
to the sanctifying of the whole man, until the seed
thus implanted receives its fulness of growth in
resurrection, or in the change without death; for
the Holy Spirit, having quickened this eternal life
in our spirits in baptism, will, if unimpeded, so
develop this life that in due time He shall quicken
our mortal bodies also by His own indwelling life

Psa. xxxvi. 9. and power. Is He not the "fountain of life" whence
must flow all manifestations of spiritual life, which
culminate in resurrection and eternal glory? Wherefore, the very possibility of our translation lies in
the fact of our being already partakers of the life of
Christ, so that translation becomes not the miraculous
but the normal and triumphant outcome of that en-
grafted life, and itself receives its crown in transfiguration. "The last triumph of the Spirit will be
the full transfiguration of the body itself into the
image of Christ. Nor is this change to be regarded
as something wrought upon the body in the way

simply of outward or foreign power, as though a
stone were transformed suddenly into a winged bird.
The glorification of the believer's body is the result
of the same process which sanctifies his soul."*

In short, is not this the conclusion of the whole
matter, that the resurrection, change, and translation
of Christians are the *consummation* of the work of
the Holy Spirit in them, and that this work has its
origin in the great mystery of the taking of the
manhood into God in the Incarnation of God the
Son? Not that the members of Christ will ever
become deified, though they be made partakers of
a divine nature. The difference between the Divine
Head and the human members must ever remain
one of *personality*. For whereas, in the Incarnation,
a divine Person took upon Himself the nature of
man, human persons, in regeneration, are made
partakers of the nature of God.

These thoughts lead up to the conclusion that
there is nothing transcendental, or mad, in the idea
of the translation — as the world in its unbelief
considers it to be. For why should not the Holy
Spirit, operating at first in the spiritual centre of
man's being, and then saturating the soul with
heavenly life, proceed to assert such mastery over
the body also, that it will no longer remain a slave
or a tyrant, but will become an instrument responsive
to the working of the indwelling Spirit? Thus the
Holy Ghost, dwelling in the recesses of the inner
man, shall in the resurrection and in the change shine

2 Pet. i. 4,
R.V.

* Note at the end of *The True Definition of the Church.*
1858.

forth (as the lamps hidden in the pitchers of Gideon and his followers, after they were broken), with the result that the body will become spiritual and heavenly, and be no longer animal or psychical. As "our God " is a consuming fire," this change will be the final and perfect manifestation of the purifying power of the Holy Spirit in man, in triumphing over the body of mortality, in fashioning it into a spiritual body and transfiguring it into the image of the risen and glorified Christ. Then the qualities of etherealism, incorruptibility, and supernatural motion will be communicated to the body together with liberation from the pre-existing laws of matter which had trammelled it in the mortal condition. The first result of this inworking of the Spirit will be to effect a conscious change in those who are accounted worthy of it, for the throb of an immortal life will assure them that they have been changed. The new life will permeate their whole being and cause them to experience the swallowing up of death in victory—"this corruptible" (in the case of the holy sleepers) having "put on incorruption," and "this mortal" (in the case of the living saints) having "put on immortality." The living saints who attain this prize shall be so filled with the Holy Ghost, that their bodies shall at once put on incorruption without passing through the deep degradation involved in death.

In this world, the action of gravitation is to draw material bodies downwards towards the centre to the earth; but when changed from mortality into immortality, the saints shall no longer be bound by

Heb. xii. 29.

See 1 Cor. xv. 42-49.

1 Cor. xv. 54.

this law; for, in the new and spiritual creation, another power of attraction will draw them upwards to the centre of the universe, even to the throne of God and of the Lamb. The natural law of that regenerate or resurrection life is to rise from the earth upward to God, and so may be said to include or involve translation. This translation is a normal action following the law of the new, spiritual, and heavenly life. An illustration of this is afforded by the burnt offering under the Law. The Hebrew word "alah," which is used for it two hundred and sixty eight times, means neither "burnt" nor "offering," but literally, "that which goes up." Moreover, in the case of the burnt offering, the condition of the flesh was entirely changed. It had to be consumed by fire, for it was contrary to nature for the flesh to ascend; but after it had undergone the change caused by the action of the fire, an upward tendency became, as it were, the law of its being—its *fumes* ascending to God as a sweet savour. This idea of change through the action of fire brings before us in a type that which will come upon those who shall be changed by the Holy Ghost into the spiritual and immortal condition, and who, on receiving a baptism of fire, shall be filled to overflowing with the Spirit of God. By this change our bodies will then become luminous and glorified, being fashioned like unto the glorious body of our Lord Jesus Christ; and the words of our Lord will be fulfilled: "Then " shall the righteous shine forth as the sun in the " kingdom of their Father."

See Phil. iii. 21.

Matt. xiii. 43.

The truth here enforced is this: that the change and the translation are the ultimate results of the indwelling and inworking of the Holy Ghost: and the raising of the dead, the change of the living from mortality to immortality, and the rapture of both in one body to meet the Lord in the air, should be regarded as due to the normal, and not to any abnormal action of the same Spirit, the Lord and Life-giver. That same Holy Spirit, who is in Christ and in the members of His mystical Body, maintains their living union, until this union, from being a heavenly mystery, becomes an accomplished visible fact, in Christ descending from heaven, and in His saints ascending to meet Him in the air.

Though the change about to be effected by the Holy Ghost in the faithful among the Baptized has been principally dwelt upon in this chapter, yet it must be remembered that all the exhibitions of divine glory hitherto manifested in man are the work of the Holy Ghost. Although in the time of Moses the Holy Ghost was not yet given, and, strictly speaking, did not dwell *in* man, still, it is recorded that the skin of Moses' face shone so brightly 2 Cor. iii. 7. from his communion with God, that the children of Israel could not stedfastly behold his countenance; and this must have been due to the action of the Spirit of God. When the Lord Jesus Christ, who had received the Spirit without measure, was transfigured on the mount, even whilst in mortal flesh like unto our own, it was the Holy Ghost who beamed forth from Him, having altered the fashion Luke ix. 29. of His countenance, as He prayed. Again, when

Stephen, the Christian protomartyr, appeared before
the hostile Jewish Sanhedrim, his face appeared to
the stedfast onlookers as it had been the face of an
angel, and it is twice recorded that Stephen was
"full of the Holy Ghost." It is the same Spirit
who is the Author of transfiguration and of ultimate
glorification, whether it be in Christ or in His
saints; for, when the Lord ascended into heaven
and reached the presence of the Father, He became
the glorified Man by virtue of the indwelling Spirit
of glory, by whom He had been raised from the
dead, and through the reception after His ascension
of that glory which, as God, He had with the
Father before the world was, and of which He had
divested Himself on His assumption of human
nature. Thus glorified, He appeared to His surviving apostle John in Patmos. Therefore it is that
the glory of these great acts is rightly ascribed to
God the Holy Ghost. It remains, however, to be
added that, after the firstfruits have been raised
or changed they may not appear at once in the full
glory of the first resurrection, but may have to
await the perfecting of the *whole Church*. Moreover, the resurrection or change of the firstfruits
may precede by some time their rapture. We read
that the two witnesses, after their resurrection,
"stood upon their feet," and thus waited in the
presence of their enemies for the call to ascend.
And as regards the general hope, the dead in
Christ rise *first*, and afterwards "we which are
"alive and remain" are "caught up together with
"them." Others have to be prepared to carry on

Acts vi. 15.

Acts vi. 5.
Acts vii. 55.

Rev. xi. 11, 12

the testimony, and these are necessary links between
those who go before and those who follow after—
Ex. xxvi. 1-6 even as the golden hooks and the blue loops on the
edges or selvedge of the curtains of the Tabernacle
connected them with each other.   Nevertheless, the
glory of the resurrection condition is *in* the raised
or changed saints, though it may not be manifested
at once in them, as also it was not in the case of
the risen Lord Himself during the forty days succeeding His resurrection.   Thus from the examples
which we have cited we learn that there may be a
visible glory *without* immortality, and a veiled glory
with immortality, both being due to the action of
the Holy Spirit of God.

It is to be feared that the great fact of the Holy
Ghost *dwelling in the Baptized* is not sufficiently
realized by the majority of Christians; for too many
do not apprehend the distinctive glory of the Christian
dispensation.   It is not the forgiveness of sins; it
is not the assurance of personal salvation; it is not
the hope of everlasting life.   These blessings might
be and were attained in the former dispensations,
and assuredly they are not withheld from us in this
era of peculiar grace, in the dispensation of the
Spirit.   But there is a " glory that excelleth," and
that is our *personal inhabitation by God*.   The covenant
of God with the Baptized is not only that He is to
be *with them*, but also that He is to be *in them*—yea,
2 Cor. vi. 16. to dwell in them according to His promise: "I will
" dwell in them, and walk in them."   But great and
wonderful as this privilege is, it is not all that is
involved in the glory that excelleth; of this the

climax is something far higher, for this indwelling
of God is not vouchsafed to Christian men merely
as individual solitary units, but as members of the
one grand fellowship of the Body of Christ. Wherefore, we should not look upon our bodies as so many
separate temples of God, even though we be, both   1 Cor. iii. 16.
individually and collectively, the temple of the Holy
Ghost; but we should regard ourselves as members
of the One, Holy, Catholic, and Apostolic Church,
the household of God, the Body of Christ, the temple
of the Holy Ghost. In this Body the Spirit of God
dwells, and manifests His glory in those gifts and
ministries which are bestowed on the different members for the profit of all.

As regards the details of the translation, or the
means for carrying it out, no conjectures are hazarded,
for this is beyond the compass of the mind of man,
and is still among the hidden things of God. His
ways and manner of working are past finding out,
and only such glimpses of His presence can be
obtained as He is pleased to reveal. His working
is certain not to be according to the forecast of our
finite minds; therefore all constructing of systems
and mapping out of future events should be avoided,
and it should suffice us to take heed to our Lord's
warning to watch and pray, that that day may not
come upon us unawares and as a snare. Although
the translation—like some of the other great mysteries
of God—is beyond our comprehension or power to
explain, it is nevertheless a glorious hope that we
should accept and rejoice in by faith,—that faith
which giveth us the "victory that overcometh the   1 John v. 4, 5.

" world," which is obtained by him " that believeth
" that Jesus is the Son of God."

A practical question arises from the contemplation
of this solemn yet joyful subject, and that is: If
the Holy Ghost be the Author of these wondrous
results in us, both now and hereafter, and if His
work be so essential to our salvation and sanctification, should not we, who have been baptized into
Christ, give earnest heed to St. Paul's admonition,
written in his earliest epistle, "Quench not the
" Spirit"?   It is certain that none of us can really
cherish this unworldly and heavenly hope of translation without the presence and grace of the Holy
Ghost, nor can we attain to its realization without His
indwelling power, first in our spirits, and souls or
minds, and finally in our mortal bodies.

I Thess. v. 19

While the glory of the Christian dispensation is
apparent in the gift and indwelling of the Holy
Ghost, so will the judgment of Babylon, or apostate
Christendom, be manifest in that fearful and evil
day, when the Spirit of God shall no longer strive
with man, but, having been quenched, shall withdraw
Himself from the earth. Then shall come inconceivable sorrow and tribulation; for godless men,
being left to themselves and bereft of the Spirit,
shall give themselves up to work iniquity and become
exposed to the storm of the wrath and righteous
indignation of God. From this fearful experience,
from this time of anguish and misery, good Lord,
deliver us!

Psa. xxviii. 9.

O Lord, " save thy people, ... and lift
" them up for ever."   ·

CHAPTER V.

Scriptural Examples of Translation of the Living: Enoch and Elijah.

Is it an incredible thing to say that translation is not a mere theory, nor an abstract idea, but that, by the mercy of God, it has become a *reality*, when there are two cases of translation enshrined in Holy Scripture for our encouragement and meditation? It is there recorded that two men did not die—only two among the thousands of millions who have lived on the earth. One was translated during the Patriarchal, the other during the Mosaic, dispensation. A brief reference has already been made to these two cases of translation; but they deserve careful consideration in all their details by those who are entertaining the hope of being changed into the likeness of the Lord, and translated into the future kingdom of God without seeing death.

I. The first case is that of *Enoch*. It is recorded in the fifth chapter of Genesis with the utmost brevity. "And Enoch lived sixty and five years, "and begat Methuselah: and Enoch walked with "God after he begat Methuselah three hundred "years, and begat sons and daughters: and all the "days of Enoch were three hundred sixty and five "years: and Enoch walked with God: and he was   Gen. v. 21-24.

" not; for God took him." Twice it is here stated
that "Enoch walked with God." On this there
is a short commentary in the epistle to the Hebrews.

Heb. xi. 5. " By faith Enoch was translated that he should
" not see death; and was not found, because God
" had translated him: for before his translation he
" had this testimony, that he pleased God." * Enoch
was the son of Jared, and the father of Methuselah.
He was translated at the age of three hundred and
sixtyfive years, which was young for an antediluvian,
and he was the only representative of the Patriarchal
dispensation to whom this exceptional privilege
was granted.

The first point that deserves investigation is the
character of Enoch. Its analysis brings, in the first
instance, into prominent relief his singular *faith*.
This is the feature singled out by the inspired writer
of the epistle to the Hebrews. Enoch comes second
in that grand roll of the heroes of faith—Abel, the
protomartyr being the first. "By faith Enoch was
"translated that he should not see death." This
great honour, even his exemption from death, is
ascribed to his faith; and, looking at the context,
it is evident that his faith was in the living God
and in His promises; for we read—"But without

Heb. xi. 6. " faith it is impossible to please him: for he that
" cometh to God must believe that he is, and that
" he is a rewarder of them that diligently seek him."
We are not told whether Enoch had any idea of
the way in which the reward of his faith would

---

* "Pleased God" is the rendering given by the Septuagint for the expression "walked with God," in Gen. v. 24.

come; but as "the secret of the Lord is with them Psa. xxv. 14.
"that fear him" *(cf.* Amos iii. 7), it is credible that
Enoch may have had some premonition of his
translation, that he laid hold of it by faith, and
that he pleaded for the grace and preparedness of
spirit indispensable to its attainment.

Besides faith, Enoch exercised *diligence.* He was
one who, for three centuries, diligently sought the
Lord. "Diligence," from its Latin derivation, implies *activity springing from love.* We do a thing
heartily when we love to do it; and so, with an
earnestness flowing out of love, Enoch sought God
because he loved God. He sought the presence,
the companionship, the guidance of God; and so
God was not only found of him, but was proved
to be the rewarder of those who diligently seek Him.
The Greek word (τοῖς ἐκζητοῦσιν) brings out a latent
beauty; for the true force of the verb used is *to
seek out*, the adverb "out" implying labour, zeal Heb. xi. 6.
and diligence in seeking for the precious treasure.
Hence, diligence should be a marked feature in the
conduct of those who desire the change without
death, and subsequent translation.

Combined with this diligence or earnestness flowing out of love, the patient continuance of Enoch
in well-doing is apparent, for he walked with God
for three hundred years. Our lives rarely extend,
as the Psalmist writes, to fourscore years; but very
few men could claim to have walked with God
uninterruptedly from their birth to their death, hence
the record of this patriarch who walked with God for
the space of three hundred years is most exceptional.

If, as it would appear, Enoch was converted to
God at the age of sixty five, the first portion of
his life may have resembled that of the generality
of men, or at least it may not have been up to its
subsequent standard of purity and devotion; for
the Scripture distinctly states that, *after* he begat
Methuselah at the age of sixty five, he walked with
God three hundred years, and was translated at the
age of three hundred and sixty five years. Now,
what does walking with God imply? The answer
may be given in the words of the prophet Amos—
"Can two walk together, except they be agreed?"
It implies constant companionship and intimate
intercourse. Enoch was of the same mind with God;
he loved what God loved, and hated what God hated;
in a word, he was a holy man, a saint of God.*

In applying the description given in Hebrews xi. 6
to Enoch's character and conduct, it may be concluded that, as he is the person alluded to in the
previous verse, he was not only a man of faith but
also a man of prayer and devotion, so that he pleased
God. He "was translated that he should not see
"death. This, it is stated, was his *reward*, and it
gives the explanation of the brief statement in the
book of Genesis, that "he was not, for God took
"him." "By faith he was translated"; so that the
power by which he was able to walk with God

Amos iii. 3.
cf. 2 Cor. vi.
14-18.

Heb. xi. 5.

* The paraphrase of the Palestine Targum is as follows :—
'And Hanok worshipped (or served) in truth before the
"Lord. And Hanok served in the truth before the Lord;
"and, behold, he was not with the sojourners of the earth,
"for he was withdrawn, and he ascended to the firmament
"by the word of the Lord."

and to please God was the same as that by which
he attained to translation.

Bearing in mind the translation of Enoch, the
allusion to him in the New Testament is the more
interesting from his recorded prophecy of the second
coming of the Lord. St. Jude writes: "And Enoch   Jude, 14, 15.
" also, the seventh from Adam, prophesied of these,
" saying, Behold, the Lord cometh with ten thousands
" of his saints, to execute judgment upon all, and
" to convince all that are ungodly among them of
" all their ungodly deeds which they have ungodly
" committed, and of all their hard speeches which
" ungodly sinners have spoken against him."* Thus
the patriarch Enoch was a prophet, and the subject
of his witness was the coming of the Lord as King
and Judge; and the denunciation of future judgment
upon the ungodly. It would appear that he must
have been—as was Noah subsequently—a preacher of
righteousness in an ungodly age; and he would
doubtless be subjected to the scorn and persecution
of the unbelieving sinners by whom he was surrounded; for, before the flood, the earth was filled
with violence and iniquity. Trials and difficulties,
such as fall to the lot of all men in this present
mortal life, must have been experienced by Enoch,
but probably special trials accompanied the faithful
testimony which he bore to those around him, not
only by his consistent and righteous manner of life
in walking with God—which would involve the
observance of all the external duties of religion in
worship and sacrifice—but also by his verbal protest

* See Appendix III.

against a world of ungodly sinners. It is evident, from St. Jude's statement, that the ungodly deeds and hard speeches of sinners against God abounded: in other words, it was an age of unrighteousness, of unbelief, of blasphemy, of swearing, of murmuring; an age in which mankind displayed the characteristics which St. Paul applies to the heathen in the opening chapter of his epistle to the Romans. Against all this Enoch must have given his witness; and, though the account of him is so brief, yet, together with his prophecy of the coming of the Lord with myriads of His saints to execute vengeance upon wilful sinners, it cannot be doubted that he uttered at the same time a call to repentance.

It is worthy of note that this preacher, this prophet —the earliest on record in the dim past—announced the coming of the Lord, and, by implication, the resurrection of the dead and the change of the living in the case of the ten thousands of saints whom the Lord should bring with Him.*

Enoch was living amongst adversaries, enemies of that God with whom he walked; and his righteous soul, like that of Lot in Sodom in later times, would

---

* The initial doctrine of a first resurrection may be contained in the prophecy of Enoch—"Behold the Lord cometh *with* ten thousands of his saints." Whence does the Lord get this army of holy ones if not by resurrection? And since there are men upon the earth for whose judgment these come, how can the truth of a *first* resurrection be evaded? It does not affect the argument that this prophecy of Enoch is mentioned only by St. Jude, for it must have been known by others, and must have been an accepted tradition in the time of St. Jude.

be vexed with the filthy conversation of the wicked. It is therefore improbable that Enoch would have received any different treatment from that which the saints of God have always suffered at the hands of a scoffing and unbelieving world. St. Paul, referring to the case of Isaac and Ishmael, lays it down as an abiding experience, that "as then he that was born Gal. iv. 29. " after the flesh persecuted him that was born after " the Spirit, even so it is now." St. Paul, in like manner, admonished the ardent Timothy—"Yea, " and all that will live godly in Christ Jesus shall 2 Tim. iii. 12. " suffer persecution." Our Lord speaks to the same effect: " In the world ye shall have tribulation." John xvi. 33.

The wicked have always felt that the life of a righteous man, with higher aims and hopes than their own, implying condemnation of their unlawful deeds—as did the lives of Enoch, Noah, Lot, and Daniel—is a witness too burdensome to be tolerated. This suggests the question: Was Enoch's translation an escape from the dangers by which he was surrounded? If it was, then his rapture was a particular mark of the divine favour, conveyed by the unprecedented reward of exemption from the pains of death.

That translation was then an unheard-of thing on the earth is evident from the special remark in connection with Enoch, that "God took him." Until they recognized that the Lord had done a new thing, the tidings would probably be received by his circle of acquaintances with scorn and incredulity. Nevertheless, to the antediluvian age, his sudden disappearance was a testimony of future

H

immortality, as was Elijah's to his age, and as the
ascension of the risen Christ is to our own.   Thus
Enoch's manner of life and the wonderful reward
which he received, should encourage those saints
who, in these last days of the history of the Church
and of the world, are diligently seeking the Lord,
and looking and praying for a similar reward.

II. The second example of translation recorded
in Holy Scripture, is that of the prophet *Elijah*.   As
more than two thousand years had elapsed since
Enoch was translated in the antediluvian era, the
memory of it may have become dim, being obscured
by vague tradition or myth.   But the time had come
when God would again vindicate His covenant, and
by the translation of Elijah, give witness to apostate
Israel and to all living under the Mosaic dispensation, that He is ever the same God,—the living
God of Israel.

Before considering the actual translation of Elijah,
his previous history must be adverted to, for there
are more details given of his life, with its varied
experiences, trials, and difficulties, than there are of
the life of Enoch.   There are many points which
excite a peculiar interest; such as Elijah's sudden
appearance without any concurrent mention of his
parentage, his relations with king Ahab, his prayer
and sacrifice on mount Carmel, his slaughter of the
priests of Baal, his flight from queen Jezebel, his
journey to mount Horeb, and his denunciation of
king Ahaziah.   Elijah had, like Enoch and Noah,
to bear witness against the prevailing wickedness
with which he was surrounded; yea, he had to

reprove even kings for the Lord's sake. Elijah
bore witness against the despot Ahab, especially in
the matter of the spoliation and murder of Naboth;
he excited the wrath of the idolatrous queen Jezebel;
he reproved the whole nation of Israel, as well as
Ahaziah, the king of Israel. From his whole
history it would seem to be a law of God's providential dealings with men that those who attain to the
highest rewards in His kingdom are called upon to
do an exceptional work of witness, involving special
trials and self-sacrifice during their time of probation.
The persecutions which Elijah endured were many
and great. Being in imminent peril of his life, after
his unique sacrifice on mount Carmel, he fled into
the wilderness from the revengeful pursuit of Jezebel;
and so many had been the martyrdoms inflicted at
her instigation upon the worshippers of Jehovah,
that Elijah supposed that all the prophets of the
Lord had been slain, and that he was the only
prophet who survived in Israel. In this spirit he
answers the Lord twice to the same effect: "And
" he said, I have been very jealous for the LORD
" God of hosts: for the children of Israel have
" forsaken thy covenant, thrown down thine altars,
" and slain thy prophets with the sword; and I,
" even I only, am left; and they seek my life, to
" take it away." But the Lord reproved the prophet,
revealing to him that He had seven thousand hidden
saints in Israel even at that time, who had not bowed
the knee to Baal. It seems strange that, after the
boldness which Elijah had displayed on Carmel,
such depression and weakness should come over him

Psa. cv. 14.

1 Kings xix. 10.

1 Kings xix.
10, 14, 18.

1 Kings xix. 4.
that "he requested for himself that he might die;
" and said, It is enough; now, O LORD, take away
" my life; for I am not better than my fathers."
But the Lord pitied the weakness of His servant,
for, as in the case of Moses, He relieved him of part
1 Kings xix. 16.
of his burden, and told him to go and anoint Elisha
to be a prophet in his stead. Again, shortly before
2 Kings i. 9.13.
his translation, it would seem as if Elijah's life were
in danger from Ahaziah, king of Israel, who sent
several companies of fifty men to take him, yet his
translation can hardly be regarded as a literal
escape from threatened death, as shall be the trans-
Luke xxi. 36.
cf, Rev. iii. 10.
lation of those who shall "be accounted worthy
" to escape all these things that shall come to
" pass." Had the rapture of the prophet taken place
shortly after the events on mount Carmel, when
Jezebel threatened his life, it might have been interpreted in this light; but, as it was after this that
the episode on mount Horeb occurred, the prophet's
translation must have taken place some years later,
since it occurred after the death of Ahaziah, the
son of Ahab.

After a life full of trials, the day approached when
Elijah was to be taken up into heaven; and an interesting account is given of his last earthly journey
2 Kings ii. 1.11
with his minister, Elisha.

(1.) They started from Gilgal, which is specially
associated with the Israelites as their first halting
place in the promised land after the capture of
Jericho, when the nation here renewed their covenant of circumcision after the wilderness parenthesis,
and when the Lord Himself declared that the

reproach of Egypt had thus been rolled away.* Josh. v. 9. From a spiritual point of view, this would indicate the recalling of the Baptized to their baptismal covenant with its obligations and privileges, this being the necessary starting point in any true spiritual revival in the Church, such as can lead on to the attainment of translation.

(2.) The second place they reached was Beth-el, the spot hallowed by Jacob's vision. It was the Gen. xxviii. 12-22. place where Jacob anointed the stone on which he had slept, calling it the house of God and the gate of heaven, and where the patriarch renewed his vows for the payment of tithes to the Lord. The meaning of "Beth-el" is the house of God, and spiritually these occurrences speak to us of the ordinances of the Lord's house, of worship, of anointing with the Holy Ghost, of prophetic visions, and of the obligation of tithes in the Christian Church.

(3.) The third place they came to was Jericho. Jericho had been captured in a miraculous manner on the entrance of the Israelites into the promised land, and it was said of it, "the city shall be accursed, Jos. vi. 17. even it, and all that are therein, to the LORD." Hence it was a city of destruction; yet it was noted for its pleasant situation, its bitter water, and those palm trees which gave it the name of "the city of Deut. xxxiv. 3.

---

* Some think that this is another Gilgal higher up in the mountains, than Gilgal which was in the plain of Jericho, because of the expression, 2 Kings ii. 2, " They went down " [from Gilgal] to Beth-el." (See *Smith's Dictionary of the Bible*—Article, Gilgal, 2.) Gesenius however accepts the ordinary site of Gilgal.

palms." The fate of Jericho symbolizes that of the spiritual Babylon, which is to be destroyed; whilst Isa xxv. its palm trees set forth a ministry which will go forth in power to deliver the Church in the last Rev. vii. 9-17. days, and ultimately the "great multitude" of the saved also, who come out of the "great tribulation" with palms in their hands, and in token of victory, wave them before the throne of God.

(4.) The two prophets next descend from Jericho to the river Jordan, which Elijah smites with his mantle, and they go over *dryshod*, and reach the territory of Reuben, on the other side of Jordan. Jordan has long been an acknowledged type of death; so that in the dividing of the river and the going over dryshod, a type is afforded of victory over death, of the change into immortality without death, and of subsequent translation. The river Psa. cxiv. 5. Jordan, which "was driven back," reminds us of the passage of the ark of the covenant through its divided waters. Its waters may also point to repentance and confession of sin, seeing that it was the place of John's baptism, and that these acts are necessary precursors of deliverance to be wrought by God; and from this point of view it should be noted that, in the journey of the Israelites, the crossing of the Jordan preceded their arrival at Gilgal.

This remarkable journey which Elijah and Elisha made before their solemn parting, was sevenfold in 2 Kings ii. 1-11. its stages, as may be gathered from Holy Scripture. 1, They set out from Gilgal; 2, they went down to Beth-el; 3, they came to Jericho; 4, they two went on (*i.e.*, from Jericho into the plain, the modern

Ghor); 5, they reached the bank of the river and stood by Jordan; 6, they went over the Jordan on dry ground; 7, "they still went on." At length an eighth stage was reached, but by Elijah alone; when, by his translation into the invisible world, he entered as it were upon a new octave in his journey. For as they still went on and talked, there suddenly appeared a chariot of fire and horses of fire, which parted them both asunder, and Elijah was caught up from the side of Elisha by a whirlwind into heaven. The inspired account is as follows:—
"And it came to pass, as they still went on, and talked, that, behold, there appeared a chariot of fire, and horses of fire, and parted them both asunder; and Elijah went up by a whirlwind into heaven. And Elisha saw it, and he cried, My father, my father, the chariot of Israel, and the horsemen thereof. And he saw him no more: and he took hold of his own clothes, and rent them in two pieces." It may be that king Joash referred to this event when, weeping over Elisha on his deathbed, he exclaimed: "O my "father, my father, the chariot of Israel, and the "horsemen thereof." *2 Kings ii. 11, 12.* *2 Kings xiii. 14.*

Thus the Lord vouchsafed to His faithful servant the great reward of translation, thereby proving Himself in the case of Elijah, as in that of Enoch, to be the rewarder of those who diligently seek Him. Truly the ways of God are as far above the ways *See Isa. lv. 9.* of man as the heavens are high above the earth; for, whereas Elijah asked that he might die, the Lord gave him exemption from death, with life more abundantly; and therefore, in this result, he was better than his fathers. This event occurred under the legal dispensation, and so far as we know, no other example of translation occurred during its course.

There is a particular interest attaching to Elisha as an eye-witness of the translation of Elijah, and Elijah laid great stress on the necessity of Elisha *seeing* his translation as the condition for the reception by him of a double portion of the same Spirit.

2 Kings ii. 9, 10.
"And it came to pass, when they were gone over, that Elijah said unto Elisha, Ask what I shall do for thee, before I be taken away from thee. And Elisha said, I pray thee, let a double portion of thy spirit be upon me. And he said, Thou hast asked a hard thing: nevertheless, if thou see me when I am taken from thee, it shall be so unto thee; but if not, it shall not be so."

That the unbelieving children of Beth-el identified Elisha with Elijah's translation is evident, for they mocked the prophet, saying, "Go up, thou bald head;

2 Kings ii. 23.
" go up, thou bald head." This derisive expression may perhaps have been personal mockery at the baldness of the prophet; but more probably they were alluding to the fact that he had been bereft of his official head. Perhaps they had previously known by hearsay that he had been warned of the approaching removal of his master from his head; and now, in tones of contempt and unbelief, they bade him perform the same marvel, and rise into the air and be carried up into heaven. This may have been their meaning in the taunt, "Go up, thou bald head," in which case it was the mockery of unbelief in the translation of

Elijah into heaven, and evinced contempt for God's chosen witness to that great act of almighty power.

There is one peculiar feature in the narrative which merits attention, namely, that the fact of Elijah's impending removal or translation was known beforehand. How could this be? It could only have been by revelation from God Himself. Elijah knew it; Elisha knew it; and the sons of the prophets at Beth-el and at Jericho knew it; for they addressed Elisha in these words: " Knowest thou that the 2 Kings ii. 3. " LORD will take away thy master from thy head " to-day?" The emphasis in the original Hebrew is on the word " to-day." " And he said, Yea, " I know it [or, I also know it]; hold ye your peace." Many interesting questions are suggested here as to the schools of the prophets, their organization, and studies, and the revelations they received, which are not strictly relevant to this subject. The following remarks, however, from *The Speaker's Commentary* are apposite: " Clearly, independent revelations had been made to the two ' schools ' at Beth-el and at Jericho, and also to Elisha, with respect to Elijah's coming removal. But it is not clear that even Elisha knew his master was to be ' *translated.*' "

Should not we then, who have been baptized into Christ, hope and pray that, when the Lord is about graciously to fulfil His promise to give this great reward of translation to some in the Christian Church, He may vouchsafe to His Church some intimation of the coming event. For surely our standing in Christ Jesus and our spiritual Christian privileges are greater than were those of the sons of the

prophets at Beth-el or at Jericho, B.C. 900; therefore
we have every encouragement to cherish the hope
that some premonition will be given to the Church
of what God is about to do; according to His distinct
Amos iii, 7. promise through the prophet Amos: "Surely the
" Lord GOD will do nothing, but he revealeth his
" secret unto his servants the prophets."

As observed already, nothing is known of the details
of Enoch's translation; nothing more is recorded than
that " He was not; for God took him ": whereas, in
the case of Elijah, we read of a " chariot of fire, and
" horses of fire," and that " Elijah went up by a
" whirlwind into heaven."   Here the two great
symbols of the Spirit—wind and fire—are conjoined.
They are the same which were manifested on the
day of Pentecost, when the Holy Ghost was given;
so that it may be confidently maintained that the
Holy Ghost was the Divine Agent; by whom Elijah's
body must have been made capable of sustaining the
rapture by a whirlwind into heaven.

From the narrative of the translation of Elijah,
Christians by common consent, and apparently in
all ages, have held that his rapture was by means
of a fiery chariot, but they do not lay sufficient stress
2 Kings ii. 1-11 upon the statement that " Elijah went up by a whirl-
" wind into heaven."   The chariot and horses of
fire suddenly appeared and parted Elijah and Elisha
asunder, whence it may be concluded that Elijah
must have been instantaneously caught up into the
chariot by a supernatural power; but the fact which
the Scripture emphasizes in connection with the chariot
and horses of fire, the action of a *whirlwind*, is some-

what overlooked. There is nothing contradictory in
attributing the rapture of Elijah to the twofold agency
of the fiery chariot and horses, and of the whirlwind;
both seem to have been necessary factors in his sudden
translation from earth to heaven; and it may be that
the rapture of the saints will be effected in like manner
by a similar twofold action: first by the power of the
Spirit of God, and, secondly, by the instrumentality
of the holy angels and the chariots and the horses
of fire. In the Book of Canticles, or the Song of
Solomon, which is prophetic of the experiences of
the Church, it is written: "Or ever I was aware,
" my soul set me among the chariots of my princely
" people." *cf.* 2 Kings vi. 17.

Cant. vi. 12 (R.V.)

What, we may ask, was the reason or rationale
of the translation without death of Enoch and
Elijah? Their translation would, in each case, be a
signal testimony to the existence of the living
God to the generations, not to say to the dispensations in which Enoch and Elijah respectively
lived. Occurring as they did at great intervals—
some two thousand years elapsing from Enoch to
Elijah, and nearly three thousand years from Elijah
to the present date (A.D. 1904)—they were marked
evidences of the interposition of God in the affairs
of men, as well as of His divine care for the preservation and recompense of His saints, and they would
encourage the faithful in the assurance that God
was a rewarder of those who diligently sought Him
and kept His commandments. The translation of those
two saints would also be a reminder of the existence
of the spiritual and invisible world, of the hope of a

future life, each translation being a fresh protest
on behalf of God, against a forgetful and unbelieving
world, and against the sentence of death which man
had brought upon himself. They would also furnish
historical types to the Christian Church of what the
Lord would do in the latter days; so that these two
cases of translation, one from each previous dispensation, might be a pattern to those who, according
to the revelation and promise of the Lord, shall
rejoice in the same hope in the last days.

Many interesting questions arise when we consider
the condition of the translated and the place to which
they were removed. In considering these problems,
we must not give way to speculation, but must adhere
to Holy Scripture, which is our only trustworthy
record, and on which we are dependent for our
knowledge of these supernatural events.

Enoch and Elijah were mortal men of like passions
with ourselves, but they were translated by God from
earth to heaven; the question therefore arises—Into
what condition and into what sphere or place were
they introduced by this act of God?

It is evident from the brief account of Enoch in
the Book of Genesis—"He was not; for God took
"him"—and from that in the New Testament—he
"was translated that he should not see death"—that
he did not die. As the inspired record tells us that
he has not died, we cannot doubt that he is kept
alive by the power of God, awaiting the development
of the divine purpose, and a further measure of life
and of the glory that is to be revealed.

There are no details given as to the place

Gen. v. 24.

Heb. xi. 5.

to which Enoch was translated. And after his translation we hear no more of Enoch. He remained hidden in "the secret place of the Most "High," safe from the power of death. And the fact that he was translated that he should not see death, whilst avouching his attainment of the reward of immortality, does not necessarily imply that his body at once attained to the resurrection condition, but rather that it was supernaturally reserved against that day when Christ having been raised as the Firstfruits of glorified humanity, it should become possible for a like change to pass upon His saints.

Psa. xci. 1.

In Hebrews xi. Enoch appears among the list of worthies of whom it is said, "These *all*, having ob- "tained a good report through faith, *received not the* "*promise* [*i.e.*, in actual possession]: God having "provided [foreseen] some better thing for us, that "they *without us should not be made perfect.*" This word implies the carrying off a prize actually obtained. The perfection here spoken of is evidently that of resurrection, which includes the change of those who are alive and remain unto the coming of the Lord.

Heb. xi. 5, 39, 40.

In the case of Elijah's translation he could not have borne the contact with the supernatural agency of the chariot and horses of fire, and the tremendous force of the whirlwind carrying him up "into heaven" (whatever that may mean), unless some change had suddenly passed over him, in the twinkling of an eye.

Although it is said of Enoch, that "God took him," and of Elijah, "that he went up by a whirlwind into "heaven," it is not said into *which* heaven. St. Paul specifies "the third heaven,"* to which he was caught up, in or out of the body, and to this these saints may possibly have been translated. If God conveyed them to a special place in the heavens, there to await the residue of the changed and translated ones, and to come down with the Lord in the air to meet them, this cannot conflict with the glory of the ascended Christ. Elijah certainly could not enter where Christ, our High Priest, entered on His ascension to heaven—to the right hand of God.

In whatever sphere among the many mansions in the Father's house Elijah may have been kept by the power of God for some eight hundred years, until his wonderful reappearance in the vision on the Holy Mount at the transfiguration of our Lord, it is not to be supposed that he had received an immortal resurrection body any more than Enoch. Nor had he reached the eternal glorified condition, though he now appeared in glory in the vision on the Mount Tabor. He could not have received a fully glorified body before the glorification of God Incarnate, and John vii. 39. at that time Jesus was not yet glorified. Whatever change Elijah underwent when carried up into heaven, it is clear that this change fell short of the ultimate glory to be revealed in the saints.

There are many Jewish traditions in connection with Elijah. By some Christians it is believed that

* The idea of the seventh heaven, a phrase in common parlance, is not a Scriptural revelation, but a Mahommedan conceit. The Scripture speaks of the "heaven of heavens" (1 Kings viii. 27, 2 Chron. vi. 18), and of "the third heaven" (2 Cor. xii. 2), but not of seven heavens.

he will again personally appear on earth before the advent of the Messiah, whilst others have imagined that he will yet suffer martyrdom, and go through the ordeal of death, in order to justify the unbelief of those who assert that all men must die. The following quotation will shew that this opinion has been held in the Church: "Both the Latin and the Greek fathers commonly couple Enoch and Elijah as historic witnesses to a possibility of a resurrection of the body and of a true human existence in glory (Irenæus iv. 5, 1; Tertullian de Resurr. Carn. 58) and the voice of early ecclesiastical tradition is almost unanimous in regarding them as the 'two Rev. xi. 3. ' witnesses' who should fall before 'the beast' and afterwards be raised to heaven before the great judgment. This belief removed a great difficulty which was supposed to attach to their translation; thus it was sought to be made clear that they would at last discharge the common debt of a sinful humanity, from which they were not to be exempted by their glorious removal from the earth."*

The case of Moses is peculiar, and though not a case of translation, still, as he appeared with Elijah on the mount of transfiguration, it has its affinities therewith. Moses, even while in mortal flesh, on his descent from Mount Sinai, had manifested a glory from his communion with God, and his face shone Ex. xxxiv. 29- so that the children of Israel could not stedfastly 35. behold his countenance because of its overpowering 2 Cor. iii. 7-13. brightness; but he had died and had been buried by

* *Smith's Dictionary of the Bible,* Volume I., page 940.

Jude 9. God; and about his body a dispute had arisen between the Archangel Michael and the Devil.*

We have no warrant in Scripture for assuming that Moses had been raised from the dead, and therefore we infer that it was not in an immortal resurrection body that he appeared in the vision with Elijah on the mount. Our Lord, who was transfigured, was still in a mortal body of common humanity, like unto our own in all things—sin only excepted—and as soon as the vision of glory faded from the disciples' sight, He became what He had been before. It was a vision, but a vision of a complex character. It was a revelation by God to the disciples of that which the natural eye could not see. It was a momentary glimpse of heavenly realities invisible to the eye when dimmed by the things of the world, but visible to the spiritual eye illuminated by the Holy Ghost. Our Lord Himself calls the transfiguration *a vision*, and to this definition we adhere, but, in so far as it involved realities, there is no need to suppose that either Moses or Elias, if really present, was in an immortal or resurrection body. This was

Mark ix. 1, 2. a vision of the kingdom of God coming with power,

2 Pet. i. 16. as our Lord declared it to be; a vision " of the power " and coming of our Lord Jesus Christ," but it need

---

* In the *Palestine Exploration Quarterly* for April, 1904, there is the republication of an old book, printed in London A.D. 1657, and which gives an account of the supposed finding of the sepulchre of Moses. It is written in a reverent spirit, and professes to give an account of this discovery as it occurred in 1655, " by certain Maronite Christians who were keeping herds of goats on Mount Nebo, otherwise called the Mountain Abarim."

not have been more than a vision. The Lord's own condition of mortality at the time and the proposal of St. Peter to make three tabernacles for the Lord and for Moses and Elias, are arguments against their having received bodies of immortality.

St. Paul was caught up to the third heaven, and saw 2 Cor. xii. 1-5. and heard much which it is not possible for a man to utter, but he remained mortal, and came back to earth again, and he alludes to it as among "visions " and revelations of the Lord" which he had received. 2 Cor. xii. 1.

It need not however be denied that, through the divine interposition, Moses and Elias were really present on the holy mount foreshadowing the time when the kingdom of God shall come with power, when the King Himself shall be again seen in " his majesty." Moses and Elias might be symbolic 2 Pet. i 16. representatives of the raised and changed saints, who shall come with the Lord at His appearing and kingdom. The correspondence between St. Mark's narrative and the words of St. Peter in his second epistle, is noteworthy, not only for what they state as to the vision of the transfiguration, but as connecting the apostle Peter with St. Mark's Gospel. The vision of the transfiguration was doubtless brief. Jesus was praying, and so may have been kneeling or standing on the ground; so that the two men, Moses and Elias, who stood by Him would also appear on the ground, and not in the air. It is difficult to shake off our preconceived ideas, derived it may be from pictures, like that of Raphael in the Vatican, but those great masterpieces of art are often full of solecisms and unscriptural conceits.

I

We reiterate that there is no authority for saying that Enoch, Elijah or Moses had received their immortal resurrection bodies, and the following reasons may be adduced in support of this hypothesis. Christ is distinctly called the firstborn of every creature, the firstborn from the dead, *the beginning of the creation of God*, the first sample of the new and spiritual eternal and glorified creation of God.* Christ alone possesses immortality. He hath brought life and immortality to light. Before His resurrection from the dead, resurrection life may be said not to have been manifested, although whilst still in mortality the Lord said, "I am the resurrection "and the life." The Lord Jesus was the first to receive a resurrection body when He was raised from the dead in the power of an endless life, so that before His rising from the dead, resurrection life may be said not to have been obtained by man.

Life and immortality are the promises of God to every generation, and all Divine *promises* are to the faithful absolute certainties. But a promise is not *a completed gift*, and the free *gift* of God is eternal life in

Col. i. 15, 18.
Rev. xiv. 14.

John xi. 25.

* " This condition of immortality, man by his sin forfeited so entirely, that God in mercy withheld it from him until the way could be made open to its being again received and beneficially possessed. But now are life and immortality brought to light. Now, *for the first time*, man regenerated in his whole being, walks the earth. Now *first hath man obtained that immortality* which it was God's eternal purpose to bestow upon him. The mortal body hath put on immortality, the corruptible flesh and blood, have put on incorruption. And in this Man, at least—this, the God-Man—whose resurrection we this day (Easter Day) celebrate, is fulfilled the saying that is written, Death is swallowed up in victory."—*Readings upon the Liturgy*, Vol. ii. p. 140; on the resurrection of our Lord.

Christ Jesus our Lord. Although Himself "the Life" as God, He, as Man, *asked life* of the Father, and *He gave it Him*, even length of days for ever and ever. To suppose that Christ *gave* it to any of His saints, however privileged, before He *received* it Himself on behalf of all men, would make the asking and receiving needless.

Psa. xxi. 4.

We must be jealous to maintain the pre-eminence of our Lord in all things, that He is the first risen, immortal and glorified Man; the Firstborn among many brethren, for in all things it behoves Him to have the pre-eminence—

"For He, tho' glorified, as yet alone,
Bears the whole Church before the Father's throne."

He was literally the first man who, having died, had been raised from the dead in the power of an endless life, never again to die, "the firstborn from the dead."

Col i. 18.

A few persons in the two previous dispensations rose from the dead, but they returned to death and corruption. The case of the saints who were raised and came out of their grave after the Lord's resurrection, presents some peculiar features. It appears that they rose when our Lord died, but that they did not come out of their graves till after His resurrection, and that they then went into the holy city and appeared unto many. What became of them afterwards we are not told, whether they died again, or whether they formed a sort of first of the firstfruits, and were the Lord's bodyguard accompanying Him up to heaven. There is a beautiful tradition concerning them that, invisibly to beholders on earth, they were translated at the

Matt. xxvii. 52, 53.

Lord's ascension, accompanying the King of glory to the realms above, affording evidence to the heavenly hosts that, as the Father hath life in Himself, so had He given to the Son to have life in Himself, even eternal resurrection life.

The ascension of the risen Lord cannot properly be regarded as an instance of translation, for it was His own personal act, whereas *translation*—the rapture of men from earth to heaven—is an act of GOD, not of those who are the subjects of translation. The Lord Jesus Christ said of Himself, " I ascend unto my " Father, and your Father; " it is also written, " When " he ascended up on high, he led captivity captive." Therefore the ascension of our Lord is not parallel with the translation either of Enoch or of Elijah, or with that of the raised and changed saints who shall be caught up to meet the Lord at His appearing. Nevertheless it has affinities with both, as well as specific differences. It was not necessary for Enoch or Elijah to die, God having willed that they should not die, but should be translated—transferred from earth to heaven—an object lesson, as it were, of His gracious purpose in His perfected Church. Our Lord's death was necessary, for He came to die for mankind, and His resurrection was also necessary, as also was His ascension to God's right hand, though in each case it was *an act of His own will* in union with that of His Father. "I lay down my life and " take it again." "I ascend unto my Father." Thus there is a clear difference between the personal act of our Lord's ascension and the act of God in translating the risen and changed saints.

John xx. 17.

Eph. iv. 8.

When the firstfruits are changed into the Lord's likeness, they will doubtless be in a higher condition than Enoch, Elijah, or Moses were or are, if the change that will have passed upon them shall be an absolute one from mortality to immortality, even though an interval occur after the change and their rapture to meet the Lord in the air. The 144,000 are seen with the Lamb on Mount Zion; what this place is or what condition it implies we do not know. It may be that as the experiences of Christ personal shall be reproduced in Christ mystical, so those of our Lord during the forty days between His resurrection and ascension may in measure be reproduced by the firstfruits when they have received their change.

A great interest attaches to the condition of our Lord's body during the forty days of His sojourn on earth after His resurrection. He had been raised from the dead in what was truly a resurrection body, for it possessed glorious qualities: immortality, incorruption, the power of being visible or invisible, apparent capacity to pass through material substances, and the power of instantaneous movement from place to place, according to the action of His will. All this we learn from His appearances to His disciples— nevertheless the GLORY was not yet manifested in Him. This doubtless burst forth from Him, when He reached His Father's presence, and, as perfect Man, risen and ascended, received the fulness of the Holy Ghost, the Spirit of glory. After His baptism our Lord received the Holy Ghost without measure, as symbolized by the dove, not as the apostles who afterwards received the Spirit in the form of divided tongues of fire. After His ascension He received in our flesh the full glory proper to His Godhead, which He had laid aside in order to become man. He will hereafter reveal all the glory which it is possible for a creature to reveal, as the Son of Man, and also all the glory of His Godhead, which He resumed not at His resurrection, but after His ascension.

Where the Lord passed most of the forty days on earth we are not told, but the circumstances of that time, and His condition then, may offer some analogies to the condition of the firstfruits after their change and before their full and final glorification. When translated these will probably have passed from their present mortal condition and will be immortal. They will in that case have outrun all the previous types, for this condition (which is the hope of all who are in Christ to be attained at the first resurrection), is the groundwork of ultimate glorification. But the glory probably will not appear at once in them, as individuals. It is quite possible, as we have seen, that glory might be manifested in a *mortal* body, whilst on the other hand it is possible that glory might for a season remain *latent* in an immortal body.

There is another point of resemblance, and yet withal of divergence, between the Lord and His firstfruits; for, whereas with the risen saints who had died, there shall be those who have never tasted death, and whose bodies therefore have not experienced dissolution; in the case of our Lord, though He Heb. ii. 9. tasted death for every man, yet His flesh saw no Psa. xvi. 10. corruption, in accordance with the prediction of David, to which St. Peter referred on the day of Pentecost. Acts ii. 27-31. And St. Paul, in his first sermon at Antioch, in Acts xiii 35-37. Pisidia, insists on this as a true mark of Christ's Messiahship and of the special intervention of God, as implied in the words, "Thou shalt not suffer thine "Holy One to see corruption."

Thus the fact that our Lord was not immediately glorified after His resurrection is not without significance in its bearing upon the case of His saints at His coming, and suggests the possibility that an interval analogous to His forty days' sojourn on earth may occur between the resurrection and change of the saints, and their rapture into the presence of their Lord in His glory.

In his first epistle to the Corinthians, St. Paul throws light upon the nature of the change that shall be imparted to the translated: "We shall 1 Cor. xv. 51-"not all sleep [*i.e.*, die], but we shall all [*i.e.*, the 54. "raised and the living] be changed, in a moment, "in the twinkling of an eye." And he goes on to say that this corruptible must put on incorruption, and this mortal must put on immortality. The change is 1 Cor. xv. 42-indicated earlier in the same chapter, when he states 46. that the body which is sown in corruption, dishonour, weakness—being a psychical or natural body—is raised incorruptible, glorious, powerful, and is now a spiritual and heavenly body. But for a time the glory may be latent and not yet manifested—the body may be immortal and spiritual, yet it may not be forthwith glorified. The great seed of all future life is hidden in *regeneration*, which we have already received. The life is in us even now, but it is hidden: "Your life Col. iii. 3.

" is hid with Christ in God." Regeneration, effected in our spirit in holy baptism, exists as an earnest of the same change in our body also, and in the resurrection it will be manifested in all its fulness in our whole being. And we in Christ who have received since our baptism the seal of our heavenly inheritance, already possess a measure of the Spirit of glory which should be manifested even in this present condition of mortality in the partial exercise of the gifts and powers of the world to come. But the full inheritance of glory which is the hope of the Church is yet future, and it is the present work of the Captain of our salvation to

Heb. ii. 10.   bring the many sons unto this glory.

And this leads to the consideration of a kindred point, namely, what will be the occupation of the firstfruits during the interval between their change and rapture, and their subsequent full and corporate glorification with the whole Church? Activity is essential to life, and pre-eminently to immortal life and to the manifestation of love, which is ever flowing forth in action and blessing. On this subject we could have no possible thoughts save such as may be gathered from Holy Scripture; and again we may study the analogy suggested by the experiences of our Lord.

The Lord spent the intermediate time of forty days in teaching His apostles and in convincing them by many infallible proofs of the truth and reality of His resurrection, in preparing them for their future work and mission that, armed with the strength of God, they might go forth against the idolatries of the great civilized nations of the ancient world.

We cannot presume to state definitely the work which the Lord may entrust to the firstfruits after their change and rapture; but it may be conjectured that they will be used to help their brethren who shall be passing through the great tribulation. This is the intimation of Holy Scripture; for the firstfruits on Mount Zion and their work seem to be foreshadowed in the prophecy of Obadiah: " But " upon mount Zion shall be they *that escape*" (rendered *deliverance* in A.V.); while their allotted work is indicated in verse. 21—"And *saviours* shall come " up on mount Zion." May not therefore the firstfruits form a company elected of God to bring a special blessing to their suffering brethren? It indicates the true humanity of the Lord, that He waits for His fellow-workers, *i.e.*, for those who, according to the divine mystery of Incarnation, are necessary to Him for the carrying out of the full purpose of God, not only in the Church, but also among mankind at large.

Obad. 17, 21. (See Marginal reading and R.V.).

The firstfruits will have had the pre-eminence in being caught up, as the *man child* unto God and His throne. They are seen with the Lamb on Mount Zion, and it is from this place of vantage that we may conceive that they will go upon behests towards the Church and the world at large.

> " Oh! the saviours on Mount Zion,
>   Who beside the Lamb shall stand!
> Faithful followers, close companions,
>   Robed in white, a priestly band;
> First to wake the song of gladness
>   None beside might understand."

The historical types of Enoch and Elijah, as examples of translation in their respective dispensations, are appropriate to the times in which we live, which, by thousands of godly persons in the Church at large, are believed to be the last days. It is moreover according to analogy and precedent that the Christian era should be distinguished at its close in the same manner as were the two former dispensations. But of course the change and translation of a number of living saints which will accentuate the Christian dispensation will be on a much larger scale, for it will not be merely that of a typical individual, but may be of many thousands, who will bring up the company of those first raised from the dead to the mystic and prophetic number of one hundred forty and four thousand. Thus shall the glory of the dispensation of the Spirit, which has the glory that excelleth, be vindicated in this particular. The Church, having been warned of coming dangers and having been promised the translation of her risen and living saints, should be earnestly watching and praying for the fulfilment of this promise, that those who thus watch and pray may escape the coming storm of tribulation and judgment which shall overwhelm the world. From what has been suggested, certain inferences may be gleaned which have their bearing on the change and translation of the first-fruits :—

(1.) What the first step may be in their being hidden in a certain *condition* or removed to a *place of safety* on Mount Zion cannot, as yet, be clearly understood.

(2.) It may be that some preliminary hiding in the Lord's secret place or pavilion might take place even whilst they are in a condition of mortality. The prophet Habakkuk speaks of "the hiding of his "[God's] power," or as the original Hebrew may be rendered, "the hiding-place of his power." Hab. iii. 4.

(3.) The Scripture intimates that the dead in Christ will be raised FIRST and the living changed suddenly: "We shall not all sleep [die], but we shall all be changed, in a moment, in the twinkling of an eye." Each of the changes may be in a moment, without necessarily being the same moment. An interval long or short might intervene between the two events. The raising of the dead in Christ occurs *first*—then, possibly after an interval, (the Greek word is ἔπειτα, rendered *then* in A. V., but it also means afterwards—thereafter) the holy saints who are still in mortality, will be changed into the immortal condition, and both will (it may be after a shorter or longer interval) be *simultaneously* caught up, or translated to meet the Lord in the air, and so shall we ever be with the Lord. 1 Cor. xv. 51-54. 1 Thess. iv. 16, 17.

(4.) It does not necessarily follow that after the dead are raised or the living changed, the glory should appear in them directly, looking at the analogy of our Lord during the forty days before His ascension. "When Christ, who is our life, shall be manifested, "then shall ye also be manifested with him in glory." Col. iii. 4. (R.V.)

It is more or less generally acknowledged that Elijah is the Scriptural type of a ministry which shall prepare the way of the Lord for His return. This type has its primary application to the ministry of John the Baptist, but it is not exhausted therein, having a germinating and future application to a spiritual ministry of warning and preparation in the last days of the Christian dispensation. Elijah was a witness to the covenant of God having been broken by Israel; with twelve stones he repaired the altar of the Lord which was broken down, as a witness to the unity of Israel; and in answer to his prayer that the people might know JEHOVAH to be God, the fire of the LORD fell and consumed the evening sacrifice; he was persecuted by Jezebel, and had to flee for his life into the desert; he took refuge in the caves of Horeb, and finally obtained a miraculous change from earth to heaven through translation (as it may be correctly termed) by the whirlwind, and the chariot and horses of fire. All these circumstances offer a sufficient analogy to the last days of this dispensation in which our lot is cast, and should lead us to look for his spiritual antitype, and for a similar way of escape from those things which are coming on the earth.

1 Kings xviii. 36-38.

Drawing a practical lesson from the *characters* of Enoch and of Elijah, it may be concluded that those who shall attain to translation in the last time, must be persons of godly lives, who bear witness against the prevailing evil, and who are willing to endure persecution and the loss of all things rather than deny Christ. Our Lord says in connection with the rapture of the saints, that " who-" soever shall lose his life shall preserve it." Does not this indicate that those who would attain translation, must be willing to count all things but loss,

Luke xvii. 33.

Phil. iii. 8.

for the excellency of the knowledge of Christ Jesus their Lord, and to give up their own lives also, in order to attain the prize of their high calling? We should daily watch, and earnestly pray for the blessed appearing of the Lord, crying: "Come, Lord "Jesus, come quickly." Oh that the confidence of the Psalmist may speedily be the blessed experience of the Church:

"The LORD . . . . maketh my feet like hinds' 'feet, and setteth me upon my high places." "Let "thy salvation, O God, set me up on high," even on thy holy hill, Mount Zion.

Psa. xviii. 33.
Psa. lxix. 29.

CHAPTER VI.

The Search for the Translated.

A UNIQUE and characteristic feature, which is common to both the recorded instances of translation, is the *search* which was made for Enoch and Elijah after their disappearance. It is remarkable that this quest should have occurred, and that it should be expressly mentioned in each case, though Scripture refers with such marked brevity to the translation of Enoch.

Gen. v. 24. In the Book of Genesis, it is written: "And he "[Enoch] was not; for God took him"; which is explained with more detail in the epistle to the Heb. xi. 5. Hebrews: "By faith Enoch was translated that he " should not see death; and was not found, because " God had translated him." Not found by whom? Naturally by those who searched for him. No particulars of Enoch's translation and of the search made for him are mentioned; but human nature is always more or less the same; and, given similar circumstances, men will act in the same way, even though it be at the interval of centuries. Surrounded as Enoch was by the ungodly, they would be unable to account for his sudden vanishing from the midst of them, much less for its miraculous cause, and they would receive the statement of his instantaneous disappearance with unbelief and scorn. Even Enoch's relatives and immediate friends would be slow to believe in the phenomenon, although possibly warned of it beforehand; and they would certainly be among those who would seek to find the missing saint. But their labour was lost; their search was vain; they could not find him, because God had translated him.

Of the search made for the prophet Elijah by the sons of the prophets, a detailed account is given in the sacred narrative: "And they said unto him " [Elisha], Behold now, there be with thy servants " fifty strong men; let them go, we pray thee, and " seek thy master: lest peradventure the Spirit of " the LORD hath taken him up, and cast him upon " some mountain, or into some valley. And he said, " Ye shall not send. And when they urged him till " he was ashamed, he said, Send. They sent there- " fore fifty men; and they sought three days, but " found him not. And when they came again to " him, (for he tarried at Jericho), he said unto them, " Did I not say unto you, Go not?" It is a striking fact that the suggestion and action came from those sons of the prophets who dwelt, not at Beth-el, but at Jericho. Its foundations had again been laid, apparently a short time before in the days of Ahab, by Hiel, the Beth-elite, notwithstanding the curse which Joshua had left on anyone who should attempt its rebuilding; therefore it seems remarkable that there should have been a school of the prophets there, as well as at Beth-el, which was the chief seat of the court and of the idolatry of Jeroboam, king of Israel. Possibly this prophetic school was

2 Kings ii. 16-18.

Josh. vi. 26.
1 Kings xvi. 34.

under the supervision of Elijah. These sons of the prophets had evidently received some premonition of the coming event, and had set themselves to watch, probably on this (the west) side of the Jordan. They may, perchance, have seen some sudden, brilliant, transitory, meteoric flash on the horizon on the other side of the river, which had been allotted to the tribe of Reuben, and they were accordingly eager to suggest the search for Elijah. The reason they advanced savours of unbelief. They did not deny that some extraordinary event had taken place, but they appear to have doubted the fact of the *translation*: for, in proposing a search for the missing prophet, they imputed a capricious or injurious action to the Spirit of God, 2 Kings ii. 16 whereby he might suffer loss; suggesting that the Spirit of the LORD might have taken up Elijah, and cast him upon some mountain, or into some valley. The tidings had gone abroad that something exceptional had happened; but even the sons of the prophets were slow to credit the possibility of that which their own lips had declared, and, in the strength of the flesh, they requested permission from Elisha to search for him who was said to have been translated from earth to heaven.

Elisha at first refused to accede to their request, being assured of the power and faithfulness of God, of the reality of the phenomenon which he had witnessed, and therefore of the futility of their search. But they were persistent; they would take no refusal. " They urged him till he was ashamed." They (as we should say) worried him, until he felt forced to give way; and he said, "Send." The men whom they sent are described as "strong men" *(sons of strength,* margin), and a band of fifty went forth to scour the valleys and the mountains. How this episode brings out the old lesson of man refusing to believe in the acts of God,— even though He should graciously afford foreknowledge of them— and also of man's self-will in presumptuously striving to interfere with the action of the Spirit of God; for if He had carried Elijah to any particular locality, it was not for them to seek to know the secret of God in so doing.

However, the fifty men did not give up their search readily. For three days they adhered to their purpose. On the first day the search, arising from unbelief, was unsuccessful as in the similar case of Enoch; nor was it more successful on the second day; but when on the third day it was also vain, the seekers gave it up in despair, and reported to Elisha their want of success. He gave them no sympathy, but rather a gentle rebuke—"Did I not say unto "you, Go not?" He might have added: "You have wasted your time and energy. I assented to your going against my better judgment; I had faith in the promises of God and in their fulfilment in Elijah's translation; hence I said to you, 'go not?'"

Thus, neither Enoch, nor Elijah, when sought for, were to be found on the earth. In considering the search made for these translated persons, it is worthy of remark that the same spirit of unbelief was manifested in the somewhat analogous case of the resurrection of our Lord. How the great acts of God

K

throw the unbelief of man into marked relief! Christ
had told His disciples in plain and nonfigurative language, that He would rise from the dead on the third
day; yet, when His resurrection occurred, not one
of His followers was able to believe and accept the
joyous fact. The disciples had not understood " what
" the rising from the dead should mean"; though
the Lord's prophecy of this new and great event must
often have been discussed among them, as well as
among the female followers who companied with
the Lord. These faithful women, who were "last
at His cross and earliest at His grave,"* seem to have
forgotten, or not to have grasped His explicit statements, that on the third day He would rise again
from the dead; therefore they came early on the
first day of the week to embalm His body, and to
carry out the sepulchral rites which had been hastily
begun on the eve of the sabbath. They were
startled at not finding the body of the Lord; but
even then they did not apprehend the truth that
He had risen from the dead. On the contrary, they
thought that He had been taken away to some other
place; that they must search for Him and find Him;
and in their anguish they exclaimed, " They have
" taken away the Lord out of the sepulchre, and we
" know not where they have laid him." Even when
Mary addressed the Lord in answer to His question,
" Why weepest thou?" she did not in the least know
to whom she was speaking. "Jesus saith unto her,
" Woman, why weepest thou? whom seekest thou?

Luke xviii. 34.
Mark ix. 10.

John xx. 2.

John xx. 15.

* Eaton Stannard Barrett *Woman*, Part I.

" She, supposing him to be the gardener, saith unto
" him, Sir, if thou have borne him hence, tell me
" where thou hast laid him, and I will take him
" away." In her first lamentation, she speaks of
them, in the plural; now, in speaking to the gardener,
as she supposed Him to be, she addresses Him in the
singular—" If *thou* have borne him hence, tell me   John xx. 15.
" where thou hast laid him, and I will take him
" away." It was something of the same failure to
apprehend or grasp by faith what the Lord had
said, that led her to wish—like those who sought
for Enoch and for Elijah—to institute a search for
the missing beloved one, who in this case had been
removed, not from the earth by translation, but from
the tomb by resurrection. But even a greater spirit
of incredulity was manifested by the eleven apostles,
" for as yet they knew not [understood not] the   John xx. 9.
" scripture, that he must rise again from the dead."
The Lord had often told them that this would occur,
but they had not apprehended its meaning or reality;
hence they could not at first believe in His resurrection, and not improbably, had circumstances permitted, they also would have instituted a fruitless
search to find the missing body of their Master. No less
than three times did our Lord rebuke them after His
resurrection for their unbelief. Even of those who
beheld the risen Lord in Galilee, it is said, " But   Matt. xxviii.
" some doubted." Yet, as it was necessary that   16, 17.
the Apostles should go forth to the ends of the earth
to witness to this great event, upon which the
Christian faith depended, the Lord shewed Himself alive to them during forty days after He was

Acts i. 3.
1 Cor. xv. 13-
19.
risen from the dead, and *convinced* them "by many "infallible proofs" that His resurrection was a great reality, and the very foundation of His Gospel.

In analysing the reasons which led the men of old to institute a search for the translated saints, it seems clear that it was due principally to latent or active unbelief, though other motives may have been intertwined therewith. The searchers must obviously have heard of the reported translation; they may have been familiar with previous intimations of it; in the case of Elijah, they may have received definite forewarnings of its expected occurrence; but, when the translation had become an accomplished fact, they could not credit it, and sought to evade the acknowledgment of this supernatural act by a solution of the difficulty derived from a natural cause.

How inherent is the unwillingness of fallen man to believe in what he considers to be an unprecedented, an uncalled for, a supernatural act of intervention in mundane affairs on the part of God. There is an innate fear in sinful man of coming into direct contact with the living God, if by any means he can escape from Him. It was this spirit that was in Adam after his fall. He fled from God, and hid
Gen. iii. 10.
himself among the trees of the garden. "I heard "thy voice in the garden, and I was afraid, ... "and I hid myself."

When God does His mighty works and gives testimony thereto, He makes an appeal to *faith;* but, if men have not this faith, they are unable to discern the workings of God. Unbelief has been one of the

most flagrant and ineradicable sins of the human
heart since the fall of man.   Alas! unbelief has
also been one of the pervading sins of the Christian
Church; it is a spiritual sin which has eaten as
a canker, and caused her to forget her heavenly
calling.   This same unbelief holds good of the
promise and hope of the translation of the saints.
It has been foretold; it is declared plainly in the
pages of the New Testament.   We should therefore *expect* it; we should be *watching* for it; and
to treat this promise of God with neglect or forgetfulness, betrays an unbelief on the part of Christians,
which must entail spiritual loss.

See John iii. 18, 36.

Now, judging from the analogy of Holy Scripture,
how will the tidings be received by the world when
the Lord takes a step forward in the perfecting of
the Church, in the fulfilment of His purpose towards
the redeemed, by raising the dead in Christ, by
changing the living saints, and by translating both
as a body of firstfruits into His presence, or hiding
them in His secret pavilion?

Psa. xxxi. 20.

Persons will everywhere be missed.   There will be
gaps in families, in society, in shops, in the army, in
the legislature, in every position and rank of life,
for a great multitude of people in various social
positions will suddenly disappear.   We have been
startled of late in reading in the public journals that
many thousands of persons disappear in one year in
the city of London, but this disappearance will not
be like that of one solitary person here and there,
for it will be the disappearance of a multitude, and
these disappearances will probably be simultaneous.

This cannot be identified with the isolated removals of a few individuals occurring at some intervals of time; this will be that of a number of godly persons who were professedly looking for a great act of God in change and translation. What a number of complex and difficult legal questions will arise— What about their property, their wills, their heirs? How long will the courts of law wait before taking legal action? A set of problems will be created that never arose before, and probably will never arise again. Will their disappearance, as it is gradually realised, be received with incredulity and ridicule? Will it be a nine days' wonder? Will it soon be forgotten and ignored, or scorned with the hostility of unbelief? Will a few paragraphs in the daily journals consign the mystery to oblivion in the midst of the crowding and terrific events that will then distract the tempest-tossed minds of men?

What about the search made for the missing ones by anxious friends? When will it be made? How long will it be continued? When will it be abandoned? The raised saints may have risen without noise, and the changed may have disappeared secretly and quietly as in the dead of night. We can hardly think that a great trumpet will be blown literally, and be audible to the careless and the ungodly mass of mankind, at least not at that early stage of these divine interventions.

Looking at the only two cases of translation on record, it is to be expected that a search will be made for those who will be the privileged subjects of the coming translation; for the event cannot but cause excitement and surprise, even among those who are most callous in an unbelieving world.

To those who shall search for the translated first-fruits, it might be said by the faithful witnesses of their rapture—"Seek not for those whom God has translated; the faithful dead are not here, they are risen; the living watchful saints are not on earth; they have been changed and taken into the clouds, having been translated; send not forth your fifty strong men to endeavour to find them; for they shall not be found; they are not cast upon some mountain, or into some valley. They stand on Mount Zion with the Lamb, and none can climb that hill but those who are specially privileged to do so."

It may be imagined, though it were vain to attempt to predict what must necessarily happen on the occurrence of such an unprecedented and unlooked for event; for it cannot be denied that comparatively few Christians are looking for the Lord's coming, or have any real desire for it. The irreligious, of course, openly say that they prefer that things should continue as they are, while "the religious world" for the most part are opponents of what they term millennarian views, maintaining that Christ's kingdom is already set up, and only requires to be extended until the earth shall be filled with the knowledge of the Lord. The Papal claim to reign as vicegerent of Christ, and Protestant missionary efforts are alike embodiments of this idea. The Lord Himself has warned us that His advent will come as a snare "on all them that dwell on the face of the earth," Luke xxi. 35. and, it may be feared, on the majority in the Church

Matt. xxv. 5. also; for "while the bridegroom tarried, they [the "ten virgins] *all* slumbered and slept," even the five wise virgins as well as the five foolish virgins who had not sufficient oil in their vessels with their lamps.

That the title of our treatise — *The Church's Forgotten Hope* — is only too true may be inferred from the fact that, among the millions of the Baptized, there are but few—as it were a sheaf that could be waved in the hand—who earnestly watch and pray for the promised privilege of being translated without seeing death. Of this small minor-Isa. x. 19. ity it might be said in the language of the prophet Isaiah, "And the rest of the trees of his forest shall "be few, that a child may write them." Translation, the hope of the Church, has its special connexion with the change, and is necessarily connected with the first resurrection, which has also been almost entirely forgotten.

The hope of translation is not only forgotten, but translation is not even desired, nay, the thought of it is almost repudiated by many godly persons, as the following extract from the writings of a popular divine will serve to prove:—

"Although for us there is no translation to heaven, and the chariot of fire comes no more to snatch us away from the slow pain of dying, yet the still small voice which speaks to us, in the ascension of Jesus Christ, of the calmness of faith, of the glory which shall be revealed in us, has a power to lift us as in a chariot of triumph above the fear of death. With such bright hopes set before us in the Gospel, and falling asleep in Jesus, assured that God will bring us with Him, we feel that dying is better than an uninterrupted continuance of life. Dying in the shadow of the Cross, our life, like that of Elisha, burning itself out in its own white ashes on earth in silence and repression, we are more blessed than Elijah, transported in his chariot of flame. The experience of death will enhance the bliss of immortality, more than all the rapture of translation."*

The writer of this earnest quotation evidently regards the fiat of death, pronounced upon Adam and his descendants as irrevocable, and that it must unalterably continue the same. He would not have penned the above, had he had a true conception of the glorious hope held out to the Church, which is not "an uninterrupted continuance of life" as we know it here on earth, but a sudden deathless transition from this mortal existence to immortal life. Rather than cling to the "experience of death" to "enhance the bliss of immortality," our faith should grasp the truth that the Lord is ready to send forth His chariots of fire for us, were we only ready to step into them. This *change* truly is more blessed, more glorious, as well as more exceptional than *death*.

The following extract from a sermon preached nearly fifty years ago, by the Rev. William Dow, manifests a different spirit, and it may form a fitting sequel and antidote to the last quotation, and an appropriate conclusion to this chapter :—

* Extract from *The Garden and the City*. Rev. Hugh Macmillan, D.D. Chap. viii., Elijah and Christ, p. 189.

"There is a great act of God to which all things now look forward. It is the sending again of Jesus Christ from the right hand of His Father. And that will take place as surely as did His resurrection. Men shall expect it as little as they expected His resurrection. The world shall be rolling on in its old course; as it was in the days of Noah; as it was in the days of Sodom. It shall come upon an unconscious generation. But His saints shall hear His voice. They shall awake at His voice, who slept in the dust; and they shall come with Him in the day of His appearing. And we which are alive and remain shall be caught away. From the housetop, from the field, from the bed of rest, His saints that are alive and look for Him shall be caught away; friend from his friend, brother from beside his brother, workman from beside his fellow-workman. They shall be caught away; they shall be missed; and no one shall know whither they have gone. They have gone with their glorious bodies, to meet Him who is coming, with the risen ones. And then He shall come with ten thousands of His saints, to judge the world which would not have Him to reign over it, to avenge the blood of His holy ones on them that dwell on the earth, and to rule the nations with His rod. Be wise therefore now; be instructed, while the day of long-suffering waiteth. ' Kiss the ' Son, lest he be angry. Blessed are all they that ' put their trust in him.'"*

* *Discourses on Practical and Doctrinal Subjects*, first series, p. 391. By the Rev. William Dow. M.A. Edinburgh, R. Grant & Son, 1853.

CHAPTER VII.

The Translation of the Saints, not as Individuals, but as one Body.

"LET the peace of God rule in your hearts, to Col. iii. 15.
"the which also ye are called in one body."

While the apostle enjoins the saints at Colosse to
let the peace of God rule in their hearts as individuals,
he points out that this is not merely for their selfish
or separate enjoyment, for he bases his injunction
upon an indisputable fact:—"To the which also ye
"(collectively) are called *in one body*." Though it
is true that the mystical Body of Christ cannot be
filled with the peace of God save as it rules in the
hearts of the individual members, yet its fulness
can be attained only in the unity and organization
of ONE BODY.

The definite statement of the hope of translation
made by St. Paul in his earliest Epistle (that to the
church of the Thessalonians, A.D. 54), was for the 2 Thess. i. 1.
benefit of the Church of Christ as one body. It
speaks of those who sleep in Jesus being raised from
the dead, of the living being changed, and of both
being caught up together to meet the Lord in the
air. Hence, the first revelation in the New Testament
Scriptures of the Church's hope, vouchsafed some
twenty years after our Lord's ascension, intimates

that it is not as individuals, but as a united company of saints, raised and changed, that the Baptized can attain to the reward of translation.

St. Paul's epistles abound in definite teaching as to the mystical Body of Christ. Nowhere does the apostle so distinctly expound the organization of the Church *as one body*, with her ministries, gifts, and memberships as in his first epistle to the Corinthians. The twelfth chapter of that epistle contains a special revelation of this divine truth. The apostle enlarges upon the unity of the Body of Christ, and upon the mutual relations of those who form this body as members of Christ, and as members one of another. He also refers to the same subject in other epistles; for to the Romans he writes—"We "being many, are one body in Christ," and to the Ephesians and Colossians he repeats the same truth. This mystery "which was kept secret since the world began," and was probably among the abundance of revelations vouchsafed to the apostle at his rapture into the third heaven, the Baptized have almost entirely forgotten, both in theory, in doctrine and in practice. They have curtailed the boundless horizon of God's truth and become narrow, individual, and it may even be said, *selfish*, in their desires for personal salvation. It is a spiritual sin which the Baptized should confess, and it is a matter for thankfulness that among a small remnant such a confession has found utterance. On the feast of All Saints, the penitent acknowledgment ascends to heaven, that—"We have been anxious for our "own personal salvation; but we have lost sight

Rom. xii. 5.
Eph. iv. 4-16.
Col. iii. 15.
Rom. xvi. 25, 26.

" of the Body of Christ, and forgotten that it is only
" as one body, and not as individuals, that we can
" be received into glory." *

With the removal of apostles at the beginning
of this dispensation, this great catholic truth faded,
like that of the hope of the translation, from the
memory of the Baptized as a doctrine, and as a
HOPE. The recognition of these high and esoteric
truths seems to depend upon the presence of apostles
in the Church of Christ, and it would seem that
this fundamental and essential ministry needs also
the aid of prophets inspired by the Holy Ghost.
In the outburst of spiritual utterance which occurred in Scotland in the year 1828, almost the
first utterance was—" Where is the Body?" It
would appear as if the Lord were powerless to work
without His body, and that the Church could not make
progress unto perfection and enter into the Kingdom
until she again recognised her relationship to Christ
as His mystical body, of which He is the Head.

This essentially apostolic doctrine pertains primarily to the personal ministry of apostles, and it
is their office to teach or to remind the Church that
she is the BODY of Christ, and should bear witness
to this truth as a practical reality. As it was through
apostles that this truth was revealed to the Church
in her youth, so the revival of that ministry was
necessary to bring the same to remembrance and
to manifest it in its integrity, for this corporate truth
has almost been forgotten since the first century.

* *The Liturgy and other Divine Offices of the Church.*
Office for the Feast of All Saints. (Pitman.)

The Son of God was made Man for us men and for our salvation. He is perfect God and perfect Col. ii. 9. Man, and "in him dwelleth all the fulness of the Eph. i. 22, 23. "Godhead bodily." The Father has given the Church to the Son as His mystical Body and divinely ordained instrument for carrying out His purpose. The strength of our Lord lay in the fact that He and His Father are one; the strength of the Church consists in Christ being one with us, the Baptized, and in our being one with Him, although this oneness does not imply that men merely as *individuals* can be one with the Son of God, but that the Church being the Body of Christ, being one with Him, each particular member by virtue of this membership, becomes one with the Lord Himself.

A baptized man who is *not abiding in the unity of the Church* may not boast of his being united to Christ, as a separate individual; for the Holy Ghost, who has effected and preserves the union of the Church with Christ, unites the individual to Christ by incorporating him into the One Body. By His divine power and action in the sacrament of Holy Baptism a believing man on earth is spiritually united to the Lord, who sits at the right hand of the Father, and this union implies incorporation into the visible Church. The Holy Ghost comes, not as it were separately to each individual baptized person, but as the common gift of God to all who are members of that corporate Body, the Church, to whom the gift was given. And that gift comes to the Church from the Father through Jesus Christ, who has received the Spirit without measure, " for " it pleased the Father that in him should all fulness Col. i. 19. " dwell."

Christ was perfected as a man in and by Himself; but this is not true of any baptized man taken individually. As units we are weak, and we become powerful only as members of Christ. And it is in the unity of the Body that we shall reach ultimate individual perfection. The Church shall attain to resurrection, change, translation, and ultimate glory, not as an aggregation of separate units, but as ONE BODY.

Thus the glorious truth of the Church being the Body of Christ, and of Christ being her Head, shines forth, both in doctrine and practice: there is one Head, not many heads: there is one Body, not many bodies: and Christ, the Head, has a fulness which filleth every member of the one Body with all needful grace. No man can be a Christ in himself; no one member can contain the fulness of the Head; but, as the apostle Paul teaches,— " unto every one of us is given grace according to Eph. iv. 7 " the measure of the gift of Christ."

The thought is prevalent among many Christians, that where the Church is spoken of in Scripture as a " Body," nothing more is intended than a mere figure of speech, or a similitude; that as in other places she is compared to an army, or to a temple, so, from the compactness of her organization, or her unity of action, she may be compared to the human frame and called a *body*. But the converse of this is the truth; for the Church, though last in manifestation, is first in the Divine intention; so that our bodies are but types of that wondrous reality, the Body of Christ, which was, according to the eternal counsel of God, to be manifested in due time, and was foreshadowed in the prophetic language of Messiah—"a body hast "thou prepared me" (*fitted me*, margin).

Heb. x. 5.
Psa. xl. 6.

"All the elect form one single family, one single body under Christ their head, in which distance of time or place has no *locus standi*. No member is insignificant to another. Closely joined together is every part of the edifice which Jesus Christ is building on earth to the glory of the Father. All future believers, the righteous, the saints—however far apart they may dwell—are *our brethren;* they have the same nature, which was also borne by Christ Himself, and we share their joy and sorrow. The '*Communion of Saints*' which we confess in our creed must infuse in us a lively sympathy with the whole Church for her future trials and blessedness as well as for the adversity or happiness that she experiences at the present time.

"Can anyone love JESUS CHRIST, and be filled with zeal for His honour, without at the same time observing with deepest interest the order and progress of His GREAT WORK since His Incarnation, which He shall accomplish; and without, on the wings of faith, also 'hasting unto the coming' of that blessed day, when He shall put all enemies under His feet, . . . ?"*

2 Pet. iii. 12.
1 Cor. xv. 25.

As the Church has been created by God a

---

* Translated from "*Exposition des prédictions et promesses, faites à l'Eglise pour les derniers temps de la gentilité,*" par le Père Lambert. Paris, 1806.

spiritual body, she will be dealt with *as a body* according to the law of her creation and being; so that for any number of members to separate themselves from the organic unity of which they have been made integral parts, or to think of attaining separately to a condition of glory, would be to violate the law of their corporate being, seeing that they are divinely knit together into a living unity. We might as well conceive of a hand or a finger subsisting by itself, apart from our body, as that Christians should enter separately into that coming glory which has been promised to the whole Church as one Body in Christ.   Hence in resurrection, change, translation, and glorification, the Church shall be treated as an united whole, and not as a number of disconnected individuals.

Wherefore, viewing the Church in her entirety, the members must tarry one for another: for of the departed it is said that, "apart from us [the living] "they should not be made perfect."

Heb. xi. 40.
(R.V.)

This knitting of the Church into a complex unity is a creative act; it is the outcome of divine thought, like the conception and creation of matter.   The enlightened and sanctified spirit must be struck with its divine originality, its simplicity, and yet complexity, so that there is nothing left for man but to bow down and worship God, saying—Both in nature and grace "thou art great, and doest wondrous "things: thou art God alone."

Psa. lxxxvi. 10.

This truth, then, of the Church's unity is no human invention or conception; it is as far above our thoughts as the heavens are higher than the earth, even as

Isa. lv. 9.

L

God's ways and thoughts are above ours, as the
Isa. lv. 9. prophet Isaiah testifies. Moreover, this spiritual
creation of the Church as one Body was a new
departure in the divine economy of salvation. The
saints in former dispensations stood apart, as it were,
in their individual integrity; but as the Baptized
are all members of Christ, and hence members one
of another, they do not stand alone, but in Him
who is their common Head.

Everything in nature advances in complexity of
organization as it rises in the scale of being. Contrast the lowest forms of animal life in the amœba, or
other jelly-like protozoan forms, with man, God's
masterpiece, in whom the functions of life are dif-
ferentiated, yet united and harmonized. The human
body is not one member but many, and the harmony
and co-operation of the whole tends to its mainten-
ance in health, activity, and usefulness.

Many earnest persons have felt discouraged at the
general unpreparedness for the change and translation which exists in the Church; and they have
wondered how she can ever be made ready for translation into the presence of the Lord. And when
we think of our own unworthiness and of the difficulties attendant on our being prepared and perfected
as individuals, and on maintaining the high spiritual
standard required for sudden change and translation,
do we not feel constrained to cry out—O Lord, can
this blessed result ever be attained? With men
it is impossible; yet faith responds—But not with
Matt. xix. 26. God, for "with God all things are possible." No
one can attain to it by any efforts of his own, nor

by his own merits or righteousness. It must be the
triumph of free grace, of God's power and love, through
the action of the Holy Ghost, and through the merits
of our Redeemer: but it must also be the result of faith
and obedience on the part of the saints, for thus only
can they attain to the perfect likeness of Christ, and
to presentation before the throne of God.

If perplexing thoughts such as these have passed
through the minds of any who read this book, let
them take comfort from the fact of the essential
spiritual unity of the Body of Christ.   For, even
though each member of the Body can attain only
to his own limited share of Christ's fulness, yet the
perfect measure is attainable by all the members cor-
porately, because "the whole body" is "fitly joined   Eph. iv. 16.
" together and compacted by that which every joint
" supplieth, according to the effectual working in the
" measure of every part."

Different graces may be prominent in different individuals, even as there are many and rainbow-tinted
flowers in a garden; but it is their combination as a
whole that forms the perfect beauty of the Eden of
the Lord, which spiritually is the Church of God.
The Bridegroom goes down into His garden to   Cant. vi. 2.
visit his beds of spices and to gather lilies; but
their loveliness, and the sweetness of their fragrance
lie in their variety, while their utility for the sweet
incense or for the anointing oil consists in their
being fitly blended or compounded. Hence, since no   Ex. xxx. 22-38.
member can by himself manifest the perfection of
any grace, he needs other members of the body to
manifest that separate grace in its fulness. This
does not imply that we are to rely on our own
deficiencies being supplemented by the virtues of

others, or that we should not seek after individual perfection; but still the aggregate—the full measure of faith for example—which might be found in one thousand members collectively—could not be found in one member only; so that the fulness of the Head in any particular grace can be witnessed to, not by individuals but only by a *Body;* for in the unity of that Body Rom. xii. 3. " God hath dealt to every man *the measure* of faith."

The same argument applies to other gifts and graces.   Charity or love exists in its fulness only in the Head of the Body, the Lord Jesus Christ. No one member can possess this love in its perfection, but its fulness dwells in the Church united to Christ, as His Body.   Never can the *fulness* of the love which Eph. iii. 17-19.   is in Christ Jesus be expressed in its " breadth and " length, and depth and height," except it be manifested by the members of His Body in their corporate entity, and by being knit together in spiritual relation-Col. ii. 3.   ship to Him.   In Christ " are hid *all* the treasures " of wisdom and knowledge "; but a multitude of His members, with their varied gifts, might be chosen to *reflect* the incomprehensible wisdom and love of the only wise God, as manifested in the incarnate Son.

Again, if we instance other graces or excellencies, such as patience, meekness, self-denial, long-suffering, it is obvious that only in a corporate unity could this varied spiritual fulness be contained or expressed; for no aggregate of separate individuals could possibly *contain* the infinite fulness of the incarnate Son apart from Him.   God has therefore given to His Son a Body—His Church—to be " his fulness," even as the Eph. i. 22, 23.   apostle expresses this truth,—" the fulness of him that

" filleth all in all."   These expressions, however, point to that perfection to which the whole Church shall attain at the apocalypse of the Lord ; for then, and not till then, shall every variety of grace and loveliness, which is in the Head, find its due manifestation in the glorified members of the one Body; then, and not till then, shall the whole Body attain " *unto a* *perfect man*, unto the measure of the stature of the " fulness of Christ."

Eph. iv. 13

But if the Church, as a living though mystical and spiritual body, had no corporate, organic relationship, the view of the truth just dwelt upon would be untenable; for the above statements would not hold good of ten thousand unconnected saints, however advanced in holiness they might be individually; nor in strictness are they applicable to the saints of the Patriarchal, or of the Mosaic dispensation, who had no spiritual organic mutual relationship.   This blessed condition proceeds from the great central mystery of the Incarnation, by virtue of which, through *baptism* into her living Head by the Holy Ghost, *the Church is the Body of Christ.*   It may be necessary to guard this doctrine practically, so that it may not be perverted and become an excuse for idleness: but that, on the contrary, out of love for all the members and in view of our common fellowship, we should each one be stirred up to greater diligence, and emulate St. Paul in giving up ourselves more unreservedly for Christ's " body's sake, which is the church," that all the members may " obtain the salvation which is in Christ Jesus, with eternal glory."   *Nevertheless our separate*

Col. i. 24.

2 Tim. ii. 10.

Matt. xvi. 27.
2 Cor. v. 10. *responsibility remains,* for every man shall be judged and rewarded according to his own works.

If therefore the truth under review be rightly apprehended, it will constrain us to magnify the Lord for His wisdom and grace in beholding us as one in His dear Son, and, therefore, as members one of another; for without doubt Christ will deal with His Church as a *body,* according to that immutable law of her being which He Himself has ordained. He will regard her as a unity; and, while He gathers into one the scattered grains of faith and love that are in her individual members, He will add thereto, from the treasure-house of His own love, such varied excellencies that the measure of perfection may be filled to overflowing, and thus Jude 24. He may be enabled to present His Church faultless before the presence of His Father with exceeding joy.

But if the Baptized as a whole be neglectful of their calling; if they refuse to go on unto perfection; if they let slip the hope set before them, will not the Lord be justified in separating a company, known by the name of "the firstfruits," to whom He can award the earnest of that prize which is the dower of the whole Church? That He can do so without severing the unity of the body is set forth in the figure Rev. xii. 1-5. of the man child born of the woman, who is seen in the Apocalyptic vision, and is caught up to the throne of God. The man child having been already referred to in chapter iii., in regard to its sudden escape from imminent danger, it may here be considered in its relation to the firstfruits as a whole, and in its symbolism of an united *company.*

It has frequently and dogmatically been asserted (especially in the Roman section of the Church Catholic), that the woman in the vision of Rev. xii. represents the Blessed Virgin Mary, and the child her Divine Son, this idea being embodied in countless paintings and sculptures, and closely connected with the *cultus* of the mother of our Lord. It is, however, an untenable interpretation, and inconsistent with the details of the vision. The symbol of the crown of twelve stars is most inappropriate to the Blessed Virgin, whilst it is perfectly clear in connection with the Catholic *and Apostolic* Church. She is, or ought to be, clothed with the sun, having put on Christ, who is the Sun of Righteousness; she has the moon, typifying the shadows of the old law, under her feet; she wears as her crown the twelvefold apostleship; and she may fitly be regarded as yearning for the birth of her firstborn son, though, as the time of her delivery draws near, she experiences the antecedent pangs of travail.   Rev. xii. 2.

As regards the man child it should be remembered that the unborn child is part of the mother, yet distinct from her, so that this emblem may well set forth a company within the Church, yet in some aspects distinct and separate from the Body at large.* In due time the woman comes to the birth, crying and paining to be delivered. But a terrible danger is imminent, for a great red dragon is seen standing before the woman ready to be delivered, to devour

* See Appendix IV., *Remarks on the Man Child*, by the Rev. G. S. Faber, M.A., in the *Sacred Calendar of Prophecy*.

her child as soon as it is born. Thereupon at the birth, the Lord intervenes, and the child is caught up unto God and to His throne: and thus a definite act of translation succeeds the birth of this symbolical man child.

This figure enfolds several thoughts akin to those we have considered; for the man child—organically constituted with the various members proper to a human body—symbolizes a company or body corporate; and its deliverance from the threatened danger is effected by its rapture to the throne of God. The woman being in childbirth pains indicates a time of sorrow preceding that great tribulation Rev. iii. 10. under Antichrist "which shall come upon all the "world, to try them that dwell upon the earth." * The child, then, as part of the parent, yet distinct from her, sets forth a company, separate yet one; a miniature representation of the mother; not a schismatic body, but a special election within the pale of the Church—One, Holy, Catholic and Apostolic. This elect company, is appropriately symbolized by the man child of Rev. xii. and by the sealed and the firstfruits of Rev. vii. and xiv. They are those who are first ready for the Lord's appearing; nor need it be doubted that they will be the first to attain the resurrection, change, and translation, as an earnest of the ultimate fulfilment of the hope of the whole Church, when as one body she shall attain to her

* It is true that the Church's citizenship is in heaven, but the visible Church is on earth, and the experiences of the woman described after the birth of the man child are upon the earth.

perfect glorification and bliss. In His firstfruits, mystically numbered as one hundred forty and four thousand, the Lord may be pleased to recognise that measure of grace and suffering, viewing them as a company—which He shall approve and reward with the great prize of translation.

In discussing the translation of Enoch and Elijah under the Patriarchal and Mosaic dispensations, we contrasted the greater glory of the number who shall first be translated under the Christian dispensation, viz., the mystic 144,000, with that of the two persons translated during the previous 4000 years; and, if the thought be repeated in this place, it is because the 144,000 are regarded not as separate individuals, but as *forming one body*, and translated as such. The dead in Christ shall be raised first, and then [*afterwards*, Greek], the living shall be changed. We merely point out that these acts are distinct, and may be successive. On this last supposition it is impossible to say what interval may intervene between the two events, but the Scripture is clear that both the raised and the living saints shall be caught up *together* in the clouds to meet the Lord in the air, and that it is as one body that they will be so translated.* This special point is emphasized in this chapter, and its apprehension

---

* It would seem from Rev. ix. 4 that there are some of the sealed on the earth during the blowing of the fifth trumpet, and that they are preserved from the surrounding judgments, for the locusts from the pit are commanded to hurt " only those men who have not the seal of God on " their foreheads."

should purge us from a selfish and individual spirit, and make the truth, that we are members one of another, more practical, and infuse us with a deeper catholic love and tenderness for the whole Body. But this act, wonderful as it is, will not be a final act. The gathering of the firstfruits, of the twelve times twelve thousand, as an earnest of what is yet to come, will only be the initial step in the fulfilment of God's purpose to manifest His glory in the whole Body of Christ, and it seems probable that, to whatever measure of glory the firstfruits may attain, the Body will not be complete and fully glorified until the other companies are gathered, and all are united.

Many persons have extremely misty and undefined ideas about the future, and those who do not carefully study the Holy Scriptures are apt to entertain the current notion of one great day, called "the Day of Judgment," in which, as they suppose, a multitude of events will take place in an incredibly short space of time. But God's works, as seen in Creation in Providence and in the Church, are generally of gradual development, and it would appear reasonable to infer that the final day of judgment must occupy some considerable time. As there will be different periods of resurrection, so may there also be of judgment, according to the axiom, "Every man in his own order." That every one will not be judged simultaneously is evident from St. Peter's words, "The time is come that judgment must *begin* " at the house of God: and if it *first* begin at us, " what shall be the end of them that obey not the " Gospel of God?" The Lord's visitation of His

1 Cor. xv. 23.

2 Peter iv. 17.

Temple is with a view to judgment, and the casting out those who defile it.   But it must not be forgotten that Christ is the Son of Man, and that He has respect to the weakness and the circumstances of men, and *as Man* deals with us as men.   We are dealing in this treatise with the winding up of the history of the Church at the end of this dispensation, and with the progressive acts of the Lord which characterise it—not with what is popularly called the end of the world.

The coming of the Lord for which the Church should even now be waiting as an instant hope, may be regarded as a progressive event, as indeed the Scriptural figure "the day of the Lord" implies, with its collateral suggestions of the morning star, the herald of the dawn, ushering in the morning; the rising sun; the noonday sun in its might; and the evening sunset; all these various figures suggesting various periods of the day, during the course of which events will be progressive. Rev. xxii. 16.
Mal. iv. 2.
Judg. v. 31.
Zech. xiv. 7.

The following reasons are adduced for believing that the resurrection, change and translation of the saints may be viewed as *progressive* :—

(1.) The fact that the Head of the Body has Himself entered into glory before His mystical Body, suggests that certain members in closest contact with the Head shall be raised and changed before their fellow members; for since the Head of the Body has ascended, why may not the members of His Body ascend also—raised, changed, and translated—" every man in his own order"? 1 Cor. xv. 23.

(2.) The parable of the labourers in the vineyard Matt. xx. 8.

hints at the same truth; in this the award of the
wage begins from the last—the penny signifying
the reception by faithful and accepted servants, of
a reward, which is the image and superscription of
Christ as revealed in resurrection glory.

(3.) Further light may be derived from the consideration of the annual feasts of the Jews, which
favour the thought of *progression* in the acts of God
that will wind up this dispensation, of which they
are divine and prophetic types.

In chapter ii. reference was made to those feasts
and to the presentation of the wave sheaf or omer,
as types of the resurrection and translation; and the
firstfruits of barley harvest was specially considered
as being typically significant of the risen Christ, as
the Firstfruits, and secondarily of the rapture of the
firstfruits of the Christian Church. It may however
be asked how it comes to pass that the result of the
labours of apostles in sealing and perfecting the
saints should be typified by the firstfruits of the
barley rather than of the wheat harvest, wheat being
pointedly symbolical of apostolic doctrine? The
reply seems to be that the barley harvest connects
itself with the preaching of the Gospel for a witness
among all nations, answering to the feeding of the
multitudes with the five barley loaves and two fishes
(these last setting forth the two sacraments of life),
this great work being concluded with the gathering
of the twelve baskets full of the fragments that
remained over and above. The preaching of the
Gospel has witnessed throughout this dispensation
to Christ the Firstfruits,—the original wave-sheaf

1 Cor. xv. 20,
23.

Mat. xiv. 15-21.

of that Easter morning, when the Crucified became the Risen One,—who commissioned His apostles to preach to every creature the Gospel of Salvation through faith in His blood, and baptism in His Name. Those who believed and were baptized were anointed with the Holy Ghost through the laying on of the apostles' hands, whereby they were " sealed unto the " day of redemption," that they might form the earnest of the first company of the firstfruits of the Church. For the fulfilment of their hope they are waiting still.

Eph. iv. 30.

The Feast of Weeks, or Pentecost, with its offering of two wave-loaves, the firstfruits of the wheat harvest, comes next. These two loaves, under a larger aspect, appear to be a type of the Church as a whole from Pentecost to the coming of the Lord, and yet appear to have a prophetic application to the time of the end, when a second company, chiefly through the ministry of the Two Witnesses, shall be brought forth and perfected in a corporate manner. Although the Church at large is described by St. James as a kind of firstfruits of God's creatures, yet there may be elections within this catholic election of which the leading one is that of the " firstfruits unto God and to the Lamb," to be followed by a second company intermediate between the firstfruits and the general harvest of the Church, symbolised by the firstfruits of the wheat harvest.*

Jas. i. 18.

Rev. xiv. 4.

After these feasts comes the Feast of Tabernacles,

* On the possible relation of the two bands of firstfruits to each other, see chapter ii., pp. 48, 49.

or Harvest-home of Ingathering, which typifies a third body of Christians to be gathered and perfected, and added to the other two companies which have gone before. This Feast sets forth the great multitude who have come out of the great tribulation, having washed their robes and made them white in the blood of the Lamb; and these three different companies in the Church, treated as corporate unities, will ultimately be combined into one, into one glorious and perfect Church.

The great idea to be apprehended is that the perfecting of the Church, whether by resurrection, change, or translation, will occur in *stages*, principally in three defined stages — each of which comprises a corporate unity — and that they shall merge into one ultimate unity; it being certain that the perfected Church *as a whole* will attain to the first resurrection.

Lev. xix. 9.   Stress might be laid on the *gleanings* of the harvest, seeing they are alluded to in the Law; but whether the gleanings will be added to the harvest, we cannot determine from the statements of Holy Scripture. The gleanings may suggest those who, although outside the threefold ingathering, are left behind for a season, not as rejected, but for the sake of others, Lev. xix. 10.   of "the poor and the stranger." They may also constitute the intermediate link whereby God unites two different dispensations, so that, in effect, they overlap each other. They may constitute the few " in the corners of the field," whom the Lord will yet use, and they may be employed for the conversion of God's ancient people, to whom, in the end of the dispensation of the Church, the Lord will turn. The antitype must be fulfilled, but in what way the Lord will perform His wondrous counsel, we cannot at present discern.

(4.) An historical type of progression in God's providential dealings with His chosen people is afforded by the *three* periods or epochs of the restoration of the Jews from captivity and their settlement under Zerubbabel (B.C. 536), Ezra (B.C. 458), and Nehemiah (B.C. 445). Under the decree of Cyrus the first return from Babylon took place, and was memorable for the setting the brasen altar on its bases, and for laying the foundations of the Temple; sixteen years later came the decree of Darius to Tatnai that he should cease hindering the Jews in building the house of God; sixty-two years after this the decree of Artaxerxes was issued, when a larger company of the Jews returned under Ezra; the result being that, thirteen years later, the wall of the city was built and dedicated by Nehemiah, the whole period equalling ninety-one years, or from B.C. 536 to B.C. 445.

Ezra i. 1.

Ezra. vi.

(5.) While speaking of a threefold act of God in winding up this dispensation, and seeing the prophetic type of it in the three feasts of the Jews, and in the three epochs in their restoration and settlement after their captivity in Babylon, we must note that three companies are distinctly outlined in the Book of the Revelation, where that of the sealed and firstfruits is seen in chapters vii. and xiv. among the earliest of those redeemed from the earth, and standing on Mount Zion. These have an antitypical relation to the firstfruits of the barley harvest.

In chapter vii. only two companies are mentioned
—the sealed 144,000 and the great multitude—but
from other portions of the Apocalypse we learn that
there is another company—that constituting the
two witnesses—which, as the second or intermediate
one, may have affinities with both the above.

As regards this second company called the "Two
Witnesses," "two prophets," and also "two olive
trees," it is evident from these titles that they have
a great work of testimony to fulfil for God in the
power of the Holy Ghost, which will doubtless be
of a ministerial character.   But as they are also
spoken of as "two candlesticks" (which according
to Rev. i. 20, sets forth churches or congregations)
it would appear as if there were churches associated
with them in this work of testimony.   And as it
seems to be an unfailing rule of divine action, that
those who have to carry on a work already
begun, should be prepared for this by those who
have had part in its previous stage, it appears
probable that those of the second company who
will be entrusted with the great work of witness-
bearing, will have been previously prepared for it
by those who have gathered the *first* company of
firstfruits.   Those headed up by this second ministerial
company of the Two Witnesses will doubtless be
those, who at that crisis, will rally round the remaining ordinances of the Church.   The Two Witnesses
will also succeed in preparing that final band of
witnesses of whom our Lord may speak as "the
Matt. xiii.   angels of the Son of Man" who shall be the reapers
39-41·   of the great harvest.   This final band will begin their

testimony after that the Two Witnesses have been slain by Antichrist. If the Two Witnesses are to have any part in the *reaping* of the harvest it is evident that they are taken away before any portion of the harvest is *gathered in*. Those who constitute the Two Witnesses form a second band of firstfruits (typified by the firstfruits of the wheat harvest) and are therefore distinct from the general harvest of the third company. In this harvest, all the rest of faithful Christian people, who have not attained to the honour of being among either band of firstfruits, will be found. Of these, the departed will be raised from the dead, and those still living and enduring to the end, will be caught up to meet the Lord in the air to join the other two companies—Christ's body mystical being thus completed.

And here it may be helpful to remember that the literal Israel, whose experiences St. Paul declares were ensamples or types to the Christian Church, received their inheritance in the promised land in *three* stages. Two and a half tribes received their allotted portion from Moses "on this side Jordan "eastward," toward the sunrising, on condition that all their men of war should go armed before the Lord to battle, "until the children of Israel have inherited "every man his inheritance." The remaining nine and a half tribes received their inheritance in the time of Joshua; first, two and a half of the remaining tribes received their allotments, and finally, through the urgent command of Joshua, and his rebuke of their slackness, the remaining seven tribes took possession of the portions already assigned to them by

1 Cor. x. 1-11.

Num. xxxii. 20-42.

Jos. xviii. 1-5.

M

lot. This offers a striking analogy to the three
companies of the Baptized, and suggests that the
second company may have affinity with the harvest
as well as with the first of the firstfruits.

The same idea of a threefold company is brought
Rev. xii. before us in the twelfth chapter of the Book of the
Revelation, revealing the rapture of the man child
and the two flights of the woman into the wilderness.

Rev. xii. 17. It may be that "the remnant" mentioned in that
Lev. xix. 9, 10. chapter typifies the gleanings of the harvest which
Lev. xxiii. 22. were left in the corners of the field (cf. Rev. xi. 13).

Our thoughts have been in a measure restricted
to the consideration of the firstfruits, who first reach
translation as one body, because this great event is
the immediate hope set before us; but it must never
be forgotten that the wave sheaf does not content
the husbandman, but that his heart rejoices in
it as being an earnest and pledge of the whole harvest
for which he longs. The greater grandeur of the
perfecting of the Catholic Church must never be
lost sight of, for in God's good time she shall
embrace and attain her true hope,—the hope of resurrection and translation,—being at last perfected as
one glorious Body. Nor must we forget the history
and experiences of the Church Catholic during the
past eighteen centuries. Where, it may be asked,
are those saints who have fallen asleep during the
Christian dispensation to find their due and relative
position? Many who lived in the early days of
the Church, who were sealed by the first apostles,
and, as lights in the world, witnessed a good
confession, will find their place among the first-

fruits. And may not some in subsequent ages be
found in the merciful judgment of God, to have
reached the spiritual standard of the firstfruits, thus
attaining to that honour without having received
the outward sealing of the Holy Ghost by the
hands of apostles? Surely the mystical number
of the sealed may not be limited to a literal 144,000,
or to those gathered at the conclusion of this dispensation. Eighteen centuries cannot have been
barren in producing eminent saints of the Most
High; and doubtless the noble army of martyrs will be
represented among the band of the firstfruits. Again
—will not some who have lived in previous ages, but
did not attain to the same high degree of faith,
holiness and devotion, find their place in the second
company, of whom the remnant will be brought
forth under the Two Witnesses at the end of the dispensation? And lastly, shall not the great majority of
Christians, even of those who have been saved during
the ages, who have had faith, and yet have not been
distinguished for piety or gifts, find their place in the
harvest, the feast of ingathering, and so be gathered
into the garner of the Lord? What holds good now,
and is true of the Church as a whole, must have been
true in past ages; therefore the question arises,—If
there be only *three* companies or elections among the
Baptized, must not those who have gone before
necessarily find their respective places among one
or another of these three companies? They cannot
enter into glory as mere units or individuals, for the
same general law must apply to them as to ourselves,
inasmuch as they also have been baptized into the

Body of Christ. From all this it may be inferred that each company will be gathered out of all the sections of the Church Catholic, from Pentecost down to the sounding of the seventh trumpet.

For if the symbol of the firstfruits of the barley harvest had its first prospective application to the saints in the first apostolic age, and subsequently to those in these last days, and possibly to others from intermediate ages, whom the Lord may gather as firstfruits on Mount Zion, may not the two other symbolic feasts have a similar threefold prospective application?

It is in this spirit that the cry of holy supplication ascends, "We pray that the time may speedily come when we, and *all Thy saints in all generations* who have been elected to this glory, may stand with the Lamb upon Mount Zion, a holy firstfruits redeemed from among men, without fault before the throne of God." And in remembrance of the saints of all dispensations who have departed in the faith, the ancient apostolic prayer, and suffrage of past centuries is uttered: "May they rest in Thy peace, and awake to a joyful resurrection."

All that has been advanced tends to prove that there must be *stages* in the attainment of the resurrection glory by the Church, which is the mystical Body of Christ, the Temple of the Holy Ghost, the Bride of the Lamb; for each of these figures embraces the whole Church. Moreover, as God works in nature and in grace by degrees, there is nothing contrary to the analogy of the faith in the suggestion that He will complete the work of perfecting His Church by stages, and that these will follow one

another in a threefold sequence, as may be gathered
from the Scriptural analogies which have been adduced.

The threefold constitution of the Tabernacle, of the
temple of Solomon, and of the temple of Ezekiel,
point in the same direction.   The Holiest place or
oracle, the holy place, and the court surrounding the
temple, constitute a threefold unity.   In the building
of Solomon's temple—a type of the glorified Church—
one part would probably be completed before the
other parts; yet it could be described only as a *part*
of the temple: in like manner applying this simile
to the firstfruits of the Church, these cannot constitute
the whole Church.

When the first resurrection has been accomplished
in all who are Christ's at His coming, in all its
various stages, then its full glory will appear
in the whole Body *as one*.   The time must come
when the full number of the elect, even of the
individual members of the body, shall be completed;
and the whole Church shall in a moment be filled
with the glory of God, even as the Shechinah glory
of the Lord filled the temple of Solomon when it   2 Chron. vii. 1, 2
was dedicated or presented to God.

As the Lord shall come *with all His saints*, they
must previously have been raised or changed
and been gathered unto Him.   St. Paul beseeches
the Thessalonians "by the coming of our Lord   2 Thess. ii. 1, 2.
" Jesus Christ, and by our gathering together unto
him," not to be " soon shaken in mind."   The Lord
is the central point of attraction to His raised and
changed saints; and, the first resurrection having

been completed in all its stages, the whole Church, as
the Bride of the Lamb, shall be manifested as the
spiritual living temple of God complete in all its
parts, the eternal habitation of God through the
Spirit.

The more this subject is considered in the light of
revelation the clearer will the truth appear that the
Bride embraces the whole Church; for Scripture
teaches that if a few early ripened ears are waved
like an omer or sheaf of firstfruits, and escape the
great tribulation, the great mass of the Baptized,
the great multitude of the saved in the last days,
will have to go through it as an act of necessity,
and of mercy also.

Many of our brethren think that the Church as a
whole will be translated in the first instance and
escape the great tribulation; but comforting as this
may be to our preconceived opinions, we believe that
it is not according to the teaching of Holy Scripture,
and that the present condition of the Christian Church
and of Christendom does not justify the anticipation.
If the firstfruits constituted the whole Church it
would form but a small band, while there would
remain the difficulty of dealing with the great
multitude who come out of the great tribulation, and
who, having washed their robes in the blood of the
Lamb, must, with their waving palms, ultimately
form part of the Church Triumphant.

The gathering of the three separate companies and
their ultimate union in one Body, leads on to the next
great step in the development of God's wondrous
purpose, and that is the marriage of the King's Son,

or, as it is termed in the Book of the Revelation,
" the marriage of the Lamb."   But, before this can
take place, the Bride who has been chosen from out
of the race of sinners for whom Christ died must be
prepared; she must make herself ready, even as
Esther had to undergo a year's purification, viz.:
" six months with oil of myrrh, and six months with
" sweet odours."   And it will be a matter of universal
rejoicing when it is announced that " the marriage
" of the Lamb is come, and his wife hath made
" herself ready."

The Scriptures indicate that it is the CHURCH, and
not Israel after the flesh, who is to be the Bride of
the Lamb; and that she is formed not of any one
section of the Church, but of the whole body of the
faithful Baptized; now, since there can be no schism
in the body, the three companies must be united
before the marriage takes place; hence the rapture
of the firstfruits, or of the man child, though a step
towards this result, will not constitute the marriage
of the Lamb.

The Bride must be ONE in her visible unity,
distinct from those who will be *guests* at the
wedding feast.

Among these guests may be the queens and virgins
mentioned in the Song of Solomon, or, as it is expressed in the royal bridal psalm, "the virgins her
" companions that follow her shall be brought
" unto thee."   In the Apocalypse, a special blessing
is pronounced on those who are the guests at
this heavenly solemnity:—"And he saith unto me,
" Write, Blessed are they which are called unto

Marginal references:
Rev. xix. 7.

Esther ii. 12.

Rev. xix. 7.

Rev. xix. 9.

Cant. vi. 9.
Matt. xxii. 2, 3,
10.

Luke xiv. 15,
16.
Cant. vi. 8.
Psa. xlv. 14.

Rev. xix. 9.

" the marriage supper of the Lamb." These would appear to include guests, who do not form part of the Bride. There will also be present the FRIENDS of the Bridegroom, one of whom will be the Lord's forerunner, John the Baptist, who thus designated himself. Again, many godly but un-baptized persons, who are on that account not members of the Body of Christ, and therefore can-not form part of the Bride, may yet find their places in this glorious retinue among the companions of the Bride or the friends of the Bridegroom.

John iii. 29.

The gathering of the first company of those who shall form the Bride, is the present matter before the Church and concerns the immediate future. This is the great event for which the Holy Ghost has been seeking to prepare her, and to which the visible Church has not yielded herself; but the Lord still stands at the door and knocks, graciously granting time for repentance, that the Church may attain this blessed hope, without incurring the great tribulation or chastisement of the Lord, who loves His whole Church, and would rather perfect her by His love, than by the fire of His jealousy.

Rev. iii. 20.

We close this chapter with an extract from a book by Père Lambert (written almost one hundred years ago), with reference to the end of this dispensation, and to the attitude of humiliation and confession which the saints of God should then maintain.

" The proceedings of God, even when most severe, are always accompanied by mercy. The history of Religion teaches us that during the most miserable periods of time

and amidst universal transgression, the Lord always
reserves to Himself certain precious remnants, which
stem the tide, and, as by a miracle, escape the general
infection.   Therefore, with the drawing near of Divine
judgment on apostate Christians, a certain number of
faithful souls who please God, will be found among
them.   *One of their chief characteristics will be that they
search and inquire into the purposes of the Lord* in all
the events of their time, entering into His plan, praising
His counsel, deeply humbling themselves under His hand,
after the example of the prophet Daniel (Dan. ix. 20), con-
fessing their own and their people's sins, making a sanctified
use of their personal trials, and of the public distresses
that they witness, and which may overtake themselves
at any moment.   For they know well, and sorrowfully
confess, that they also have had their part in the mass
of transgressions which have provoked the righteousness
of God.

"If we be destined to see this day of tribulation which
Thy prophets, O Lord, have described so fearfully, or should
these great sufferings be reserved for another generation,
may we, O my God, be united in spirit with Thy then living
children, and with them, and like them, say: 'Lord, we have
sinned before Thee, we have transgressed Thy holy laws,
we have added pride to disobedience.   No humiliation, no
chastisement can be too great for our going astray.   If
therefore, the great storm of Thy fury should descend all
at once upon us, we could only put our mouth in the dust'
(Lam. iii. 29), and say to Thee, 'Righteous art Thou, O Lord,
and upright are Thy judgments.'   The fire of Thy vengeance
shall devour the godless and purify the earth which they
have corrupted.   Thy will, O God, be done, but let Thy love
to us be present at all times.   If Thy justice strike us let
Thy mercy accompany it.   Let the invisible, mighty hand
of Thy grace sustain us in the terrible crucible wherein
Thou shalt refine Thy children.   Let the blood of Thy Son
sprinkle the knife wherewith we shall be sacrificed."[*]

* Translated from "*Exposition des prédictions et promesses,
faites à l'Eglise pour les derniers temps de la Gentilité,*" Par
le Père Lambert.   Paris 1806.

CHAPTER VIII.

The Translation : The Subject of the Testimony of the Two Witnesses.

———

MANY students of prophecy believe that the initial stage of the first resurrection and of the translation of the raised and changed saints will be the subject of the testimony of the Two Witnesses, who are portrayed in the eleventh chapter of the book of the Revelation, and this development is intimately connected with our general subject.

A few thoughts on the subject of witness may form a fitting introduction to this chapter:

(1) What is the meaning of the word "witness" as applied to a person?

The Greek word for witness is μάρτυρ "martyr," which in its primary sense means one who gives testimony to a fact of which he had been an *eye-witness*. The word, however, soon attained a secondary signification which became the one currently adopted. Thus the word *martyr* is popularly employed to denote one who gives up his life in witnessing faithfully to that of which it is his duty to testify, and this secondary idea of confession unto death has superseded the original idea of *witness*, pure and simple. In human affairs, the office of a witness is necessary, responsible, and honourable. Our Lord Jesus Christ calls Rev. iii. 14. Himself "the faithful and true witness;" and

these qualities of faithfulness and truth are the two
essentials in all testimony that merits the name of
witness for God. "A faithful witness will not lie;   Prov. xiv. 5.
"but a false witness will utter lies"; and among the
six things that are an abomination to the Lord, is
"a false witness that speaketh lies." The main   Prov. vi. 19.
proposition in Paley's "Evidences of Christianity,"   See Ex. xx 16.
is as follows: "That there is satisfactory evidence
that many professing to be original witnesses of the
Christian miracles passed their lives in labours,
dangers, and sufferings, voluntarily undergone, in
attestation of the accounts which they delivered,
solely in consequence of their belief of those
accounts, and that they also submitted, from the
same motives, to new rules of conduct." Human
life is in effect based on witness; and at every step
even in things mundane, *faith* is latent and is
indispensable; and if this holds good of the life that
now is, how much more must it be true of that
which is to come. "If we receive the witness of   1 John v. 9.
"men, the witness of God is *greater*."

(2) The witnesses are plural; their number is
specified, for the Lord Jesus calls them "My two   Rev. xi. 3.
witnesses." The reason for this duality will be
found in the law of Moses. Duality or plurality
of testimony was a recognized principle of the Law,
the production of two (or three) witnesses being
necessary for the condemnation of the accused, in
capital charges. The testimony of one single witness was not sufficient to ensure conviction: hence
it is written: "The murderer shall be put to   Num. xxxv. 30.
"death by the mouth of witnesses: but *one witness*

"shall not testify against any person to cause him
"to die." Again, "At the mouth of two witnesses,
"or three witnesses, shall he that is worthy of
"death be put to death; but at the mouth of *one*
"witness he shall not be put to death. The hands
"of the witnesses shall be first upon him to put
"him to death, and afterward the hands of all the
"people." Two points arrest our attention here: the
number and the responsibility of the witnesses; for,
if the witnesses were false, their guilt would be
aggravated by conspiracy and malice prepense.
Moreover, it being harder to suborn two men than
one man, the number of *two* at the least, was
meant to be a guarantee for eliciting the truth, and
for the protection of the accused. The character of
a false witness has always been held in abhorrence;
so that the judicial murders of the innocent Naboth
and of the spotless Saviour of mankind, through
false witness, have ever been regarded as crimes
of the deepest dye. The sin or crime of false
witness was expressly forbidden by the ninth
commandment, and the wisdom of the Law in this
matter is applied to dealings in the Church by the
Master Himself. In regard to His own mission,
Christ appealed to the Law, saying, "It is also
"written in your law, that the testimony of two men
"is true;" and the Lord subsequently said to His
apostles concerning the Spirit of truth which
proceedeth from the Father, "He shall testify of me:
"and ye also shall bear witness." St. Paul, in
writing to the Corinthian Church, lays down the
rule, "In the mouth of two or three witnesses shall

Deut. xvii. 6.

Ex. xx. 16.

See Mat. xviii. 15-16.

John viii. 17.

John xv. 26, 27.

2 Cor. xiii. 1.

"every word be established"; and he instructs
Timothy to the same effect: "Against an elder   1 Tim. v. 19.
"receive not an accusation, but before (under) two
"or three witnesses." Thus the apostle establishes
the principle of duality in witness-bearing, as an
axiom of the Church. God has given to it this
twofold character: so that witness-bearing is not a
simple or single, but a complex or double thing.

There are many examples of this duality to be
found in Holy Scripture. Caleb and Joshua were   Num. xiv. 30.
the only *two* of the twelve spies who bare witness
to the faithfulness and mercy of God, and they
were the only two of the *numbered* thousands of
Israel who, having come out of Egypt, crossed the
Jordan into the promised land. Moses and Elijah   Luke ix. 28-31.
were the two messengers from God who, at the
transfiguration of our Lord, represented the law and
the prophets, or the law and its restoration, being
respectively, the builder and rebuilder of God's
holy altar. After these two had finished speaking
to Jesus of His approaching death, God the Father
Himself witnessed of His beloved Son in the
hearing of Peter, and James, and John, whom alone
Jesus had taken with Him, as witnesses to the   See 2 Pet. i.
Mount of Transfiguration. Thus, this glorious vision   16-18.
embraced a threefold witness—from heaven, from
Hades, and from earth. Likewise in the case of
the ascension of the Lord, there was the double   Acts i. 10
witness of two angels, the "two men" who stood
near the disciples in white apparel, and substantiated
its reality to the eleven apostles, themselves "wit-   Acts x. 41.
" nesses chosen before of God."

Again, the two tables of the Law were a witness for God, and were put into the ark which was called the ark of the testimony (or witness) over which were the two overshadowing Cherubim. At the return of Israel from Babylon, the governor Zerubbabel was helped by the high priest Joshua, and encouraged by the ministry of the two prophets Haggai and Zechariah, the latter of whom had a vision of "two olive trees," designated as "the two "anointed ones, ('sons of oil,' margin), that stand "by the Lord of the whole earth"; Christ's two witnesses being similarly described in the apocalyptic vision.

Zech. iv. 3, 11-14.

Rev. xi. 4.

(3) It is certain that the testimony of these two witnesses, will be to some special act of God, for our Lord speaks of them as "*My* two witnesses." Not only will their office be one of testimony, embracing the duality which is the recognized principle in all true evidence, but they will have a special mission from the Lord Jesus. In this connection it may not be inappropriate to ask:—Will the just God require from men that which He has not first given to them? Has He ever brought judgments on mankind without first sending them warning? Therefore, if He is about to give a witness which shall leave men without excuse, it will be a twofold witness, that every word may be established.

See Mat. xxv. 14-30.

"It is but natural that we should ask ourselves *whether the Lord has not given His Church some remarkable sign, to announce such important events.*

"Hitherto a revolution—a change—has *never* taken

place among God's people, without being preceded
by forerunners—messengers—to lead intelligent and
pious persons to be watchful and mindful.   When
the Lord causes a universal flood, He warns the
guilty by the building of the ark.   The revolutions
or changes among the people of God and their
intimations generally stand in relation one to the
other. *The greater the importance of the former, so
much the greater and more wonderful will be the
harbingers thereof. .   .   .   .* Would it not be
contrary to the order of God, that an astonishing
change should suddenly take place in the world,
without there being a previous and supernatural
announcement of the same, which would encourage
every upright devout heart to give heed thereto?
So to this revolution—which in the eyes of most
Christians appears to be so unlikely and impossible
—the greatness and the nature of the precursor
must correspond." *

Shall not God have His two witnesses according
to His own unchangeable law?   God is truth, and
His witnesses can testify only to the truth, the
whole truth, and nothing but the truth.   They can
give only that light which comes from Him who is
"the true Light;" therefore they are set forth in the   John i. 9.
double figure of the two olive trees, and of the   Zech. iv. 11, 12.
candlesticks or lampstands.

The corresponding prophecies of Zechariah
and in the Apocalypse suggest on the one hand

* Translated from *"Exposition des prédictions et promesses,
faites à l' Eglise pour les derniers temps de la Gentilité,"* par
le Père Lambert.   Paris, 1806.

the *ministerial character* of Christ's two witnesses
(anointed ones), and on the other hand that their
testimony goes forth from, or in connection with, two
Churches or ecclesiastical centres (candlesticks).

(4) The natural question arises: " *Who will be
the two witnesses ?* "

It was an early patristic suggestion that Enoch
and Elijah would be the Two Witnesses, and modern
students of prophecy have offered many other
interpretations.   Mr. Elliot gives a list* of many
witnesses for the truth of the Gospel in the Eastern
Church, and also in the Western Church, from the
year A.D 600, and he pursues the same line of
enquiry through mediæval history.   Other commentators have indicated the Waldenses and Albigenses
as the Two Witnesses, on account of their having
suffered cruel persecution by the Church of Rome in
the middle ages, because of their faithful witness
to primitive truth.   But these interpretations are
unsatisfactory and inadequate; and it is sufficient to
state that, if these portions of Scripture have any
application to the past, according to the historical
school of commentators, there is a well-grounded
assurance that they must have a wider fulfilment in
the future, for it may be regarded as certain that
this testimony is still future.   In some form or other
the two witnesses seem to represent a special
ministry of testimony, of preparation, and of warning,
with the putting forth of supernatural action in the

* Rev. E. B. Elliot, M.A., *Horæ Apocalypticæ*.
Vol. ii., p. 215-297.

Christian Church at the close of this dispensation,
—a ministry which the Lord will send forth to the
Church Catholic before His *manifested* apocalypse.
Must not these two prophets or witnesses then have
some ministerial relation to our Lord Jesus Christ
Himself, to whom, as Head of His Church, God
gave this revelation, and of whom it is written that
"the testimony (or witness) of Jesus is the spirit   Rev. xix. 10.
"of prophecy?"

The pouring out of the Spirit on the seventy elders   Num. xi. 24-29.
who were to assist Moses, with the special position of
Eldad and Medad, who remained in the camp, was
analogical of events still future; for the Lord, at
the beginning of this dispensation, after sending
forth His twelve, "appointed other seventy also, and
"sent them *two and two* before his face into every   Luke x. 1.
"city and place, whither he himself would come."
Hence this dispensation may *close* in a similar manner,
first, with a twelvefold witness, and then with that of
seventy chosen witnesses, who shall go forth two and
two into the cities of Christendom, to utter a call to
repentance, before the coming of the Lord to take
account of His servants.   The Two Witnesses then
may represent a ministry of seventy special messengers
connected with the Christian Church, and as they
are called "two prophets," this would imply the
restoration and manifestation of prophetic power
shortly before the close of the dispensation of the
Spirit.

(5) A most important question now arises, viz:—
to what shall the Two Witnesses testify? They must
have some work to do which will justify their name.

N

They must witness to something, to some fact, to some event. It is clear that they must witness to some work of God, else how would their name be justified, when they are called by the Lord "My "two witnesses"? They must witness not to an act of God in past ages which had already been accredited, but to some recent act, or to a then present act, or to coming judgments—or to the conjunction of all three—as connected with the conclusion of the present dispensation.

Judging from analogy and from the circumstances of the case, there is one great act of God which lies in the immediate future which is certain, and is of such splendour and magnitude as to justify a special witness being given to a careless and unbelieving Church, which has forgotten the great hope of her high calling. This great act of God is RESURREC-TION and TRANSLATION. The testimony of the two witnesses would run on these lines; they would witness to the existence of the living God, to His abiding providence, symbolized by the wheels of the Cherubim full of eyes; to His great salvation; but chiefly to that salvation as manifested in certain recent marvellous acts, viz: in the resurrection of the dead, in the change of the living, and in their joint translation to meet the Lord in the air. This testimony to the realization of the early hope of the Church and to the fulfilment of the Lord's promises would appeal to faith, and would be a rebuke to unbelief and indifference, whilst it would mark the close of this dispensation and the introduction of the next, even that of the kingdom of God.

The Christian dispensation began with a witness to *resurrection*.   To the cardinal fact of Christ's resurrection the *two angels*, whom the women saw sitting the one at the head and the other at the feet where the body of Jesus had lain, gave witness, saying unto them, "Why seek ye the living among the dead? He is not here, but is risen." Luke xxiv. 5, 6.

The witness to the resurrection of Christ, as the foundation of the Christian faith, had to be borne to the Jews and to the world at large; and, since all men could not come into contact with Christ Himself, the account of His resurrection as an historical fact had to be brought to them as a testimony to faith; and to this end specially chosen and reliable witnesses were necessary.

Hence the apostles were commissioned for this great work by the Lord Himself, who said to them: "And ye are witnesses of these things;" and that Luke xxiv. 48. the twelvefold apostleship should not lack one of its number, Matthias was chosen to complete the Acts i. 21-26. number as a witness of Christ's resurrection. St. Peter testified to Cornelius that they—the apostles —were the witnesses "chosen before of God," to Acts x. 41. whom Christ had shewed Himself openly after He rose from the dead. St. Paul the apostle of the Acts ix. 5, 6. Gentiles could also personally testify to the risen Christ as a living person.   There is thus a twofold development of the apostolic ministry in the apostleship of the circumcision and in the apostleship of the uncircumcision, the two being headed up in Peter and Paul, a striking duality being thus imparted to the first ministry of the Church, the ministry of apostleship.

The special witness at the end of this dispensation will be to RESURRECTION, but not as at the beginning to the resurrection of one man only—the Man Christ Jesus—but to that of thousands, as well as to their translation together with the living and changed saints. At the beginning of this dispensation the witness was to the resurrection of Christ—Christ personal—whilst at its end the witness will be to the resurrection of those members of His Body who have been accounted worthy to obtain the first award of this prize, or of change without death and of subsequent translation. Its object will be to awaken slumbering Christendom to its privileges and responsibilities, and to warn men beforehand of the judgments of the Lord, which precede His apocalypse and the establishment of His kingdom upon earth. These mighty events, both past and future, may well afford sufficient reasons why God should send forth His Two Witnesses to those upon whom the end of this age will then have come.

When Elisha accompanied Elijah on his last journey, Elijah's promise that a double portion of his spirit should rest upon Elisha was conditional on the latter being a witness of his translation. As in the sequel Elisha was an eye-witness to the translation of Elijah, and was thus qualified to testify thereto, so will the translation of the first-fruits be the principal subject to which the Two Witnesses will give evidence from personal knowledge.

The majority of unbelieving Christians will find the testimony of the Two Witnesses difficult to receive, for the resurrection to which these will testify

will probably be known only to a limited number,
as in the case of our Lord's resurrection; so that
faith will be required in the hearers of the testimony
to this event, even as St. Peter said of the risen
Christ: "Him God raised up the third day, and   Acts x. 40, 41.
"shewed him openly; not to all the people, but
"unto witnesses chosen before of God, even to us
"(the apostles), who did eat and drink with him
"after he rose from the dead." Faith is ever
necessary in order to apprehend the supernatural
acts of God, and to accept them to our salvation, in
a spirit of meekness.

But the Two Witnesses are "clothed in *sackcloth*,"   Rev. xi. 3.
which indicates great humiliation and sorrow for sin.
Doubtless the special sin which, as the burden of their
testimony, calls for repentance and confession, will be
that the Baptized have rejected the grace of God in His
previous work of mercy and in the proffered deliverance from the great tribulation, which was meant for
the acceptance of *all*, and not merely of the *firstfruits*.
Nevertheless they witness to the salvation which God
has already accomplished, as a hope and encouragement to those who are still in the furnace of temptation and tribulation, and testify that as God has saved
many *from* the great tribulation, so He can deliver
also a great multitude *out of it*, by His power and
grace, by the same means, viz., by the resurrection of
the sleeping saints, the change of the living, and the
translation of both, as already manifested in the case
of the firstfruits.

In the revelation which the Lord Jesus gave to His
Church, through His apostle John, terrible judg-

ments are pronounced upon Christendom and upon
the earth.   Hence, warnings of these stupendous
coming judgments, as well as testimony to the great
acts of God already accomplished, must form part of
their message to Christendom, if not to the world
at large.

Let us endeavour to realize what might happen
in actual daily life as the result of this witness.
Supposing that to-day God raised and changed some
of the firstfruits of the Church—whether it might
be ten, or a hundred, or a thousand—that He gave
to some persons infallible proofs of the reality of
this wonderful act, and that these were bidden to
bear witness to it in the populous cities of Christendom, at the same time denouncing fearful judgments
about to fall on the inhabitants of the earth, how
would such a startling declaration be received? Would
not the world say—"The prophet is a fool, the
"spiritual man is mad!" A very short time might
elapse before these witnesses would be brought
before the magistrate for causing a tumult and an
obstruction, and they would doubtless be fined or
cast into "the common prison," like the apostles
of old.   But, when liberated, the messengers would
continue their cry: "This is our witness: God
is the living God; and, according to His eternal
purpose, He has begun to shew forth His mighty
power in raising many from among the dead. It
is an earnest of the setting up of His kingdom;
it is the prelude to great tribulation and heavy
judgments.   Repent ye therefore and believe the
Gospel." But their testimony would not stop here,

Hosea ix. 7.

Acts v. 17-33.

for as we have seen they must also testify to the cognate miracle of a certain number of persons having been changed into the immortal condition without death, and of having been caught up with the risen saints to meet the Lord in the air. Perhaps the witness of this extraordinary occurrence—of the change without death and of the subsequent rapture—will be more difficult to receive than that of the resurrection. Men have heard of resurrection from the dead; but, despite the express teaching of the apostle Paul, the doctrine of the change without death is unknown to Christendom generally; or, at least, in spite of the cases of Enoch and Elijah, it is regarded as inconceivable and visionary. Still, when witnessed to as a *fact*, and when shewn to be credible according to the testimony of Holy Scripture, it will arouse as well as startle the professing Church, and, shaking her to her foundations, will convict her of unbelief in the promises of God, as revealed in His holy word.

There are ever these three parts in a true and special witness for God, viz:—

(1) To testify to the acts of God, that is, to what He has done;

(2) To warn the careless and unbelieving of what God is about to do;

(3) To exhort men everywhere to repent and to "flee from the wrath to come."   Matt. iii. 7.

This is the substance of all testimony in the past, and may be traced in the witness of Noah, Elijah, Jeremiah, John the Baptist, and of the apostles at the beginning of this dispensation, and it will surely form the substance of the testimony to be borne by the Lord's Two Witnesses at the close of this dispensation, which thousands of devout Christians believe to be at the very door.

But the ministry of the Two Witnesses will, apart from their message, be such as to arrest marked attention, for it will be characterised by mighty signs and wonders. It is revealed that supernatural power will be given to them over the elements of God's Rev. xi. 6, 10 creation, and that they will torment them that dwell upon the earth. There is thus an affinity between their testimony and that of Moses and of Elijah. Like Moses they will have power over waters to turn them into blood, and to smite with various plagues: like Elijah they will employ fire to devour their enemies, and like him they will have power to shut heaven, that it rain not in the days of their prophecy.*

(6) Let us glance at the results of the testimony of the Two Witnesses. Although it ends, like all true witness for God on earth, in *apparent* failure, it is impossible that a witness sent by God and borne in His name should really prove to be a failure. Notwithstanding its apparent unsuccessful issue, their testimony shall accomplish what the Lord has decreed, and shall fulfil His eternal counsel, for it will be a solemn official protest against the Beast which rises from the sea, against the thraldom of the coming Antichrist, the darling of the democracy; and so successful shall their witness be, that through it, his full manifestation shall be for a time restrained.

* These acts may doubtless have a spiritual as well as a literal signification.

Further, they succeed in preparing a company of disciples who shall carry on their work and testimony (after they have been slain by Antichrist as the Beast from the abyss), and so shall extend the testimony of the gathered firstfruits, even as Elisha, and afterwards one of the sons of the prophets carried on to its completion the work and testimony given, in the first place, to Elijah to fulfil.

Rev. xi. 7.

See 1 Kings xix. 15-17, and 2 Kings ix. 1-10.

Having regard to the perils of the time during the rise of the last Antichrist, even that "hour of temptation" (developing into the great tribulation), that shall "try them that dwell upon the earth," those that are left on earth after the rapture of the firstfruits or first company, will derive much consolation from the testimony of Christ's Two Witnesses, through whose power they will be afforded shelter and protection, at least until the Witnesses shall have finished their testimony, when the faithful will begin to experience the full fury of the trinity of hell—the Dragon, the Beast, and the false Prophet.

Rev. iii. 10.

(vide Rev. xiii).

In these days of religious indifference, Christians can live in freedom, without undergoing open persecution. To true believers in the present time, the knowledge of the resurrection of Christ, coupled with that of the first principles of the doctrine of Christ, is sufficient to sustain the faith of all those who have not denied the Lord who purchased them with His own blood. But the faith of the great multitude of the Baptized who will undergo the fiery trials of the great tribulation will need to be specially strengthened, that the faithful may overcome the Beast, and, winning the crown of martyrdom

Acts xx. 28.

Rev. xv. 2 may stand on the sea of glass mingled with fire. This will be effected through the personal ministry of the Two Witnesses and through that of their adherents who follow them, who, amid the terrors of those days, will testify to Christian men, that they are Heb. xiii. 5, 6, 8. not forsaken by the living God, but that the Lord is still their helper. The knowledge imparted to them by the testimony of these two prophets, that many thousands of their fellow-Christians have received the reward of their faith and hope by having been raised from the dead, or changed without death, and translated into the presence of the Lord, shall 1 Tim. vi. 12. doubtless embolden the survivors to " fight the good fight of faith " even unto the end.   Indeed, viewed practically, what testimony could be more helpful at such a crisis?

(7) In considering the subsequent persecution which the two prophets shall endure because of their testimony, it is patent that the witness which they will bear must be a painful task to flesh and blood, and one involving the highest courage, faith and self-sacrifice.   Their testimony will be unacceptable to the mass of the Baptized, and will be generally rejected, notwithstanding the miraculous signs with which it will be accompanied, so that it will appear to the world to end in failure and disaster.

The duration of the testimony of the two witnesses for a period of one thousand two hundred and threescore days, terminates during the last phase of the antichristian power.   At this stage of his development, Antichrist is described in the Apocalypse as Rev. xi. 7. " the beast that ascendeth out of the bottomless pit"

(the *abyss*, Greek), who shall make war against
Two Witnesses, and shall overcome them, and kill
them, but not until they shall have finished their
testimony. It is revealed that at the close of the
testimony of the Two Witnesses, the people triumph
in their martyrdom, as in the case of previous prophets who made unwelcome announcements from
God, and endured cruel persecution even unto death,
for our blessed Lord in His indictment of Jerusalem,
described the reception she was wont to give to
her prophets, saying: "O Jerusalem, Jerusalem, thou
" that killest the prophets, and stonest them which
" are sent unto thee!" The Two Witnesses will
thus meet with the usual fate of the messengers of
God, viz., REJECTION, ending in their violent death.

When the Two Witnesses shall have sealed their
testimony with their blood, "they that dwell upon
" the earth shall rejoice over them," because these
two prophets had tormented them on account of their
wickedness. But their triumph will be brief, for "after
" three days and an half the Spirit of life from God
" entered into them, and they stood upon their feet;
" and great fear fell upon them which saw them.
" And they heard a great voice from heaven saying
" unto them, Come up hither. And they ascended
" up to heaven in a cloud; and their enemies beheld
" them." Thus, by the act of God in their resurrection and triumphal ascension into heaven, their
testimony will receive the seal of the Lord. This
will take place during the Laodicean period of the
Church, to whom in her lukewarm state the Lord
Jesus Christ makes His appeal as "the faithful and

Matt. xxiii. 29-34.

Matt. xxiii. 37.

Rev. xi. 10-12.

Rev. iii. 14, 22. " true witness," saying, " He that hath an ear, let " him hear what the Spirit saith unto the churches."

It is worthy of notice that in the first allusion in Rev. xi. 1, 2. this chapter to the *city*, in connexion with the Two Witnesses, with the measuring of the temple of God, the altar, the worshippers, and the treading under foot by the Gentiles of the court for forty and two weeks, Christendom, as the spiritual Jerusalem is called "the holy city," and that afterwards, when the Two Witnesses have been slain, the city is no longer Rev. xi. 8. designated the holy city, but "the great city," as if the former name had been forfeited, and God had withdrawn from her in wrath at the rejection of His ordinances, and because of the slaughter of His Two Witnesses.

Having considered the Two Witnesses, as referred to in the book of the Revelation, we may enquire into their relation to the Feasts of the Law, in their typical bearing on the concluding events of the Christian dispensation. (See Chapters II. and VII).

The Two Witnesses and their following do not seem to be *directly* connected with the firstfruits of the barley harvest, but rather with those of the wheat harvest, which were presented in the form of two loaves waved before the Lord at Pentecost. No reference is here made to the reaping of a sheaf of Lev. xxiii. 15-21 wheat; the type consists in the bringing forth from the habitations of Israel, two loaves baken with leaven, and in waving them before the Lord on the fiftieth day after the presentation of the firstfruits of barley harvest, these loaves being declared to be the firstfruits of the wheat harvest.

Recognizing the risen Christ as the Firstfruits typified by the barley sheaf, the type of the two Pentecostal loaves may have a primary, though not an exclusive, reference to the *whole* Church which came into existence on the day of Pentecost.* Wheat is a symbol of divine truth in its highest form as ministered by those having the mind of Christ: flour is a symbol of such truth moulded into doctrinal form through the understanding. It is stated concerning the first believers, that "they continued stedfastly in the apostles' doctrine." These and subsequent Jewish believers were an election from among Israel, and were gathered by the apostles to the circumcision, who also gathered the first household of Gentile believers upon whom the Holy Spirit came down, as He had done some eight years previously, on the first apostolic band. Moreover, the Lord began to bring into manifestation an apostleship to the Gentiles,

Acts ii. 42.

Acts x. 44, 45.

* Types have various applications, and truth is both simple and complex. We have in Chapter II. spoken of the firstfruits of the Christian Church, the 144,000 being typified by the firstfruits of the barley harvest; and the suggestion in the text is only another view of the inexhaustible truth and purpose of God. And in confirmation of the application of the sheaf of barley to the firstfruits of the Christian Church, we may remark that the Lord spoke of His approaching death as the sowing of a single *corn of wheat*, which must die in order to bring forth fruit. The numerous grains of corn in a sheaf (or omer) of barley, evidently must refer to a large *number of persons*. The barley harvest comes *first*. Christ was the Firstfruits. He first obtained perfect redemption, but others will obtain in their due order, perfect redemption of body, soul and spirit, but only IN HIM. All types receive their first and full accomplishment in Christ Himself, and then in His Body the Church.

John xii. 24.

by the call and separation of Saul (Paul) and Barnabas, to whom He also committed the Gospel, and by whom many from among the Gentiles were sealed after they believed in the Lord Jesus and were baptized. So here we see two bands of firstfruits under two bands of apostles answering to the two loaves, and it is probable that the leaven signifies that spirit of separation which for eight years prevented even the Jewish apostles from discerning the full purpose of God, which was to break down the middle wall of partition between Jews and Gentiles, and to make them one in Christ. This spirit of separation on the part of the Jews, seems never to have been wholly eradicated. The leaven remained, though the gift of God was not withheld even from the rebellious. The leaven of separation in another form showed itself rampant among the Baptized in the great schism between the Churches in the East and the West, and later on when the Western Church itself split into two great divisions (known as the Roman and Protestant communions), each of which has its measure of the meal of pure doctrine, though mingled with erroneous doctrines and practices which lie at the root of separation.*

See Acts x. 1-15

Eph. ii. 13-15.

Ps. lxviii. 18.

Matt. xiii. 33.

* It is very difficult to say when the division or schism between the Eastern and Western Churches really began. There was first, the Easter controversy (settled at the Council of Nice, A.D. 325), then the dispute about the clause *filioque*, which began in the sixth century, leading ultimately to the final separation and excommunication which took place A.D. 1054. It is also difficult to affix a definite date to the Protestant disruption in the sixteenth century. As regards England, she repudiated the Papal supremacy in A.D. 1534, and the Pope published his sentence of excommunication against Henry VIII. in A.D. 1538.

Many and varied have been the efforts to restore
the unity of Christendom, but the results have been
similar to those which followed the endeavours made
from time to time to reunite the kingdoms of Israel
and Judah. God alone can reunite the broken stick.   Ezek. xxxvii.
He has overruled the evil of disruption by preserving   16-20.
a witness to the full measure of His truth in
the separate portions of the riven Church, until by
His own act of mercy He should restore her unity.
The Lord's mode of testifying to the unity of the
Church in Himself has been by apostles and prophets,
and it is, no doubt, this double witness which is in
some form to be perpetuated by the Two Witnesses,
even as Elisha received a double portion of the Spirit
to carry on the testimony of Elijah.

It is apparent, then, how these Two Witnesses and
their followers will be the instruments of God for
bringing together into unity of faith, hope, and love,
the remnant of the hidden and faithful saints in
distracted and divided Christendom, pushing the
people together—like the horns of an unicorn (margin)   Deut. xxxiii. 17.
—to the ends of the earth. The Two Witnesses will
also then be seen as symbolized in the two loaves
brought out of the *habitations*, the Churches, not
coming from only one division of the Baptized, but
coming in a Catholic spirit in the power of a divine
endowment received from their contact with the
apostolic firstfruits, as Elisha received his endowment
through Elijah. They will have been prepared
secretly by God, that on the translation of the first
of the firstfruits, they may be ready to give their
testimony to the doctrine and witness of apostles

previously rejected, and to the translation of those whom the Lord has accounted worthy of this great honour. The baking of these two loaves points probably to a secret preparation through meditation and prayer, and a perfecting through suffering.

This *second* company is not called in Scripture a gathering. Two gatherings are spoken of in Rev. vii., that of the firstfruits and that of the harvest which followed. Whatever is not firstfruits is harvest, and whatever is not harvest is firstfruits, and the Scripture suggests no other classification.

As regards the *third* great company, they come out of the great tribulation, and they form the great multitude, the *harvest* or the great final ingathering at the close of the Christian dispensation, and are distinct from the *vintage*, which is the manifestation of the wrath of God upon the finally impenitent.

Rev. xiv. 14-20.

Thus we see three companies:—

Ex xxxiv. 26.
Lev. xxiii. 9-14.

(1) Those who are the first of the firstfruits, Rev. vii. and xiv. (The firstfruits of the barley harvest.)

(2) Those who form a second company connected with the Two Witnesses. (The firstfruits of wheat harvest who form the two loaves, Lev. xxiii. 15-21.)

Lev. xxiii. 33-44.

(3) And thirdly the rest of the harvest reaped in the great tribulation.

As we have already remarked (chap. vii.), this threefold order seems to be borne out in the Apocalypse, but it is in the eleventh chapter that special reference is made to the Two Witnesses. This chapter opens with the measuring of the (spiritual) temple and of its worshippers, who are to be judged, or measured by the criterion of their accept-

ance or rejection of a special message. The Church
at large is still regarded as a heavenly polity, and
to this fact the Two Witnesses direct their appeal;
they are not concerned with measuring the outer
court—the standing and condition of those who
despise the sacraments and ordinances of the Church,
and on which judgment is to follow when the
Antichrist (the beast out of the abyss) shall be
revealed and shall tread the holy city (Christendom)
under foot for forty and two months. Owing to the   Rev. xi. 2, 3.
juxtaposition in the text of this period of forty two
months with the 1260 days of the ministry of the
Two Witnesses, some have supposed that these periods
are one and the same; others have thought, however, that such is not the case, but that, while
the 1260 days mark the prophesying of the Witnesses, the forty two months mark the succeeding
period of the brief triumph of Antichrist, when after   cf. Rev. xiii. 5.
warring against the Two Witnesses and at length
slaying them, he will for the space of three and a
half years overcome the saints—these two periods
making up one prophetic week (of years), namely,
the seventieth week of the prophet Daniel.

There can be little doubt that the seventy weeks
spoken of by the prophet Daniel, are weeks of years,
periods of seven years each, and by some profound
students of prophecy it is considered that the times of
the Gentiles* occupy a parenthetical space between the
sixty ninth week and the seventieth week, the latter

* The times of the Gentiles are generally reckoned as
dating from Nebuchadnezzar, cir. 580 B.C., who was the
head of gold of his fourfold metallic and prophetic image.

o

half of the seventieth week being the period of the brief despotic career of Antichrist and the conclusion of the Christian era.

The period intervening between the sixty ninth and seventieth week is undated, and no created intelligence knows when it will end. But with the coming of the Lord and the translation of the firstfruits or the rapture of the manchild, the seventieth week will begin, the events of which are mapped out into periods of time. With this "week" the Christian dispensation will conclude; after which God will revert to His ancient covenant people, the Jews, and restore them to their own land, Christ's kingdom being proclaimed at the sounding of the seventh trumpet, and the Jews becoming the acknowledged channel of blessing to all the nations of the earth.

In connexion with the duration of the ministry of the Two Witnesses, viz: 1260 days, we may offer the following remarks on this prophetic measure of time which is mentioned five times in the book of the Revelation and twice in the prophecy of Daniel, B.C. 537. This period is supposed to be one of three years and a half, and is described in different formulæ. It may be termed (as by the prophet Daniel) a time, times, (generally taken to mean two times) and the dividing of time, or forty two months, or 1260 days, all of which periods may be taken as arithmetically synonymous. A prophetic year is 360 days, consequently the first expression equals $360+360+360+180$, the equivalent of 1260 days, or forty two months, the duration of each prophetic month being

Dan. vii. 25.
Dan. xii. 7.

thirty days. The measure of three years and a half is expressly mentioned in the epistle of James with reference to the drought in the time of Elijah, which lasted for the space of three years and six months, and seems to point to that part of the Elias testimony of the last days which will devolve upon the Two Witnesses, who will have power to shut heaven in the days of their prophecy. There is also an analogy — but not an identity — between this measure of time and the three days and a half mentioned in Revelation xi., as the interval between the death of the Witnesses and their resurrection, when the Spirit of life from God entered into them, and they stood upon their feet. The ministry of our Lord on earth lasted three years and a half; so that this prophetic period may be regarded as significant in connexion with the events which wind up the present dispensation, when the Church's experiences may be analogous to those of her Lord. May these glorious events soon take place and give us an abundant entrance into the everlasting kingdom of our Lord and Saviour Jesus Christ!

It would appear from the signs of the times as if the testimony and work of the Two Witnesses might be anticipated in the immediate future.

James v. 17.

Rev. xi. 11

> "But soon the word of witness
>   Shall sound from land to land,
> And in the hour of darkness
>   The wise shall understand:
>
> "When through the fires of judgment,
>   And through the waves of strife,
> The saints of God returning,
>   Shall pass from death to life."
> —E. W. R.

CHAPTER IX.

Testimonies to the Hope of Translation during the Christian Dispensation.

IN the records of the Christian Church during the past nineteen centuries, there seem to be comparatively few testimonies to the special hope of our high calling in Christ Jesus — the first resurrection, the change of the living without death, and their joint translation into the air to meet the returning Lord—upon which we have been dwelling. In considering this subject, there are two phases of it which seem to be contradictory. On the one hand, God has always had His witnesses for His truth, albeit they may have been few and hidden, like the seven thousand in Israel, who had not bowed 1 Kings xix. 18. the knee to Baal, who were *left* to God, but yet were unknown to the despairing prophet, Elijah. On the other hand, when reviewing the past eighteen centuries, the Church may well be filled with sorrow and humiliation that these cardinal and living truths of revelation have been so much forgotten by the great mass of those who have been baptized into this hope of their calling.

In the first century of the Christian era, when living Apostles guided the Church, these hopes burned brightly, and afforded consolation to the primitive martyrs under their persecutions. The priority of the resurrection of the dead in Christ, the change of those who are alive and remain, and their joint translation to meet the Lord in the air, are clearly stated by the Apostle to the Gentiles. The relevant passages in his epistles have been fully quoted (Chap. I.).   Most of the Apostles refer to the Lord's return, and St. John received a clear vision of the first resurrection, while the whole book of the Apocalypse rings with the hope of the coming of the Lord.   At the same time it must be acknowledged that the hope of attaining to bodily immortality without death, soon lapsed from the memory of the Baptized. St. Paul himself was forced to accept the inevitable fact of his departure; St. Peter also was conscious that he should shortly put off his earthly tabernacle as the Lord had shewed him.

1 Thess. iv. 14-
17.
1 Cor. xv. 20-57.
2 Cor. v. 1-8.

Phil. i. 21.
2 Tim. iv. 6-8.
2 Pet. i. 13-15.

Passing from the apostolic age and entering upon the second century, we come upon an interesting document which has recently been discovered, "The Didaché, or Teaching of the Twelve Apostles," the date of which is supposed to be about A.D. 100, and in which there are allusions to the coming of the Lord, to the first resurrection, and to the millennial reign of Christ, but no explicit reference to the change of the living, or to the translation of the saints.* Even in the first century these hopes began to decline, and it may be said that they had died out ere the fifth century dawned.   Yet, speaking generally, the Christians of the early post-apostolic Church, from Hermas to Origen, were believers in the first resurrection and in the personal reign of Christ on the earth for

* See Appendix V.

Rev. ii. 8. a thousand years. Clement of Rome, Barnabas, Ignatius, Polycarp, who was the "angel of the Church in Smyrna," Irenæus the pupil of Polycarp, Justin Martyr (in his dialogue with Trypho the Jew, held at Ephesus) all witnessed to the first resurrection, and to the succeeding millennial kingdom of Christ. But even Ignatius and Polycarp looked forward to death as the deliverer, and hardly embraced the hope of *life without death*, and indeed many of the early Christians became passionately eager for the attainment of the crown of martyrdom, and longed for death rather than for the blessed change into the Lord's likeness without death. To the above names may be added those of Tertullian, Clement of Alexandria, and Cyprian. Many are the brilliant names of bishops, fathers, doctors, martyrs and confessors which adorn the Church's annals in the second century, and of whom it may be said that, without exception, they expected the pre-millennial advent of the Lord.

In the third and fourth centuries the same testimony exists, though without complete unanimity, a different view being held by some, to whom reference will be made. During this period, however, Lactantius, Gregory of Nyssa, and the Nicene Fathers, clung to the faith of the first resurrection, though, it must be added, that few (if any) traces of the cognate doctrines of the change of the living and of their subsequent translation can be discerned in their writings. Eusebius, Cyril, Ambrose, Chrysostom, and Hilary cannot be cited as upholders of these truths, although they were not professedly hostile

to them.   But Jerome was an avowed opposer and
a scoffer at the doctrine in question, and it gradually
fell into disrepute, until it almost dwindled away
about the close of the fourth century.   But over the
grave of Bishop Alexander, who lived about A.D.
375, and is buried at Tipasa, near Algiers, the
witness that he died expecting the first resurrection
is still to be read in the loose crumbling mosaics
which cover his grave.*   The Council of Constantinople (A.D. 381) gave some witness to the truth in
concluding the enlarged Nicene Creed with that
sentence which for centuries the Church has gone
on repeating as a formula — " I look for the
resurrection of the dead, and the life of the world
to come.   Amen."

It is clear that these truths were held after the
death of the Apostles, more or less throughout the
period during which the manifestation of the gifts
of the Holy Spirit continued to exist in the Church,
but they began to be neglected when the Church,
having lost the apostolic and prophetic ministries,
and ceasing to exercise spiritual gifts (properly so
called), fell away from her heavenly standing.   By
degrees, the truths in question became matters of
controversy; until at length they passed even into
the catalogue of heresies, being almost forgotten
until their revival in these last days; for, though
the hope of the Lord's return and of the first
resurrection survived the apostolic age, nevertheless
the thought of the concurrent change of the living
at the coming of the Lord Jesus, and of the joint

* See Appendix VI.

translation of the raised and changed saints, soon disappeared, not only as a practical living hope, but even as an abstract doctrine. The manifested presence of the Holy Ghost in the Church, and the exercise of all the heavenly ministries of Christ —especially those of apostles and prophets—are necessary to keep these hopes alive, for it is the peculiar office of the Holy Spirit to bring to the memory of the Church what Christ Himself taught, or what was subsequently revealed to the apostles; and without His manifested presence, Christians cannot fail to be overcome by the world, by its sins, its cares, and its pleasures, and thus they are tempted to let slip the special hope of their calling and the things which pertain to the revelation of the kingdom of God.

Wherefore, the failure of these heavenly hopes connected with the Lord's return and the establishment of His kingdom, must be associated with the gradual quenching of the gifts of the Holy Spirit. The gift of prophecy lingered on in the Church till about A.D. 325, the date of the Council of Niccæa, after which it was neither exercised nor desired, whilst in the Councils of the Church, diminished stress was laid on the blessed hope which was the pivot of apostolic doctrine. We are not aware of any Council in which these truths formed the prominent subject of consideration; whilst orthodoxy, heresy, controversy, and the temporal position of the Church occupied an increasingly wide horizon during the lapse of ages. Before long, indeed, the idea of the millennial kingdom of Christ became

branded as heretical, and at length, as already said,
it died out entirely; for, if men cared for religion
at all, they were swallowed up with the one thought
of their personal salvation, and became indifferent
to the grand purpose of God in the perfecting of
His Church, and in the deliverance of the groaning
creation.   Thus the Church, afflicted with heresy
and schism, entered upon the era of the second,
third, and fourth centuries, which are generally
reckoned as the age of heresies.

For this condition of things the following reasons
may be specified :—

(1) The removal by death of the Apostles—the
ordinance of God for rule in the Church—who first
revealed these truths and hopes, and earnestly proclaimed the same.

(2) The quenching of the gifts of the Holy Ghost,
the disappearance of prophets, and the gradual cessation of the voice of prophecy.

(3) The gradual decease of those faithful men who
had companied with the Apostles and witnessed
to their doctrine. These were like the elders who   Josh. xxiv. 31.
outlived Joshua, during whose lives Israel served the
Lord, but after whose death they lapsed into idolatry.

(4) The cooling of the first love, which was the   Rev. ii. 4.
precise charge of the Lord Jesus against the Church
in Ephesus.

(5) The intrusion of the power of the world into
the Church, and her establishment as a worldly
institution. This took place when the Emperor
Constantine publicly recognized Christianity as the
religion of the Roman Empire, A.D. 320.

(6) The supreme rule of pastoral bishops, aided by Church Councils, which was not God's appointed way for guiding the universal Church, or for preserving it from heresy and schism. It is true that Councils did something for the faith, chiefly as concerning the doctrines of the Trinity and of the Incarnation, but they could not set the Church right as to its *hope*, when they themselves did not entertain this hope.

Besides these general considerations, one direct cause may be cited as having tended to quench for a season the early bridal hope of the Church, and this was the influence of two men who have been held to be doctors in the Eastern and Western branches of the Church, viz.: Origen and Augustine. Most of the Fathers of the first three centuries as we have seen, had taught the pre-millennial advent of the Lord, and Origen was the first teacher of any note who questioned its correctness. He was born about A.D. 186, and died about A.D. 253. He was given to spiritualizing interpretations of Scripture, and fell into the error of ignoring its plain letter, and was thus led to explain away the truths of the first resurrection and of the subsequent kingdom of Christ upon the earth.* But Augustine, bishop

* "A formidable opponent of the views of the Chiliasts arose in the fanciful Origen. * * * * *

From this time the credit of millenarianism gradually declined, and with the exception of a general statement which occurs in the canons of the Council of Nice, A.D. 325, we hear little more of the doctrine until the lapse of centuries brought it again into discussion." *Faiths of the World*, s.v. Millennarians or Chiliasts.

of Hippo, about A.D. 390, following in his footsteps, succeeded more than any other theologian in crushing the truth; for he opposed the opinions of the so-called Chiliasts with all the weight of his authority; and, with hyper-spirituality, considered the belief in the millennial kingdom as material and carnal.

As to the school of interpretation which makes the first resurrection to be spiritual, and to relate to the regeneration of Christian souls, it will be appropriate to quote Dean Alford's comment on Rev. xx. He says—"I cannot consent to distort the words from their plain sense and chronological place in the prophecy on account of any considerations of difficulty, or any risk of abuses which the doctrine of the millennium may bring with it. Those who lived next to the Apostles, and the whole Church for three hundred years, understood them in the plain literal sense. As regards the text itself, no legitimate treatment of it will extort what is known as the spiritual interpretation now in fashion. If in a passage where *two resurrections* are mentioned, where certain dead rose at the first, 'and the rest of the dead' rose only at the end of a specified period after that first—if in such a passage the first resurrection may be understood to be *spiritual* rising with Christ, while the second means *literal* rising from the grave—then there is an end to all significance in language, the Scripture is wiped out as a definite testimony to anything. If the first resurrection is spiritual, then so is the second, which, I suppose, none will be hardy enough to maintain; but if the first is literal, then so is the second, which, in common with the whole primitive Church, and many of the best modern expositors, I do maintain and receive as an article of faith and hope."*

The popular but erroneous view, which originated with Augustine about the beginning of the fifth century, has within the last forty years been revived by Bishop Wordsworth. According to this view the "thousand years" is a form of speech intended to cover the whole period from the ascension to the second advent, which is to be the time for the final judgment and of the end of the world; consequently, we are now in the millennium, and the saints are reigning with Christ now; the "first resurrection," according to this school of teachers, is the spiritual resurrection of souls in becoming regenerate, and not the bodily resurrection of departed saints. It need scarcely be said that such a method of interpretation is purely arbitrary, and that it is sufficiently refuted by the present awful condition of Christendom which is ripening for the manifestation of the coming Antichrist.†

Alas! the Doctors of the Church have often manifested the tendency to depart from the written Scriptures, and to make the word of God of none effect by their traditions.

Succeeding to the age of heresies, there supervened a period of four centuries which has been named the age of schisms; when, alas! the Church could no longer be looked upon as *one*, but finally became broken up in A.D. 1054 into two great divisions—the Eastern and the Western.

* Dean Alford, Greek Testament; Notes on Rev. xx. 4-6.
† See *The Parousia*, p. 9: D. Hobbs & Co., Glasgow.

The Eastern or Greek Church has long prided herself on her orthodoxy, and from time to time has produced men who have left precious truth on record. But she has lapsed during the ages into many errors, both of doctrine and of practice, either identical with similar superstitions in the Roman Church, or resembling them, while she has adopted a distinctly hostile attitude towards the *doctrine* involved in the word *filioque*, which was inserted in the Creed of Constantinople, by the Pope of Rome in A.D. 1014, and led to the great schism of the eleventh century. But for centuries the Eastern Church as a whole has been stagnant and Laodicean, although of late she has aroused herself to persecute the "Stundists," who are inoffensive Bible-reading Christians, only craving more spiritual light than they can receive from the "Orthodox Church."*
As regards the hope of the Lord's second advent, and resultant events, there has been no acknowledged testimonies in this branch of the Church for centuries. God, however, has always had His hidden witnesses; and in a treatise which has lately been published †by one who has examined the writings of the Greco-Russian Church, the author states that he has discovered a few witnesses to the first resurrection, but scarcely any reference to the change of the living and to the translation of the saints.

In the Western or Roman Church, these truths have been practically unrecognized, and have even been condemned as heretical. One of the spiritual

* God grant that they may benefit by the Czar's recent ukase of religious toleration (May, 1905).
† *Stimmen aus der Kirche*, by Herr K. von Mickwitz, A.D. 1902.

sins of the Roman Church has been that of endeavouring to forestall the manifestation of the kingdom
of God, and of arrogating to her head, the Pope, the
position of Christ's vicegerent upon earth; hence,
this section of the Church has never favoured the
doctrine of the premillennial coming of the Lord to
set up His kingdom on the earth, the hope of the
change and of the translation having been generally
and officially ignored. "Throughout the dark ages,
when popery ruled with despotic sway over the
minds and consciences of men, Chiliasm was utterly
disowned, and it is a remarkable fact, that popery
has not only omitted this doctrine from her creed,
but testified against it as a heresy." *

The Papacy, in fact, adopted Augustine's notion
that the kingdom of God was already established on
earth, and identified that kingdom with the Roman
Church. This being the case, why should Romanists
look for the return of the Lord, which would only
mar their plans? Why should they, who have settled
on their lees on the earth, hope for a kingdom
of a thousand years' duration, or for the first
resurrection, or for a change of the body into
immortality without death, or for a translation from
the earth into the heavens, all of which hopes must
appear to them to be dreamy visions? Thus as the
Papacy has viewed these doctrines not merely with
apathy but with hostility, it is a matter of little
wonder that the ten centuries of papal ascendency
afford very few witnesses to the ancient hope of the
coming and kingdom of Christ.

* *Faiths of the World:* s.v. Millennarians.

Hildegardis von Bingen, who lived in the twelfth century, dying in A.D. 1178, wrote a remarkable book called *Heptachronon*, in which, after picturing the approaching corruption (decay) in the Church, he anticipates a new and better time, saying:—
" There shall then arise brave and wise men who will gather together all the old and new declarations of the Bible, and all words diffused by the Holy Ghost, and will set them forth with understanding, like as it were an ornament with costly jewels . . ."

Now, as our Lord's announcement to the scribes and Pharisees that He would " send them prophets and " apostles " is rendered by St. Matthew as " prophets " and *wise men*," and as St. Paul calls himself a " wise master-builder," may not the above prophetic forecast in the twelfth century of " wise men " arising in the Church, and of " words diffused by the Holy Ghost" (in addition to the "declarations of the Bible ") be regarded as a prediction of the restoration of apostles and prophets, such as is claimed to have taken place during the nineteenth century ? Luke xi. 49. Matt. xxiii. 34. 1 Cor. iii. 10.

From such an isolated mediæval instance it may be concluded that while many hidden saints may have longed for the restoration of the original ordinances of the Church, and have cherished her early hope through earnest study of the Holy Scriptures, their aspirations have not floated down on the stream of history.   A notable exception, however, may be mentioned.   Simeon Levita was a learned Spanish rabbi, with a profound knowledge of Hebrew, of the Talmud, and of the rabbinical writings, who, on his conversion to Christianity, received the baptismal name of Paul, and became bishop of Burgos, and finally patriarch of Aquileia, dying in A.D. 1435. He wrote a book * in which after setting forth that this world would continue for six thousand years, according to an old tradition, † he testifies plainly to the first resurrection, the change, and translation of the saints, the coming of Christ and His millennial kingdom.

But while the Church of Rome has produced many world-known saints and scholars, such as the Venerable Bede, Anselm archbishop of Canterbury, Bernard of Clairvaux, Bonaventura, Francis of Assisi, Elizabeth of Hungary, Thomas Aquinas, Catherine of Siena, Savonarola, Bellarmine, Charles Borromeo, St. Theresa, Vincent de Paul, Francis de Sales, Madame Guyon, Fenelon, and many others, there is little or nothing to be found in their writings, doctrinal or devotional, about the hope of the resurrection and of the coming kingdom; and nothing at all concerning the change without death, or the translation of the raised and changed saints to meet the returning Lord in the air.

During the spiritual throes in the next crisis of the Church—that of the Reformation of the sixteenth century—the human mind became greatly emancipated; and, the written word of God having been exhumed from the neglect of centuries, a recognition of these soul-stirring truths, with a revival of the hope set

* "Dyalogus qui vocatur scrutinium scripturarum compositus per Rev. Patr. Dom. Paulum de Sancta Maria, magistrum in theologia, episcopum Burgensem . . . . A.D. 1434."

† In the book *Sanhedrin*, "Liber Canchedrin hierosolimatanus."

before the early Christians, might have been expected. But it was an age of excited feeling and controversy, not only with Rome, but also among the various Protestant sects themselves.   Hence, in the formularies and liturgies of the Reformed Churches, a clear recognition of these special hopes cannot be found; and, although certain accepted truths are enshrined in the creeds, such as the return of the Lord to judge the world, and the resurrection at the last day, yet there is a general ignoring of the *first* resurrection, and of the change and translation of the saints.   These truths appear to have been overlooked, except in the writings of Melancthon and Luther, who in their "Chroniken"* quote largely from Levita's book, through which their attention was drawn to these truths.†

Although there are stray allusions in the works of the Reformers to the second coming of the Lord, yet, speaking generally, throughout their writings, and those of the Puritans, *the hope of it* cannot be discerned.   In the writings of Calvin, Tyndale, Latimer, Ridley, Bullinger, there is but little allusion to the coming of Christ, with its concurrent hopes; nor, notwithstanding the great intellectual and spiritual awakening at the Reformation, was the great doctrine of Christ's second advent prominently brought before the Church by the Reformers.   For it needed more than councils or bishops, or even the mighty men of the Reformation of the sixteenth century, or the giant divines of the Puritan age, to effect the great spiritual awakening of the Church to her true and

* Melancthon, A.D. 1531.   Luther, A.D. 1550.
† See Appendix VII.

P

heavenly *hope*. The Reformers appear to have tacitly adopted the later patristic view, held by Augustine in the fourth century.

There were, however, a few exceptions, of which the following case is a beautiful example. A Lutheran pastor, Johann Arndt (A.D. 1555–1625) was a burning and shining light in his day, his work *Paradise Gartlein* being widely read as a devotional book. In this work he speaks not only of the hope of the coming of the Lord, and of his longing to escape by translation those things that are coming on the earth, and to stand before the Son of Man, but of the preparation needed for it; viz., in the restoration of the ministries of the Lord—apostles, prophets, evangelists, pastors and teachers—through whose instrumentality the Church shall be prepared for her eagle flight or translation into heaven. Arndt offers this remarkable prayer:—

cf. Eph. iv. 11.

"O Thou who hast ascended up on high, and taken captivity captive, Thou hast received gifts for men; God hath set Thee as Head over Thy Church. . . . . Thou art our eternal and only Head, who fillest Thy body and Thy members with life, light, comfort, strength, victory, peace, and joy. Thou art our everlasting High Priest; Thou dost anoint us with Thy Holy Spirit; Thou givest evangelists, apostles, prophets, pastors and teachers, that Thy mystical body may be edified (built up). Oh! send forth such builders, whom Thou hast filled with the spirit of wisdom and understanding. Thou hast an everlasting priesthood, therefore canst Thou answer prayer at all times. By Thine ascension into heaven,

Thou hast led the way; because Thou, as our Head, art now in heaven, so certainly will not Thy members remain outside: Thou wilt fetch us all up. Give us the wings of the morning and the holy longing for Thee, that we may beseech Thee: Oh, when shall I go thither, where I shall see Thy face. . . . . Come, Lord Jesus, and take me to Thyself. Thou hast foretold us of the end of the world, hast revealed the sign thereof, and hast taught how we should prepare ourselves for it. Oh, my King and Lord, let me wait every day with joy for Thy coming. O, let us fly as eagles to Thee, Lord Christ; strengthen my faith, for Thou hast said—'When the Son of Man cometh, shall He find faith on the earth?' Come, O Lord! Faith and love are extinguished; the winter has continued too long; and, if Thou dost not hasten the days, no man will be saved. Ah! beautiful harvest of the resurrection of the just; what beautiful sheaves wilt Thou bring forth. Thou wilt change us in a moment from mortality into immortality; from weakness into strength."

The following striking testimony, which has come down to us from the seventeenth century, is taken from an address by John Robinson—one of the Pilgrim Fathers—to his followers, when they emigrated to America, and sailed in the *Mayflower* in A.D. 1620. "From the shores of the old world," writes Miss Bremer, "he uttered, as a parting address, these glorious words":—

"I charge you before God and His blessed angels, that ye follow me no farther than ye have seen me follow the Lord Jesus Christ. The Lord has yet

more truth to break out of His holy word. I cannot
sufficiently bewail the condition of the Reformed
Churches who are come to a period in religion, and
will go no farther at present than the instruments
of their reformation. Luther and Calvin were great
and shining lights in their times, yet they penetrated
not into the whole counsel of God. I beseech you,
remember it—'tis an article of your church covenant
that you be ready to receive whatever truth shall be
made known to you from the written word of God."*

The following extract from *Calvin's Institutes*,
A.D. 1557, on the possibility of the Lord's restoring
apostles is too remarkable to be omitted :—" In Eph. iv.
4-16, Paul shows that the ministry of men, which God
employs in His government of the Church, is the
principal bond which holds the faithful together in
one body. He also indicates that the Church cannot
be preserved in perfect safety unless it be supported
by these means which God has been pleased to
appoint for its preservation. . . . . Those who
preside over the government of the Church, according
to the institution of Christ, are stated by Paul to be,
first, apostles; secondly, prophets; thirdly, evangelists;
fourthly, pastors ; lastly, teachers. Of these, only the
two last sustain an ordinary office in the Church ; the
others were such as the Lord raised up at the com-
mencement of His kingdom, and such as He still
raises up on particular occasions when required by
the necessity of the time. . . . . though I do
not deny that ever since that period, God has some-

---

* From *Homes of the New World*, by Miss Frederika
Bremer. Vol. 1, p. 187.

times raised up apostles, or *evangelists in their stead*, as He has done in our own time." *

In the older documents of the Church of Scotland, many expressions are used respecting the ordinances of the Church, indicative of the lingering in the heart of the writer, that the Lord might at some time restore the ministry of Apostles.   For example, the following sentence occurs in *The Second Book of Discipline*, A.D. 1581, chap. ii. sec. 6.   " Sum of thir ecclesiasticall functiones ar ordinar, and sum extraordinar, or temporarie.   There be three extraordinar functiones: the office of the apostle, of the evanglist, and of the prophet, quhilkis ar not perpetuall, and now have ceisit in the Kirk of God, except quhen He pleasit extraordinarly for a tyme to steir sum of them up againe."

Later, in the seventeenth century, various eminent names could be given of those who believed in the millennial kingdom; such as Mede, Usher, Milton, Baxter, Bunyan; but none of them utter a clarion testimony to the change and to the translation, as the prelude thereto.   Nevertheless, the following quotation from Milton is full of interest:—" Now, once again by all concurrence of signs, and by the general instinct of holy and devout men, as they daily and solemnly express their thoughts, God is decreeing to begin some new and great period in His Church, even to the reforming of the Reformation itself: what does He then but reveal Himself to His servants, and as His manner is, first to His Englishmen; I say as His manner is, first to us, though we

* Quoted in *The Elijah Ministry to the Christian Church*, p. 529; by C. W. Boase.   Robert Grant, 1868.

mark not the method of His counsels, and are unworthy. Now, the time seems come wherein Moses, the great prophet, may sit in heaven rejoicing to see that memorable and glorious work of his fulfilled, when not only the seventy elders, but all the Lord's people are become prophets."*

The Rev. Richard Baxter's intense longing for the Lord's coming is evident from his prayer in A.D. 1662 :—"Hasten, O my Saviour, the time of Thy return; send forth Thine angels, and let that dreadful joyful trumpet sound; delay not, lest the living give up their hopes; delay not, lest earth should grow like hell, and lest Thy Church, by divisions, be crumbled all to dust; delay not, lest the grave should boast of victory. . . . . Return, O Lord, how long! Oh! let Thy kingdom come. The desolate Bride saith, Come! For Thy Spirit within her saith, Come! The whole creation saith, Come!—waiting to be delivered from the bondage of corruption. Thyself hath said, 'Surely I come quickly.' Amen—even so come, Lord Jesus!"

George Lorentz Seidenbecher, who died about A.D. 1664, was pastor at Unterneubrun in Saxony. He wrote on the reign of Christ and on its wonderful concomitants. For preaching on this subject, he was condemned as a heretic by the consistory of the University of Jena, and was "unfrocked." He was told that the seventeenth article of the Augsburg confession was against this doctrine. "Chiliasmus Sanctus, qui est Sabbatismus populo Dei relictus"

---

* "*Areopagitica:* A speech for the liberty of unlicensed printing." By John Milton: Nov., A.D. 1644.

was a book that he wrote in A.D. 1660, and it was condemned as heretical. Mosheim says of him:—
"The expectation of the millennial kingdom, which seldom exists in well-informed minds, and which generally produced extravagant opinions, was embraced and propagated by George Lawrence Seidenbecher, a preacher in the Saxon district of Eichsfeld; and for this he was deprived of his office."*

Jacob Tauben, another German pastor, living in the same century, also preached on the millennial reign; and the Lutherans "put him out of the Synagogue." There were others during that period — laymen as well as pastors in the Lutheran Church—who were persecuted and deprived of their professions, and even of their property, for holding these views, which were branded as heretical.† Breckling, who lived at the same period as Seidenbecher, was twice imprisoned, and for witnessing to the truth of the pre-millennial advent, his property in Germany was confiscated. It is evident, however, that while they preached the coming of the Lord and His kingdom, they made no reference to the change of the living, or to the translation of the saints; shewing that they had not laid fully to heart these truths, upon which both Luther and Melanchthon had preached, and had written in their "Chroniken." During the course of the seventeenth and eighteenth centuries, there were many godly

John ix. 22.
John xvi. 2.

* *Mosheim*—edited by Henry Soames, M.A.   Book iv. Century xvii. Section 2, part 2, page 346.

† Vide Gottfried Arnold's *Kirchen und Ketzer Historie*, second and third books.

students who gave increased attention to the prophetic
Scriptures, and a school of writers on prophecy arose,
including such men as Sir Isaac Newton, 1642;
Bishop Sherlock, 1678; Bishop Newton, 1704; Bishop
Lowth, 1710; Bishop Horsley, 1773; James Mac-
knight, 1721; Robert Fleming, and others, among
whom millennarian truth was partially revived; but
little or no emphasis was laid on the doctrine of the
resurrection, change, and translation which St. Paul
delivered to the churches of Thessalonica and of
Corinth as a chief ground of hope and comfort.

About A.D. 1699, Mrs. Jane Lead, of whom some
details are given in Appendix VIII. gives a remarkable
witness to the true hope of the Church. She distinctly
points to the restoration of Apostles and Prophets at
the end of the dispensation, for the preparation of a
bridal or Philadelphian Church to be translated
without death to meet the Lord at His return.

In *The Signs of the Kingdom of Christ* (June 1,
1699), she writes as follows, in numbered paragraphs:

VI. "The powers of eternity will make their
descent into Time, among such sanctified, prepared
souls who shall be marked and sealed with the
Father's Name of Power. . . . .

XII. "Another sign will be that, by and through
the opening of the *living testimony* which proclaims
the approach of Christ's kingdom. . . . . Then
shall a sealing go forth in the Father's Name, and
in My Name, and the Holy Ghost. . . . ."

In another publication* this passage occurs:—

* *A Message to the Philadelphian Society.*

"This only is required on our part to suffer the Spirit of Burning to do upon us the Refining Work, fanning us with His fiery breath, until all be pure and clean.

"The lost apostolical gifts will return and flow again as from their own fountain.

"Now a cry from the heavens does go forth: who shall be those angels of all the several churches of this nation, that shall go out as trumpets for the awakening the sleepy Laodiceans, that in lukewarm temper do yet remain, to come out of their traditions, formalities, confusions and divisions, into the unity of the Philadelphian Love. . . . .

"O England, England, know the day of thy visitation; for a wonderful morning light is springing. Therefore open the windows of thy mind and let it in, for then it will usher in the LORD of Glory, who hath said, 'Behold I come to reign in love's kingdom.'"

The following is extracted from another book— *The Wars of David* :—

Paragraph xxxi. "He will call some aside . . . . as He did Moses, to hear His own voice expressly out of the burning bush; as that was visible and outward, so now it will be invisible and inward, in the flaming heart of Christ's humanity.

xxxii. "Now further it was intimated to me, that when any great deliverance was to be wrought for the Zion flock, there would be a calling up such as should stand in the meek and gentle, and yet zealous spirit of Moses, to receive counsel and command; to be as God's agents, to perform all that revealed to them shall be, from the mouth of the true infallible prophet, Christ

the Lord in them : this being the needful season here-
for, to be commissioned for such principal work and
office.

*   *   *   *   *   *   *   *   *

"By way of preparation and order for this to be
accomplished in this very season of time, a royal command from the king of the superior Jerusalem is gone
forth, to stir up some heroical spirits, to lay the
foundations for the building up this mystical and
spiritual defensive wall, which has an analogy to the
building of the Jewish temple. As the ancient temple
was laid waste, so likewise the spiritual Gospel
structure, of which the twelve apostles were laid as
the foundation, with their Head Corner-Stone, has been
much demolished and decayed, so that its first pure
and primitive model has been as it were obliterated
for many generations past. In the sense of which, I
was speaking before the Lord, and mourning for so
great a lapse of this ministration, as Daniel, for some
number of weeks; after which I found a strengthening
power girding me up, and several bright clouds en-
compassing me, out of which I saw several persons,
as I apprehended to the number of twelve, representing twelve apostles, that had each one a golden reed
in their hands to measure out the lengths and breadths
upon which this edifice was to stand : who did depute
and impower some persons now living in this age of
time, for the building and raising up what the Baby-
lonish spirit has been pulling down.

*   *   *   *   *   *   *   *   *

"And as the Lord in His humiliation-state did
ordain, and called twelve disciples, that they might be

witness of His mighty deeds, as He was the Son of God and Saviour of mankind. So herefrom is understood that He will now also elect and assign twelve principal persons as the foundation-builders, who shall stand each one at his several gate, intrusted with the key thereof, to lock out and to open as they please, as directed from their principal Head: and so to go on to multiply the number of disciples till they be numberless, for the publishing and *reviving* of that more than glorious ministration, that consisteth purely of the fiery Baptism of the Holy Ghost: which all that shall find admittance through these gates, must be partakers."

An interesting example of faith in the hope of translation without death occurs in the case of John Asgill, who, at the beginning of the eighteenth century, published a book under the following title—"An argument proving that, according to the covenant of eternal life revealed in the Scriptures, man may be translated from hence into that eternal life without passing through death, although the human nature of Christ Himself could not be thus translated till He had passed through death." He thus witnessed to the hope of the change without death, and of the translation; and for writing this book he was expelled from the Irish House of Commons, A.D. 1703, and from the English House of Commons, A.D. 1707, while his book was burned by the hangman! He gave an impassioned and explicit testimony to the hope of translation without death, to meet the Lord. Details of this unique case are given in Appendix I. He hoped that he might be changed without seeing death, and he suffered persecution for his hope, but he lived to an advanced age, the Lord thus recognizing the faith and hope of His servant in unbelieving times.

Other testimonies like that of John Asgill might perchance be found hidden in the archives of the Church, if there were any possible means of exhuming the same.

The restoration of Apostles and Prophets was clearly foretold by Count N. L. von Zinzendorf (A.D. 1700-1760), the first bishop of the Moravian Brotherhood, whose name was eminent in the religious history of Germany.* His writings were of a religious character. The following is an extract from one of them :—

"The time will come when God will send men, messengers, who can lay their hands upon the children of God, and the Holy Ghost will be communicated as in the beginning. The Lord will also give prophets and the gift of prophecy, as it is foretold in Joel, and along with it the gift of healing in the blessed name of the Lord Jesus Christ. Such a work in the Spirit of God will come among Christian nations before the Lord Himself will come. Dear brothers and sisters, when you see this work, then it will be your duty to dissolve this our Brotherhood, and to join that blessed work; and, if you cannot be rulers in it, if you cannot participate in the government, then be subject and obey."

Another German pastor, Phil. Matthew Hahn (who died A.D. 1790), after speaking in his "sermons" of the glorious millennial reign of Christ, says:

* See Appendix IX.

"The whole multitude of Christians, who at the beginning waited longingly for His advent, shall, during the delay of His coming, become lukewarm and sleepy, and finally all will actually slumber. Therefore doth Jesus say in Rev. xvi. 15, 'Behold, 'I come as a thief.   Blessed is he that watcheth!' *Immediately beforehand, God will send out a call*   Rev. xiv. 6. *to the world through the teachers of the everlasting Gospel*, in order to arouse men to go out to meet the Bridegroom.   Then, in the midst of corrupted unbelieving Christendom, there will be a little gathering of those who shall believe God's word. The office and work of these messengers is to call attention to these things. *They are ambassadors who bestow the Holy Ghost*, to whom the baptizing with water is the least part of their work. (See 1 Cor. i. 17.)   They are vessels and members of Jesus, not as the hand and foot, but *as the heart and mouth* of Jesus: through whom Jesus will quicken the dead, will illumine darkness and blindness, and will strengthen the weak.

"What God did for men 1800 years ago, He can still do; and why should it be deemed unnecessary for the Church of God in these days, even as at that time, to be implanted by qualified men? . . . Is there no need for "fishers of men" to stand in a given relation to and *in the likeness of the apostles of the former time*?"

In reviewing the Protestant evangelical revival at the close of the eighteenth century, initiated by John Wesley and Whitfield, and carried on by many revered men, such as Romaine, Fletcher, Venn,

Toplady, and Hall, it is mournful to find so little testimony in their prose writings or in their hymns, to the distinctive hope of the translation. Charles Wesley was a firm believer in pre-millennarianism, and earnestly desired the Lord's coming, as may be seen in many of his hymns.

About this time there was an interesting testimony to the coming and kingdom of Christ from the pen of a Jesuit, Emanuel Lacunza, known by the Jewish name of "Ben Ezra," who was born at St. Iago, in Chili, South America, on the 13th July, 1731. He was the son of noble though not rich parents, who sent him to the college of the Jesuits, of which Society he became a member in 1747. He left the college to devote himself to the study of geography and astronomy, and finally came to Europe and resided in Italy. His only published work was entitled, "La Venida del Mesias en Gloria y Majestad," or, "The Coming of Messiah in Glory and Majesty." Ben Ezra was a truly pious man, and studied the Holy Scriptures with an earnest and single mind, and the result was—as generally happens in such cases—that the Lord led him into larger views of truth and of the divine purpose. The following is an extract from the work mentioned above, in which allusion is made to the translation of the living. In referring to the petition, "Thy kingdom come," and to Christ's millennial reign on earth, Ben Ezra writes as follows:—

. . . "The glorious advent of the Lord Jesus is a divine truth, which is as essential and fundamental to Christianity, as His first advent to suffer in the flesh . . . When that great day shall come, which heaven and earth await with earnest desire, then will the Lord Himself descend from heaven with a shout, with the voice of the archangel, and with the trump of God. Then in that moment (as I conceive it) at the Lord's contact with the atmosphere of our earth, will occur, first, the resurrection of all the saints who are accounted worthy of the resurrection *from* the dead, of whom Paul says, "And the dead in *Christ* shall rise *first*." In a moment, when this *first* resurrection of the saints of the first order has taken place, then will those few among the living, who will be counted worthy of this designation of *saints*, on account of their wonderful faith and of their righteousness, be caught up, together with the sleeping saints who have been resuscitated, and will ascend with them to meet the Lord in the air. All this is very clear and very easy to be comprehended."*

1 Thess. iv. 16.

Luke xx. 35.
1 Thess. iv. 16, 17.

1 Thess. iv. 17.

The eighteenth century closed with one of the greatest religious, social, and political convulsions that the world has ever seen—the first French Revolution, with its "reign of terror," which shook the kingdoms and institutions of Europe to their base. From the events of that time, men, especially Christian men, may learn that if they throw off God, they will be left to themselves, and will display themselves as half beasts and half devils. If man sows the wind, he will reap the whirlwind. The vice, self-indulgence, and atheism of the Court, of the nobles, and of the leading thinkers of France,

Hosea viii. 7.

* See Appendix II.

combined with the poverty, ignorance and serfdom of the masses, no doubt helped to bring about this cataclysm; but, from one point of view, spiritual good was evolved from it; for men were so appalled by its horrors, that the minds of many God-fearing persons were turned to the study of the prophetic books of Holy Scripture, and earnest evangelical preaching succeeded the lethargic, dry, moral essays of the eighteenth century, more attention being given to searching the Scriptures, and to enquiring into such truths as the outpouring of the Holy Ghost, the second coming of the Lord, and the impending close of the Christian dispensation, of which the quotations from the remarkable spiritual utterances of Père Lambert, with reference to a coming time of tribulation, and subsequent deliverance was one result. (See Chap. VIII.)

The nineteenth century has produced many well-known writers on prophecy, such as Irving, Faber, Elliott, Frere, Bickersteth, Birks, Bonar, Cumming; while pamphlets on prophetic subjects are now frequent, and have familiarized many with the too much forgotten hope of the Church. Although the hope of the translation has been almost quenched in the Church Catholic, it cannot be denied that there are devout persons who pray for its accomplishment; though, speaking generally, and looking at the three great sections into which the visible Church is divided, it is only too true that the Greek and Roman Churches do not formally acknowledge this hope; whilst in the Protestant Churches—episcopal and non-episcopal—it is very rarely preached.

Alas! these facts vindicate the title of this book, "The Church's Forgotten Hope," to which some pious persons have taken exception.

During the evangelical revival which followed the terrible events of the great French Revolution, an earnest missionary spirit was awakened, and many of the great societies were founded, such as the British and Foreign Bible Society, the Church Missionary Society, and others, whilst an impetus was given to the earnest study of the prophetic Scriptures.

At the beginning of the nineteenth century De Maistre (*Soirées de St. Petersbourg*, 1806), wrote as follows: —

"I know that Rome cannot endure the Bible Society. However, she need not disquiet herself too much about it. While the Bible Society itself scarcely knows what it is really doing, it will nevertheless effect for a future epoch exactly what the LXX. (i.e., the Septuagint) effected.

"*A fresh outpouring of the Holy Ghost belongs to the things which are most reasonably expected;* it is necessary that the preachers equipped with the new gift should be able to cite, to bring the tenour of Scripture before every nation. The apostles are no translators; they have to do with widely different matters. But the Bible Society, the blind instrument of Providence, prepares these different translations of the text (of Scripture) which the true apostles (veritables envoyés), in virtue of their legitimate mission, shall one day expound, by which they will drive infidelity from the City of God—which the

Q

terrible enemies of unity are working to establish."*

A very earnest and spiritual preacher, the Rev. J. M. Campbell of Row, arose in Scotland about 1825-1831. He preached the love of God to all men, the coming of the Lord, which to him seemed to be a new revelation, and for the preaching of which he almost apologizes to his congregation.† He was cast out by the Church of Scotland which, being steeped in Calvinism, could not endure the doctrine of the free love of God to all men, and of the universality of the atonement.

In 1820, the Rev. Haldane Stewart, believing that the end of this dispensation was approaching, and that the Church was unprepared, was impressed with the necessity for the outpouring of the Holy Spirit of God in the last days, as the "latter rain," according to the promises of Holy Scripture. He issued an appeal for prayer for this object in a tract, of which 300,000 copies were printed by the Religious Tract Society, and which was issued in 1821, its number among the Tract Society's publications being 263. Never before had there been such a testimony to the office and work of the Holy Ghost; indeed for centuries His personality and operations had been almost ignored.

In the year 1826, a clerical and lay gathering assembled at Albury, in Surrey, to search the prophetic Scriptures, during which a great increase of

* Quoted by Karl von Mickwitz in *Ein Zeitbild in wichtigen Zeugnissen*, Berlin, 1902.

† Sermons by the Rev. J. M. Campbell, vol. i., sermon ix., p. 187, 193.

light was received, causing the teaching of the
apostles on many forgotten truths to be proclaimed,
after the lapse of centuries.   The hopes, then revived,
have since been cherished by an increasing number
of persons in different parts of the Church Catholic.
To adopt Latimer's dying saying, it may be said
that "a candle has been lighted in England, which
by the grace of God shall never be put out," until it
merge in the noonday splendour of the Sun of
Righteousness.

A most extraordinary manifestation of spiritual
and prophetic power took place among the Roman
Catholic peasantry in Bavaria, in February, A.D
1828,* in the remote parish of Karlshuld in the
Donaumoos, on the river Danube, announcing that
the Lord was about to send apostles to the church,
previous to His personal coming.   It took the
Pastor and people by surprise, and created many
problems which they were unable to solve.   This,
so far as we know, was the first manifestation of
spiritual power in utterance among the Baptized
since the cessation of the supernatural gifts of the
Spirit in the early part of the fourth century.   It
occurred seven or eight years after the issue of the
Rev. Haldane Stewart's appeal for prayer for the outpouring of the Holy Spirit, and preceded similar
manifestations in Scotland and in England, which did
not take place until 1830 and 1831 respectively.

The first word spoken at Karlshuld in the power
of the Spirit was the following: "Know ye not,

* *A Chapter of Church History from South Germany,*
by L. W. Scholler, Longmans, 1894.

ye children of God, that ye are living in the last
days, in the days in which the Lord will come.
Know ye not that before the Lord comes He will give
again apostles, prophets, evangelists, and pastors, and
churches as at the beginning." What this meant
these simple German peasants could not understand,
and the movement was soon crushed by the ecclesiastical authorities, the priest being removed from the
parish to another cure.

Another testimony from the Roman Church may
be quoted. A Jesuit father, Père Ramière, in 1864,
stated his conviction of the necessity of a revival
in the Church of Christ, and thus expressed his
longings for the same, with his anticipations of the
character of the men through whom such a revival
would be effected.

"We pray God, the Father of our Lord Jesus
Christ, to raise up for Him ministers worthy of
Him, living examples of all His virtues, faithful
exponents of His love, men mighty in works and
words, men, in short, who shall be to the Church
in the last days what the apostles were to the
primitive Church and to the Christian society in
succeeding ages, new apostles, whose miraculous
influence shall lead her victoriously through all
her crises. Unless a change in the ways of Providence
has arisen, we may rest assured that it will be by
such an influence that the dangers menacing the
Church at the present time will be averted. . . . .
Let us, by our prayers, hasten the appearance of
these consoling luminaries, who shall disperse the
storms, the darkness of which afflicts our eyes." *

In a private letter, Père Ramière gave an outline of what he conceived should be the marked characteristics of the new apostles.   He wrote :—

"These extraordinary men, these new apostles whom God shall send to regenerate society, cannot be strangers to the one true Church with whom Jesus Christ has promised to abide always, even unto the end of the world.   They will be both the heirs, the successors, and the imitators of the first apostles, but they will not come to destroy what the first apostles established.   Jesus Christ cannot act adversely to Himself, for, as there is one God, and one Mediator, there is also one faith, one baptism, one authority (or rule)."

It would thus appear that although the Lord awakened His servants in different countries to the Church's need of special apostolic men, whom He would send as His messengers, yet the glorious but long forgotten hope of the Church in the first resurrection, change, and rapture of the saints to meet the Lord, received but little attention among devout persons.   During the nineteenth century, however, more thought was bestowed on these truths than had been since the apostolic age; and, although the mass of Christians are still ignorant of or indifferent to them, yet they have been witnessed to in some of the sections of the Church Catholic in such a way as has never been the case since the first century of the Christian era; which fact of itself

---

* Extract from *Apostolat de la Prière*, by Père Ramière. Page 288.   Printed A.D. 1864.

seems to be a distinct sign of the approaching end of the present dispensation. The Church of England in her formularies gives no distinct witness to the hope of the change of the living, or of the translation of the saints, and these great topics of faith and hope are rarely dwelt upon in the pulpits of the Established Church.

However, the testimonies we have been able to cite to an expected revival of Christ's ordinances and the pouring out of the latter rain at the end of the dispensation previous to the return of the Lord are remarkable, shewing, as they do, the action of the one Spirit, who dwells in the one Body, even the Spirit of Truth, who knows the end from the beginning. These testimonies have been uttered at different times and in different places, and have emanated from different parts of the Church, but they are all those of godly persons, who were living in the fear and love of God. They are not the rhapsodies of fanatics or enthusiasts, but the pious desires and previsions of sober-minded persons, and they are in strict conformity with the predictions and statements of Holy Scripture.

Some of these enlightened Christians must have had prophetic intimations or premonitions, of a time of refreshing from the presence of the Lord, in pre-paration for His coming again, since they specified the manner in which it might be expected to occur, and indicated that it would run on ancient lines, even on those of the Primitive Church, the expected revival being bound up with the work of the Holy Ghost, with His gifts and manifestations, as well as

with the fourfold ministry of the Christian Church— Eph. iv. 11.
the four divinely appointed ministerial channels for
the manifestation of the Spirit.

That there is a wide-spread feeling in the present
day of some coming change, of some great event,
or deliverer, seems undeniable. These unexpressed
longings and anticipations which have pervaded the
world at certain periods are a remarkable spiritual
phenomenon. They existed before our Lord's first
advent; for Suetonius, in the life of Vespasian, states
that, "In the East an old and fixed opinion had
become general that at that time men of Jewish
race should attain to supreme power."* Tacitus,
another Roman historian, gives a similar account of
such an expectation: "There was a belief in many
minds that in the ancient books of the priests a
prophecy was contained, that at that very time the
East would gain a predominant influence, and that
one of Jewish race would hold the supreme
power."† He mentions the general rumours and
anticipations, that existed at the beginning of the
Christian era, of some great deliverer who should
arise in the East and establish a kingdom.

As it may not be generally known how great is
the feeling—it may even be said, belief—pervading
the Mahommedan world, that a great Messiah is about

---

* "Percrebuerat Oriente toto vetus et constans opinio,
esse in fatis, ut eo tempore Judæâ profecti rerum potirentur" (Suetonius in *Vita Vespasiani*).

† "Pluribus persuasio inerat, antiquis sacerdotum literis
contineri, eo ipso tempore fore, ut valesceret oriens, pro-
fectique Judæâ rerum potirentur" (*Tacitus*, Hist. Lib. v. 13).

to appear, and how intense is the longing for his advent, an extract may be quoted from *A Talk with a Persian Statesman*, by the late Rev. W. E. Haweis, which appeared in a magazine in 1899:—

"*Mahdism* is the doctrine of the Mussulman Messiah—it is only taught orally. It is a tradition. *Mahdi* means a saviour, a deliverer. . . . .

"The Messianic or Mahdist belief is so deeply rooted in all Mussulman nations, especially the Schiites (Persian), that it has been their life and soul. Mussulman nations are crying out for him to remedy all evils. Every Friday in all the mosques, prayers are offered up, and invocations made, beseeching Allah to hasten the time of Messiah's advent. . . . .

" A vast underground agitation is going on throughout our Mussulman population, of which Europeans can gather but the faintest and vaguest idea; but one thing is undeniable, that this movement is daily and hourly gathering momentum throughout the Mussulman world. It is a new conception of a universal religion and morality, incorporating the results of modern progress, but culled severely and built up from the scattered precepts of Islamic tradition, and is shaking the old Persian regime to its foundations; and as Persia has been throughout classical time the home, and starting point of all Mussulman innovations, I think it probable that this regenerating movement will spread throughout all Mahommedan lands.

"The root of all these sects is a passionate desire for change, reform, innovation; an abiding disgust with the order or disorder of things as they are.

It is a constant protest against the narrow orthodoxy of Islam, combined with a revolt of the human conscience against the excesses of a barbarous despotism, an irresistible, but uncertain and unorganized aspiration for a national deliverance."

It may be said with truth that "the whole creation groaneth and travaileth in pain together," awaiting deliverance at the coming of the Lord, and it is a cause for deep thankfulness that in the Christian Church an increasing number of the saints are crying for the Lord's return, even if few definitely desire the change into His presence without seeing death. But we must not forget that the advent of the Lord is the pivot event on which the glorious events of the first resurrection, the change, and the translation turn, for without it they cannot take place. Hence, in recognizing the intimate connection between the translation and the coming of the Lord, those who have watched and waited for His coming may also have cherished—it may be unconsciously— a secondary hope connected with the change of the living, this event being bound up with the resurrection and change of the departed saints; for, as the apostle declares, "we shall *all* be changed." Rom. viii. 22. 1 Cor. xv. 51.

Hasten, O Lord, the time when we shall see Thee as Thou art, and be changed into Thy likeness. Amen.

NOTE (MAY 15, 1905).

The revivals which have taken place in England during the last few months have excited general attention, and have elicited approval from some of the

Bishops.   But a remarkable sign of the times is that the Archbishop of Canterbury has sent a letter to all the Diocesan Bishops in his Province, exhorting them to invite their clergy and people to unite in special prayer to God at the ensuing Whitsuntide for an outpouring of the Holy Spirit.   These brief extracts are taken from his letter :—

LAMBETH PALACE, *Easter*, 1905.

RIGHT REVEREND AND DEAR BROTHER,

In February last, as you doubtless remember, our Convocation came to an informal agreement that, in view of the present conditions of religious life in England, it would be well that the clergy and people should be invited at the ensuing Whitsuntide, to unite in special prayer to God for an outpouring of the Holy Spirit among us, and for the strengthening of our hold as Christians upon the deeper realities of our faith.

* * * * * * * *

Be such our special prayer this Whitsuntide, throughout the Church of God.   It cannot be offered to Him in vain.

I am, your faithful brother and servant
in the Lord Jesus Christ,

RANDALL CANTUAR.

The spirit of this unprecedented invitation by the Archbishop to the Bishops in the Province of Canterbury, has permeated also the Province of York, yea the whole of Great Britain.   May the Holy Ghost for which the Church in this land is beseeching God, grant her to see and confess her neglect of His grace and gifts, and, according to His office, guide her into all truth, and shew her "things to come," that she may cry for the return of the Lord, for the first resurrection, for the change of the living, and for their joint translation to meet the Lord in the air, and thus be prepared to escape those things which are coming on the earth.

John xvi. 13.

CHAPTER X.

The Revival of the Hope of Translation in these Last Days.

In the last chapter have been embodied the previsions of various saintly persons of a coming time of revival, and their yearnings for a true spiritual reformation, as the means of preparation for the return of the Lord, and for the manifestation of His kingdom; while some of them even anticipated and outlined the manner thereof, viz: by the revival of the Lord's fourfold ministry in the Christian Church. Whence arose this yearning? Was it due to their own imaginations or spiritual desires, or was it due to the working of the Holy Spirit of God in them? These godly persons grieved over the desolations of the spiritual Zion; and when God opened their eyes to see the need of the ministries of apostles and prophets to carry the Church forward to perfection and to prepare her for her Lord's appearing and kingdom, He gave His faithful servants by the illumination of the Holy Ghost, prophetic previsions of His gracious purpose to revive these ministries in the Church.

But there is another important point to consider in this connexion, viz: that not only did the Spirit of God express His yearnings for a revival of the two lapsed ministries of apostles and prophets in the midst of the Church, but that He had foretold a great spiritual revival as a herald of the Lord's return centuries before in the infallible predictions of the Holy Scriptures. This of itself is so wide a subject that it can only be briefly glanced at, and as a prelude to what follows: enough may be adduced to shew that a spiritual revival in the last days is not a thing to startle Christian men, but rather a thing to be expected according to the analogy of God's dealings with His people in previous dispensations.

That the written word of God testifies to a revival in the latter days is our authority for expecting the Joel ii. 28-32.   same. The prophet Joel declared that an outpouring of the Spirit should occur in the last days, and St. Peter quoted this prophecy on the day of Pentecost, when, speaking by the Holy Ghost, he declared Acts ii. 16, 17.   that it had been fulfilled on that very day;—"This "is that which was spoken by the prophet Joel: "And it shall come to pass in the last days, saith God, "I will pour out of my Spirit upon all flesh." And in his next discourse he made allusion to the same Acts iii. 19.   promise in speaking of "the times of refreshing" that should come from the presence of the Lord. But that these were not exhaustive fulfilments of the promise is evident from the words, "I will pour "out of my Spirit upon *all* flesh," since the Holy Ghost was poured out only upon a few thousands of persons; and therefore like other Scriptures, these must have a germinating fulfilment. Nearly nineteen hundred years of the Christian dispensation have elapsed since those events occurred, and the Church is still in the wilderness of this world, needing the help of the Spirit to enable her to look for the Lord's return, and the translation of the firstfruits before the manifestation of the coming Antichrist.

There is a distinct promise in the books of the prophets Hosea and Joel of the *latter rain*. What can this mean? Rain is a scriptural symbol of the Holy Spirit, so that this figure typifies the truth that any revival in the last days must be connected with an outpouring of the Holy Ghost. In Palestine the early or former rain came soon after the sowing of the seed in the month of Tisri (*Ethanim*, October), and the latter rain fell before the crops were ripe in the month of Abib (*Nisan*, April). The outpouring of the Spirit on the day of Pentecost was the former or early rain in the case of the Christian Church, but of necessity there must be a latter rain; and what time is so probable for this outpouring of the Spirit as the close of the dispensation, before the harvest of the Church is gathered in? Can any period between the first century and the nineteenth century be specialized when anything answering to the latter rain has taken place? In the middle ages, no doubt, there have been periods of religious excitement (as in the case of the Crusades), but even the Reformation of the sixteenth century, in which the written word of God was liberated, and the human mind disenthralled from the bondage of superstition, can hardly be cited as the period of the latter rain. Nor did it claim to be so, nor was it characterized by those marks which are specially associated with the outpouring of the Holy Ghost. On the other hand it may be asked, is there any work of God in these last days which is characterized by

Hosea vi. 3.
Joel ii. 23.

these two salient Scriptural features, the manifestation of the gifts of the Spirit, and the mission of apostles to prepare a people for the return of the Lord?

The question resolves itself into this;—How will the outpouring of the Holy Spirit be effected in the Church? Judging from the testimony of Scripture and the experiences of the day of Pentecost, there seems to be no other way than *through the instrumentality of men;* for in the Church the Holy Ghost is the Spirit of Christ, ever witnessing to the grand truth of the Incarnation of the Son of God, the Word made flesh. It will no doubt be bound up with the restoration of that fourfold ministry which, *Eph. iv. 10.* as St. Paul tells the Ephesians, the Lord on His ascension gave as gifts unto men for their edification and perfecting. The Psalmist, speaking of Messiah, had declared some thousand years before—" Thou *Psa. lxviii. 18.* hast *received* gifts for men," while the apostle Paul teaches that the risen and ascended Lord *gave* the gifts. The ascension of the Lord was to be the sign and precursor of the outpouring of the Spirit at the beginning of this dispensation, namely—as the former rain; to be followed by the latter rain, in due season. This admits of no reasonable doubt. The gifts are men, or ministries, apostles, prophets, evangelists, pastors and teachers; nor may we dissociate the gift of the Holy Spirit from this fourfold channel for the conveyance of the living water. In other words, the outpouring of the Holy Ghost will be connected with the revival of the fourfold ministry, in the Christian Church, and especially with the ministry of apostles and prophets.

Hence all these ideas, the outpouring of the latter rain, the revival of the fourfold ministry, the Elias testimony before the coming of the great and dreadful day of the Lord, are all bound up with an outpouring of the Holy Spirit, such as the Scriptures declare shall take place in the last days.

Mal. iv. 5.

In writing to the Ephesians St. Paul says that these four ministries were given for the perfecting (πρὸς τὸν καταρτισμὸν, the rearticulating, the connecting by joints as members of a body) of the saints; for the edifying (εἰς οἰκοδομὴν, temple building) of the body of Christ, till we all come unto a perfect (τέλειον, full grown) man, unto the measure of the stature of the fulness of Christ. But after the first century the theory of being perfected in this manner became obsolete, and before long the necessity of the fourfold ministry, as the means whereby the Lord, who changes not His plans or ordinances, would perfect His Church, became forgotten.

Eph. iv. 7-16.

Let us turn to the consideration of the actual facts of the case, looking at these as matters of history.

In the light of the godly yearnings for the Church's preparation for the return of her Lord, for personal conformity to His will in character and holiness, and for renewed manifestation of the gifts of the Holy Ghost, is it an incredible statement that God has heard her cry and has sent to the Church the revival which was needed, and this to a great extent in the way foreshadowed? Still, as often happens, those who cry do not always recognize the answer when it is given, and are inclined to despise the day of small things. Thus Moses,

Gideon, and David were despised, and the Lord
Himself, the Son of God incarnate, the Messiah, was
not recognized by His own generation, who stumbled
at His supposed origin, saying, "Can there any
good thing come out of Nazareth?"

John i. 46.

The first answer to prayer was that many persons
of acknowledged piety and sobriety, faithful members
of the Episcopal and Presbyterian bodies and of
other Christian communities, were supernaturally
moved to speak in prophecy and to declare the purpose of God in His Church.

Thus the truth concerning these forgotten hopes
was exhumed from Holy Scripture by the voice of the
Holy Ghost in prophecy, first in February, 1828, in
Bavaria; shortly afterwards in March, 1830, in
Scotland; and in April, 1831, in England, and ever
since the same testimony has continued and increased
in force all over Christendom like the voice of
many waters.

The first utterance in Scotland manifesting the
presence of the Holy Ghost in spiritual power, was
concerning the return of the Lord: "Behold, the
"bridegroom cometh; go ye out to meet him."
These were remarkable words to fall on the ears
of a slumbering Church, yet they are the identical
cry which the Lord foretold should be made at
midnight, when it might be least expected. The
sacred canon of Scripture closes with the Lord's
promise, "Surely I come quickly," but until that
utterance took place in Bavaria in A.D. 1828, centuries
had elapsed since the Church had responded, "Amen,
"even so, come Lord Jesus." Shortly after the

Matt. xxv. 5, 6.

Rev. xxii. 20.

utterance given above, there came another to this
effect: "Where is the Body?"—that is, where is
the Church as an organized spiritual body, with her
membership and ministries, as joints and bands knit
together to do the will of her Head, and to shew
forth the glory of her Divine Creator?   A third
utterance was the prayer in spiritual power, "Send
us apostles," the meaning of which neither those
who spake, nor those who heard, were able to com-
prehend, even as the disciples did not understand
the Lord's words when He spake of His coming
resurrection.

The revival of this spiritual though forgotten hope
of the return of the Lord is, as it were, a great
wonder in heaven, and is traceable to two concurrent
facts—the presence of apostles and the manifestation
of the gifts of the Holy Ghost in the Church on
earth.   Although it existed once for a short time, it
had faded away; so that its revival in these last
days, notwithstanding the abounding lawlessness,
worldliness, and immorality on all sides, is a unique
spiritual phenomenon.

The historical review of the preceding chapter has
shewn that it was only when living apostles were in
the Church, and when prophecy was in exercise in
the manifestation of the gifts of the Holy Ghost,
that the HOPE of the first resurrection of the departed
saints, of the change of the living, and of their
translation together to meet the Lord in the air, was
cherished by the Church; and also that the hope of
the Lord's premillennial advent, which lingered until
the beginning of the fourth century, died out when

R

the Roman Empire became Christian, and the progress of worldly Christianity seemed to point to the
conversion of the world before the Lord's appearing.
This vain expectation still holds the field, but of
late years the ancient hope has been quickened anew
in the heart of the Church, after the lapse of centuries.

Those who spake in spiritual power in England
declared certain men to be apostles whose inner
spiritual consciousness assented to the reality of the
call; and, despite the novelty, the difficulty, the
apparent presumption involved in the character of
the claim, twelve men were separated to this office
on the 14th of July, 1835.* Living apostles were in
fact in the midst of the visible Church from 1832,
when the first was called, to 1901 when the last
survivor died; and the gifts of the Holy Ghost have
now been in manifestation, and His voice has been
heard speaking through men in prophecy, for well
nigh three-quarters of a century.

It is impossible for us in this place to give details
of the development of this work of God in the

---

* It is remarkable that Halley's comet, which has long
been known as the Star of Bethlehem, is supposed to
have appeared in the East at the time of the birth of
Christ, when the wise men saw "the star in the east."
The comet would then be on its course *towards* the sun;
and on its *return*, six months later, it would be in the
zenith, above Bethlehem, about the end of December.
Josephus tells us of the next appearance of the comet
having occurred at the destruction of Jerusalem, about
A.D. 75. Since then it has come and gone twenty-three
times, ending in 1835. It may be seen again in 1910 or 1911.

Church Catholic;* it is sufficient to say that for nearly seventy years the apostles fulfilled their office, maintained the faith once delivered to the saints, and witnessed to Christendom of the Lord's return.

It may truly be said that a like work has never been conceived, attempted, or carried into practice since the removal of apostles at the end of the first century. There is no other work of revival or restoration like it on earth: it is unique; it bears the stamp of *divinity* in its originality, in its success, and, dare we add, in its apparent failure before its vindication in resurrection and translation, which may the Lord hasten in His faithfulness and mercy.

Until Christian men learn what the Church Catholic is by the constitution of God, they can never know what "the true work of God" therein has been in these days. They can see no use for it. According to the opinion of the majority of Christian men, the Churches in Christendom, Episcopal and non-Episcopal, are precisely in the condition where God has brought them, and in which He meant them to abide. Hence many regard a fourfold ministry, the sealing and spiritual gifts, as unnecessary, and not in accordance

* Those who wish to learn more are referred to the following works:—*Spiritual Occurrences in Bavaria, 1827-28: A Chapter in Church History from South Germany. The Restoration of Apostles and Prophets*, by Dr. Norton. *The Original Constitution of the Church and its Restoration: A Narrative of Events. The Church and her Organic Ministries. The Catholic Apostolic Church, its Organization and Ministries. Lights and Shadows. Creation and Redemption. Functions and Credentials of Apostles.* Some of these may now be out of print.

with the mind of God; indeed the assertion of their restoration is considered to be even blasphemous and presumptuous.

To many readers these statements will seem hard sayings, and they must remain so if the antecedent credibility of the facts alleged be rejected by those to whom the witness is borne; therefore, the definition of an *apostle* must first be given. What is the origin of the name "apostle"? How are apostles distinguishable from all other ministers of Christ? The inquiry is an important one, and may not be shelved by the commonplaces current among the Baptized; such as, that the apostles were simply the first bishops, or that they were inspired missionaries sent forth for the guidance of the infant Church, to give Christianity a fair start in the world. Such limited conceptions of the office and mission of apostles fail to convey the teachings of Holy Scripture respecting those ministers whom, according to St. Paul, God has set *first* in the Church. The inquiry is the more important, because, unless the true nature of the apostolic ministry be grasped, there can be no adequate conception of the divine constitution of the Catholic Church. "Ye are the body of Christ," writes St. Paul, "and members in particular; and "God hath set some in the church, *first* apostles, "*secondarily* prophets, *thirdly* teachers. . . . ." This whole chapter (1 Cor. xii.) deals with the spiritual endowment of the body of Christ; and if, in this divinely organized society, apostles be set first, the precise nature of their sacred office cannot be too narrowly investigated in the light of Holy

1 Cor. xii. 28.

1 Cor. xii. 27, 28.

Scripture, not to say of the earliest and best catholic tradition. Now turning to the pages of the New Testament, there are four salient characteristics of the ministry of apostleship, not shared either by their brethren of the episcopate, or by any other ministers of Christ.

I. The name "apostle" as a distinctive ecclesiastical designation.

When our blessed Lord chose the Twelve, He *named* them Apostles. This He did after a night spent in prayer; and, in His great intercessory prayer before He suffered, He describes them as the men whom His Father had given to Him out of the John vii. 6. world. The name of "apostles" became thus consecrated and restricted to those standing in a special ministry; nor—and this is remarkable—has the name been assumed by any others of the clergy as their official designation; not even by the Roman Pontiff, who, though claiming apostolic authority, has never assumed the name of "Apostle."

No doubt there are passages in which the word "apostle" is otherwise employed, but in those passages it is qualified; nor have the English translators of the New Testament failed to preserve the dis-   2 Cor. viii. 23 tinction by translating it "messenger." It is elsewhere   Phil. ii. 25. once used of our Lord Himself, but otherwise (except   Heb. iii. 1. where claimed by false apostles), it is restricted to those recognized as Apostles proper, viz., the Eleven, St. Matthias, St. Paul and St. Barnabas.*

* See Appendix X., on the Biblical use of the word "apostle."

II. The special mode of mission of Apostles.

This again is unique; for, whereas all other ministers of Christ are ordained by the imposition of
hands, it cannot be shown that any apostle was
ever thus ordained. If it be thought surprising that
John xx. 21. the Lord did not Himself lay hands on His eleven
apostles when He commissioned them, the answer
is that He would not make them to differ from
others on whom, from the Father's right hand, He
Rom. i. 5. would afterwards confer grace and apostleship for
obedience to the faith among all nations. The facts
Gal. i. 1. coincide with St. Paul's account of himself, as an
apostle ("not of men, *neither by man*, but by Jesus
"Christ, and God the Father, who raised him from
"the dead"). For neither had he been chosen by
his fellows in the Church, nor had he been constituted
an apostle by ordination at the hands of any man;
no, his mission had been direct from the heavenly
sanctuary, as the Father's gift to the Son, and as
the Son's gift to His Church, for the fulfilment of
the high functions of the apostolic ministry. But the
argument for the direct mission of apostles may be
clinched by the circumstance of the church in
Rev. ii. 2. Ephesus having *tried those who said they were apostles*,
which, in the case of ministers who could prove
their ordination, would be needless. The essential
idea connected with apostles is that they should in
some way or other receive a commission direct from
the Lord, and be sent by Himself on their mission.
No doubt the Lord may work miracles, signs or
wonders by eloquent and mighty teachers or preachers,
but these things do not of themselves form the

essential characteristics of the apostolic office, nor constitute men to be *apostles*. Many possessed all these privileges and gifts, and yet were not apostles— these, as the Scriptures clearly testify, being sent forth immediately from the Lord Jesus Christ, the Head of His Body the Church.

III. The plenary grace conferred through Apostles.

Holy Scripture narrates that by the laying on of the apostles' hands, the Holy Ghost was given. Two instances are mentioned of the administration of this rite,—on the first occasion by St. Peter and St. John, Acts viii. 16, 17. apostles to the circumcision, and on the second by Acts xix. 6. St. Paul, the apostle to the uncircumcision or to the Gentiles, who refers to it in his Epistle to the Ephesians, as the *sealing* with the Holy Spirit of Eph. i. 13, 14. promise, the earnest of the future inheritance. The apostles also laid on hands in ordination, being guided 2 Tim. i. 6. thereto by words of prophecy going before upon those admitted to the episcopate or presbyterate of the Church. In the absence of apostles, similar functions have devolved upon the pastoral episcopate, though doubtless with a diminution in the measure of grace conveyed, while the word of prophecy has ceased " to go before" upon those about to be ordained. 1 Tim. i. 18.

IV. The universal jurisdiction of Apostles.

Upon apostles alone devolves the care of all the 2 Cor. xi. 28. churches. They are Christ's elders, ruling in His absence over His great bishopric, the Holy Catholic Church. Whereas all other ministers have a limited jurisdiction outside which their authority does not extend, it cannot be shewn that this was the case with the apostles; and in fact the claim of the Bishop of Rome to universal jurisdiction, reposes on the allegation, that the apostolate "persevered" in the see of Peter. This negatively illustrates the point under consideration, but it is not relevant to our subject to discuss the Petrine claims of the Papacy. Suffice it to say, that there is no other witness in Christendom to the necessity of a ministry of universal jurisdiction, to bind the episcopate together, and thus to secure unity of faith and practice; but it has failed, because it is not *God's* way of unity. His way is His own ordinance of apostleship.

Thus the special and central mark of apostles is, that they are sent forth directly from the Lord Jesus Christ Himself, without the intervention of any human instrumentality; and this of itself distinguishes them from the other ministries in the Christian Church. Apostleship, moreover, is the first named among the four ministries which, as

Psa. lxviii. 18. cf. Eph. iv. 8, 11.

St. Paul writes to the Ephesians, the Lord Jesus Christ received as gifts for men, and gave at His ascension, viz: apostles, prophets, evangelists, pastors and teachers.

As has already been stated, fully seventy years have elapsed since the presence of apostles was indicated to the Church,* certain men having been called to the exercise of the apostolic office by the

---

* From Rev. ii. 2, may be learned the duty of the episcopate or rulers in the Church, to *try* those who say they are apostles. This, as we have seen, indicates the nature of their claim, viz.: to superhuman ordination (Gal. i. 1).

word of the Holy Ghost in prophecy, through men speaking in supernatural power; as at Antioch, when the Holy Spirit said—"Separate me Barnabas and "Saul for the work whereunto I have called them." The apostles of these last days were separated from all other avocations by the voice or command of the Holy Ghost, for the work whereunto God called them. Looking to the purpose of the presence of the Holy Spirit in the Church, to the law of the Church's organization, and to her present position in the world, it may be asked: In what other way could their call be made known during the Lord's bodily absence from His Church on earth? In whatever way the Lord might call apostles, whether by vision to the men themselves, by a direct voice from heaven, or by the word of the Holy Ghost speaking through men, it must ever remain an appeal to *faith*, something to be believed on the testimony of others who are known to be godly, intelligent, and truthful witnesses. In the present instance there is the indisputable evidence of the godly men who were used in prophecy that they were moved by a power other than the motion of their own spirit, and apart from the natural exercise of their own will, to utter the prophetic call; there is also the evidence of the apostles themselves, men of the highest integrity, having no personal interests to serve (for on the contrary their mission involved great self-denial), that in their spirits they were conscious of the call of God before it was uttered, and that they accepted the weighty responsibilities of the apostolic office and ministry in assured faith that they had received a true call from the Lord; whilst at the same time there is,

Acts xiii. 1, 2.

John xvi. 14, 15.

in abundant measure, the subjective evidence of the grace given to them, even the grace of apostleship, just as James, Cephas and John recognized it in the case of Paul; his own statement being that, when they perceived the grace that was given unto him, they gave Gal. ii. 9. to him and Barnabas "the right hands of fellowship." Their doctrine and the revival of the special apostolic truths which had been forgotten during well nigh eighteen centuries, as well as the organization of the Churches which they have planted, and which are their living epistles, as well as the grace ministered to others from the Lord through the laying on of their hands—all these things are signs of apostleship.*

It is remarkable that, directly apostles were restored to the Church, they proclaimed the full doctrine of the first apostles, and especially that of St. Paul, the apostle to the Gentiles. For Apostles preach a gospel of hope, they give emphasis to the grand truths of the first resurrection, the change of the living without death, the translation of both the raised and the changed to meet the Lord in the air; and while those gathered under Apostles are engaged in ceaseless prayer for these great prophetic events, they are in fact, as is well-known, the only organized body of Christians in the Church Catholic who are thus engaged. This truly is a spiritual sign of a spiritual work, and, as such, should have been recognized by a spiritual people if they had been abiding in their

---

* It may be observed that unlike their brethren of the Jewish apostolate, the apostles to the Gentiles, beginning with Barnabas and Paul, have been men of education and culture.

heavenly standing as members of the Body of Christ, and upheld therein through the power of the Holy Ghost. Translation, in fact, is one of the Church's grand spiritual battle cries and watchwords, which has again found utterance. Speaking generally, it may be said that before the year 1830, the hope of translation was practically unknown; Mr. Asgill, in 1703, being, apparently, the only individual who, since the Reformation had given a clarion testimony to this, the true hope of the Church. But now, thank God, the hope is current and is cherished by thousands, though these are but a handful out of the whitening harvest-field of Christendom. O, when will the Lord fulfil our hope! It must surely be fulfilled sometime; but when, where, and how? O Lord, hasten the time, shew us Thy mercy, and speedily make us partakers of Thy great salvation!   Psa. lxxxv. 7.

That the Lord's message through apostles to the Baptized in these last days was not avouched by many miracles does not nullify its TRUTH, nor lessen the responsibility of the Church and her rulers in having to recognize its DIVINE origin and essence. It was necessary at the beginning of the dispensation that the preaching of the gospel to the Jews and to the heathen should be confirmed by outward signs of spiritual power in the apostles; but to the children of God in Christ Jesus signs and wonders should not be necessary to enable them to discern the grace given by the Lord to His apostolic messengers, and to believe the inherent truth of the message of restoration and of the call to repentance which they bear. Nor is it necessary that apostles should have seen the Lord in these last days; for their testimony is not so much to the resurrection of Christ, in which the Church has not ceased to believe, as to those truths which have long lain buried in the dust of ages.

In his first Epistle to the Corinthians, St. Paul writes—"Am I not an apostle? am I not free? have "I not seen Jesus Christ our Lord? are not ye my "work in the Lord? . . . . the seal of mine "apostleship are ye in the Lord." Here he lays stress on the spiritual work which he, as an apostle, has done in organizing and confirming the Church in Corinth; and, in his second Epistle, the first of the signs of an apostle which he enumerates is that of "all patience." It was necessary, no doubt, that the first apostles should have seen the Lord in order to witness to His resurrection; and it was necessary also that some of them should have the power of working miracles, for they were the heralds to the Jews and the Gentiles or heathen, of a new dispensation needing to be accredited in a supernatural manner. It is, however, recorded of only some of the apostles that they worked miracles; whilst of Barnabas, whom the Church Catholic acknowledges to be an apostle, it is not recorded either that he saw the Lord or that he worked miracles.

In the early days of the Church, miracles were wrought to *manifest the power of the Name of the Lord Jesus;* and in an early prayer which the apostles offered, they desired of God that signs and wonders might be done in the name of His holy child Jesus. It was necessary that the Name of Jesus should be exalted among those who did not know Him, or

1 Cor. ix. 1.

2 Cor. xii. 12.

See Acts iii. 16, iv. 10.

Acts iv. 30.

did not believe in Him : for example, it is recorded in the Book of the Acts, that the Roman deputy, "when "he saw what was done, believed." The manifestation of power in Christ's name convinced him. Acts xiii. 12.

But the position of Christians at the end of the dispensation is different; they believe in the Lord Jesus; hence there is not the same necessity or scope for miracles in any spiritual work of restoration among those who should be abiding in the grace of their baptismal standing, and daily waiting for the Lord from heaven.* It may indeed be confidently affirmed that *God will not suffer miracles to be wrought to convince men of what they are bound to believe without miracles.* It was so with the testimony of the Baptist, for " *John did no miracle.*" John x. 41

What is it then, to which apostles have witnessed in these last days? Not only to the second coming of the Lord, to the promise of the first resurrection, to the change without death, to the imminent translation of the firstfruits, but also to the establishment of the kingdom of Christ on earth, as the one and only hope of the Church and of all the groaning creation. The last apostles have taken up the work where the first apostles left it, and have gone on with the perfecting of the saints and the edifying of the Body of Christ.

---

* Miracles in and by themselves are no positive evidence of truth, for both the Antichrist and spirits of devils will be permitted in the last days to do signs and wonders. (2 Thess. ii. 2-9 ; Rev. xiii. 13, 14 ; xvi. 13, 14.) (Ch. xi. *infra.*)

See *God's Purpose with Mankind and the Earth.* By Messrs. Caird and Lutz. Vol. II., p. 738.

Every reader of the New Testament must be struck with the great difference between the Church of the primitive age and the Church as we now behold her. Then she was enriched with the manifold gifts of the Holy Ghost sent by the glorified Lord to strengthen and comfort His people during His absence: now, these are in great part lost, and men justify the loss of them on the ground that they belonged to the infancy of the Church, and that they would be out of place in this her time of maturity.

Protestants allege further that, as the Church now possesses the completed canon of Holy Scripture, she does not need either living apostles or the manifestation of the Holy Ghost in His ninefold gifts, 1 Cor. xii. 7-11. or charismata, as enumerated by St. Paul. Thus the written word of God (which we cannot value too highly) is made to supersede the work of the fourfold ministry, the great gift of the ascended Christ for the ministration of the Spirit, and for the perfecting of His mystical Body for His coming.

At the beginning the Lord was able to rule and bless His whole flock by apostles aided by prophets, through whom the Holy Ghost gave continual light and guidance; now pastors alone are left—save here and there an evangelist occasionally raised up—to do the full work of the Christian ministry. The joy of the Church in the hope of her Lord's speedy return, to raise the dead and change the living saints and to establish His kingdom on the earth, has now largely merged in the expectation of death as being practically inevitable, and of the conversion of the world without the Lord's bodily presence.

In looking at these two conditions of the Church of Christ, which of them, we may ask, must be the more pleasing to God—that which He Himself ordained, or that which has arisen through loss of faith and through the strifes and divisions of many generations? Is it not plain that the Church, when still undivided, filled with the gifts of the Spirit, having all the ministries which Christ gave on His ascension,* and rejoicing in the hope of His speedy return, was in a condition to serve Him more effectually in the proclamation of the Gospel, than the same Church in her present state, broken into many antagonistic fragments, ruled by rival leaders, distracted by conflicting doctrines, destitute of spiritual gifts, with no ministry but the pastoral, and neither looking for nor desiring the advent of the Lord?

But should not the Lord find His Church on His return as He originally constituted her—equipped with the same organization and endowments? She must be prepared to meet Him, being found of Him 2 Peter iii. 14. in peace, without spot, and blameless; and, if this can be accomplished only by the ministries and ordinances which He gave at the first, then He must restore them ere His purpose can be fulfilled. He must send again the *masterbuilders;* "and they shall 1 Cor. iii. 10. " build the old wastes, they shall raise up the former   Isa. lxi. 4. " desolations, and they shall repair the waste cities, " the desolations of many generations." This is the work which the Lord has been doing in preparation for the day that is rapidly drawing near, when He

* These, with their allotted work, are fully described in Eph. iv. 11-13; 1 Cor. xii. 28.

will return to take the rule of the earth into His own hands and to fill it with His salvation.

It would be impossible to give all the reasons which lead to the assured belief that God did again give apostles to the Church; an event which many devout writers admit is quite within the bounds of possibility, not to say of probability. The following passage may be quoted from the last work of one who is known in the churches for his piety and scholarship, and which is the more weighty in the present connexion because he himself does not accept the present mission of apostles. He says—" But after the first century, apostles altogether disappeared, and the churches were deprived of their greatest strength. This, as we have already seen, ought not to have been the case; and the only probable reason by which we can attempt to explain it is that the very early apostasy from the faith and introduction of the institutions and commandments of men into the churches, caused the Lord Jesus to withhold His most precious gifts, even as He did not many mighty works in His own country, because of their unbelief! *It is, however, quite possible that He may once more send apostles for the guidance of His people amid the difficulties, perplexities and dangers of these last days.*"*

That this mode of divine intervention has been recognized from time to time by saintly men—or rather, that it has been laid upon their hearts by the Lord—in the past, is evident from their writings and prayers, many of which have been quoted in Chapter IX.

* *The Church, the Churches and the Ministries*, by G. H. Pember, M.A. Hodder & Stoughton, London, 1901.

Surely then it is a highly credible hypothesis that God would send a message to His Church in the last days to warn her of coming dangers, and to furnish her with grace to meet the hour of temptation, or to provide a way of escape from the same. Judging from past history, this procedure is most probable; for there is the sure word of prophecy which speaks of an Elias ministry in the latter days, that is, a Christian ministry in the spirit and power of Elias, which shall prepare the Lord's way before Him. Are there not many signs that the coming of the Lord is at hand? Let those who, because of these signs, profess to believe that His advent is near, tell us where to find the ministry of which Elijah was the type. If it be lacking, then the principal sign of the coming of the Lord is also lacking.

When the Lord restored apostles, the office of *prophet* was also once more brought into exercise* in the Christian Church. *Evangelists* were sent forth to warn the Church and the nations of the impending judgments, and to testify to the coming of the Lord, and to the outpouring of the Spirit to prepare His way. The *pastoral* ministry, in its threefold form of bishop,† priest, and deacon, then found its true place

1 Cor. xii. 28.

---

* A *prophet* in the Christian Church is not merely a person who speaks in prophecy; he is an ordained *minister*, whether of the episcopate or of the presbyterate, as also is an *evangelist* or a *pastor*.

† The episcopate is one, and the angels of the churches and the bishops of Christendom are *pastors* of the Catholic, i.e., universal, episcopate; but the present position of the latter is in some respects abnormal.

s

in teaching and shepherding the flock. The four-fold ministry was thus revived in its divinely appointed order, to fulfil its work for the edifying of the Body of Christ. But these apostolic messengers of the Lord, whom He sent forth for the blessing of the whole Church, were rejected by her rulers throughout her various divisions, and many of her ministers and members, who rejoiced in the returning grace of the Lord unto His Church, were expelled from their places. They could not, however, be left unshepherded—they could not be permitted to drift away from the Church ordinances; nor could their spiritual welfare and necessities be disregarded; hence it was necessary that these dispersed members should be formed into distinct congregations.

The Rev. Edward Irving, to whom, ignorantly and falsely, men have ascribed the origin of the "Catholic Apostolic Church" (which was founded by our Lord Jesus Christ, and not by man, on the day of Pentecost, A.D. 33), came to the conclusion after much earnest prayer and agonizing struggles, that this was a special work of God, and truly divine, and that the gift of prophecy was a genuine revival, and for this reason he acted as quasi-pastor to those who were cast out of their own congregations, and sheltered them, encouraging among them the manifestation of spiritual gifts. For thus yielding to the Spirit of the Lord, and for prominently taking part in God's work, he was cast out of the synagogue—if his ministry in the Presbyterian Church of Scotland may be so described.

John ix. 22, 34.

Mr. Irving himself had been an unconscious pioneer

of this work of revival, for he had vindicated the reality of the sacrament of Baptism as a means of grace, and expounded the true catholic doctrine of the Incarnation of the Son of God.* He had preached on the speedy coming of the Lord, on the necessity for spiritual gifts, on the general condition of the Church as the mystical Babylon, and on the near revelation of the coming Antichrist. He recognized the call of such of the apostles who were designated by the Holy Ghost during his lifetime, but he had nothing to do with the development of the work, for the apostles were not all called when he died in 1834, and were not separated till July 14, 1835.

The gathering of separate congregations was inevitable in the existing state of the churches of Christendom, unprepared as the latter were to receive and submit themselves to Christ's original ordinances. The altar had to be rebuilt, and the forms and ordinances of the House to be shewn to Christendom; while, by the Elias ministry of the last days, a people had to be prepared for the return of the Lord. Nor can the charge of schism lie against churches gathered under the chief ministry of Christ for rule; for, being

Heb. xiii. 10.

See Ezek. xliii. 10, 11.

Luke i. 17.

---

* It has been falsely asserted, that Mr. Irving imputed sin to the sacred humanity of the Saviour, or, at least, peccability. What he contended for was that the Son of God assumed the nature of man in its fallen condition, *yet without sin*. Being made man of the substance of His mother, He took part of the same flesh and blood as all other men with all the physical consequences of the fall, yet, being conceived by the Holy Ghost, He took our nature free from the taint of that original sin which inheres in every other descendant of the first Adam (cf. Heb. ii. 14).

apostolic churches, they claim full communion and
fellowship with all their baptized brethren. The one
question for the latter to consider is, whether apostles
have indeed been restored; and with this object, to
examine the work done by them in the light of the
Matt. vii. 16-20. test which our Lord Himself prescribes: " By their
Luke vi. 43, 44. " fruits ye shall know them."

The apostles and their work must stand or fall
by this test, and the experience of nearly seventy
years goes far to settle the question; it being a thing
impossible that such a work could have been wrought
2 Cor. xi. 13. through the instrumentality of false apostles, or
deceitful workers, posing as apostles of Christ.

As the fruit of their labours, churches have been
gathered, not only in the United Kingdom, but in
most of the other countries of Europe, as well as
in North America, Australia, and New Zealand, in
which the apostles and their fellow-labourers have
taught the doctrine of Christ, have imparted, cherished,
and directed the gifts of the Holy Ghost, and have
instructed the people in all the ways of godliness
in preparation for the coming of the kingdom of
the Lord. These churches, which recognize no other
name than that which belongs to the whole Church—
One, Holy, Catholic, and Apostolic—are distinguished
from other bodies of Christians in the following
particulars:—

(1.) In the recognition and confession of the
common sin of the Baptized, in having broken the
unity of the Body of Christ, and in having departed
from the appointed ordinances of God. The true
spirit of Catholic confession has marked all that

apostles have done. This is the first step in every
genuine spiritual work of restoration, and sorrow
for the sins of the whole Church must have lain
heavily upon them, and could not fail to find formal
expression in every approach to God. This confession of sin, this antitypical sprinkling of dust
and ashes, has been a marked feature in all their
appointed services, being fully necessitated by the
present divided and unholy condition of Christendom.
They are not accusers of the brethren, but they
confess the common sin of the Church in which
—as forming one body—they and all the members
are more or less involved.

(2.) In having recognized those ministries which
Christ gave to His Church at the first, namely,
the fourfold ministry in the episcopate and in the
presbyterate; while to the order of the diaconate
have been restored its proper functions, which were
long in abeyance, to the great spiritual loss of the
Church at large.

(3.) In giving room for the exercise of the supernatural gifts of the Holy Ghost, especially in the
exercise of the prophet's ministry in the word of
prophecy uttered during divine worship.

(4.) In having received from the apostles a liturgy
and other divine offices of admitted beauty and
catholic comprehensiveness, in accordance with which
they are enabled to seek the Lord "after the due
order." There is but little of liturgical value in
other existing liturgies that does not find a place
in "The Liturgy and other Divine Offices of the
Church," in framing which the apostles were guided

Eph. iv. 11.
1 Cor. xii. 28.

Acts. vi. 1-8.

1 Thess. v. 19.
2 Peter i. 21.

1 Chron. xv. 13.
1 Cor. xi. 34;
xvi. 1.

by the light of prophecy, especially in the opening
up of the liturgical meaning of the types of the Law.

Beginning with the office of the Holy Eucharist,
the several services rest upon no mere fancy, but
upon definite principles, somewhat obscurely under-
lying the other chief liturgies of the churches in
East and West, but now for the first time clearly
asserted, and fully demonstrated.   This remark
applies primarily to the Eucharist office, but it
applies also to such occasional offices as the
Baptismal Service, the Ordinal, and many others;
while the extension of the liturgical ritual proper
to the *full services* of Morning and Evening Prayer,
is a unique feature of the book, appealing to those
who have been taught the spiritual significance
of the daily services of the Tabernacle in the
wilderness.*

(5.) In bringing up to God, as an act of worship,
the tithes and offerings of His people: the one as
the portion of the earth's increase which He has
reserved to Himself, the other as the expression of
their thankfulness and liberality.

(6.) In recognizing all the Baptized as constituting
the one Church, and in seeking to uphold and
Rev. iii. 2.   "strengthen the things which remain" of divine
truth and order in its several divisions (Eph. iv. 1-7).

(7.) In praying continually for the Lord's coming,
and for the resurrection of those who sleep in

---

* These full daily services, as well as the larger form for
the celebration of the Eucharist, from which they spring,
are in abeyance, owing to the cessation of the full Intercession, since the decease of the last apostle in Feb. 1901.

Him, and that they themselves may have part with those who are alive and remain at His coming, who shall not die, but be changed, and thus be translated without seeing death.

1 Thess. iv. 13-18.
1 Cor. xv. 51.

They hold the common faith of the Church as set forth in the three great Creeds, commonly called the Apostles', the Nicene, and the Athanasian Creed. They believe that God's terrible judgments are about to fall upon the visible Church at large for her unfaithfulness, and upon the Christian nations for their rebellion, and that God is preparing a refuge from the storm; that there shall be a *firstfruits* who have been sealed with the seal of the living God, by the ministry of His apostles,* before the winds of His indignation begin to blow; and there shall be a *harvest*, comprising a multitude who will come out of the great tribulation, from which, had they been wise in time, they might have escaped. God sent forth His apostles to make known this work of deliverance and to revive the blessed hope that gladdened the hearts of the early saints. At such a message the heart of every Christian should be filled with joy, for no such joyful tidings have been heard since the first century of the Christian era.

Rev. vii. 1-3.
Rev. xiv. 1-4.
Rev. vii. 9-14.
Rev. xiv. 14-16.

If this work be impartially examined, it will be found to be no invention of men, but the fruit

---

* Nevertheless the power of Christ "the Apostle and High Priest of our profession" to seal some of His firstfruits —His perfected ones—out of all generations of the Christian dispensation, in the absence of apostles from the Church on earth, may not be denied.

Heb. iii. 1.

of a supernatural interposition of God on behalf
of His people.   It has not been carried on in the
wisdom of men.   Those engaged in it have followed
what they recognized to be the voice of God.   He
spake and they believed; He commanded and they
obeyed.   Nothing repugnant to Scripture or early
Catholic tradition has been introduced, no new
doctrine has been taught, no new ordinances have
been established.   What has been contended for are
the original ordinances of Christ, the original teaching
of the Lord's apostles, and the original hope set
before the Church; for of necessity she must at the
end, as at the beginning, have all things necessary
to her complete development and perfecting.   As
a living witness, that the purpose of God and His
way in His sanctuary are unchanged, a work of
restoration and of preparation for the Lord's return
was needed.   It is, in fact, God's gracious answer
to the cry of many who mourned over the desolation
of Zion, and besought Him that He would restore
Psa. li. 12, etc.   unto her the joy of His salvation, and uphold her
cf. Isa. i. 26.   with His free Spirit.

In every part of Christendom, there have been
found those to whom the news of this work of
Prov. xxv. 25.   restoration is "as cold waters to a thirsty soul."
They rejoice together in the conscious presence of
the Head manifested in the members of His Body.
They have learned to love all who bear His name;
and, as a company gathered together from the
various sections of the divided Church, they desire,
and hope, and pray, for the return of their departed
brethren in resurrection life, and for the living to

be ready for the coming of the Lord, and that with
the risen saints they may be caught up to meet
the Lord in the air.

The revived apostolate, acting in unison, delivered
a testimony* in 1838, to the chief crowned heads
of Europe.

This testimony was delivered by two of the
apostles; first to the Pope, Gregory XVI., as representing *theocracy*, and as the head over the largest
section of the Christian Church.   It was next
delivered by two other apostles to the Emperor of
Austria, the representative in Christendom of *autocracy*
and of the universal empire of the Cæsars, while
thirdly, it was delivered to the King of the French
as the representative of *democracy*, or of limited
constitutional monarchy, founded in these latter days,
not upon hereditary or divine right, but upon the
vote, the gift, the nomination of the people.

In these three official characters, the kingdom of
Christ and the authority of the Lord are represented
in a remarkable and comprehensive way; for all
spiritual and temporal authority are headed up in
these three forms of government.   The apostolic
testimony was also delivered to the patriarchs, archbishops, and bishops of Christendom in 1838, its
witness being that the Lord had begun to rebuild
His Sanctuary as a prelude to His speedy return.   It is

* This weighty document was translated into several
languages; the copy delivered at the Vatican being in
Latin. A testimony had been previously delivered in 1836
to the archbishops and bishops of the United Church of
England and Ireland, as well as to King William IV.

an unrivalled *resumé* of Catholic and Apostolic doctrine.

One spiritual feature in this apostolic work which deserves emphasis, though it may be little appreciated by the unspiritual, is that the truth of the Lord's coming, with its attendant events, is no longer a theory, nor an abstraction, nor a polemical controversial doctrine, but that it is now *a living hope*. It has been made practical; it has been brought near to the Church as within measurable distance of its realization; but truly to hope, to long, and to wait for the coming of the Lord, is a result which can only be effected by the power of the Holy Ghost. Since this work of the Lord began, a great revival of the hope of His return, and even of the translation, has been felt in many Christian communities, which must be attributed to this central movement of the Lord's Spirit. Thousands are desiring and expecting a spiritual revival, a latter rain, a great outpouring of the Holy Ghost;* and yet those thousands will not even condescend to enquire into this work of God which is characterized by so many extraordinary spiritual signs.

The question is often asked—If this work be the sign of God's visitation of His Church in these last days, why do so few accept it, why has it hitherto been rejected by the Baptized and their rulers? In answer to this, another question may be asked—Has any special message from God to His covenant

---

* Of this, evidence is given in the letter of the Archbishop of Canterbury, dated Easter, 1905, inviting the bishops (and through them the clergy) of his Province to pray for the outpouring of the Holy Ghost at the ensuing Whitsuntide. June 11, 1905. (See Chapter IX.)

people *ever* met with general acceptance ?   The old
world disbelieved Noah the preacher of righteousness,
and was drowned ; the Jews, with their rulers, were
unmoved by the Forerunner's witness to Christ, and
having rejected and crucified Christ Himself, they
were scattered and their city was destroyed.   So is
it with Christendom at the end of this age ; the
Lord's special message has thus far, for the most
part, fallen upon deaf ears.   For the things of the   1 Cor. ii. 14.
Spirit of God must be spiritually discerned, and
spiritual discernment is foreign to the present fleshly
condition of the sects of the Baptized, who are
satisfied to come far short of possessing—if they do
not actually resist—those perfect ordinances and that
full spiritual endowment which characterized the
undivided Church of apostolic times.   Hence, to a
work which bears upon the face of it every mark
of a divine origin, such terms as "delusion," and even
"imposture," have been applied by those who have
not taken the trouble to inquire into it, or who are
spiritually blind to its true features.

Alas ! we have all come short and failed in the
Lord's hands ; so that we are constrained to humble
ourselves before God, and to look to His mercy and
faithfulness to lift us out of the dust and to fulfil
our hope.   Apostles have again been removed ; but,
since our trust is NOT IN THEM, but in the living God,
who raiseth the dead, we are looking and waiting
for the resurrection ; for, as we believe that none
but apostles can do apostles' work, so do we look
forward to the apostles being raised from the dead
to finish their work, and to present the Church as a

chaste virgin to Christ, and therefore, earnest and daily prayer is made for the first resurrection.

It has often been reported that those who have acknowledged the mission of apostles, have stated that during the lifetime of these last apostles the Lord would come. Such a statement has never been made on any responsible authority. Apostles, to the loss of the whole Church, have been removed by death, and the Lord has not come; but, though the hope of those who rejoiced in their ministry has been deferred, it has not perished. With the removal of apostles, the full form of Intercession has ceased on earth; and the Church, though she knows it not, has entered upon that period which is set forth in the Book of the Revelation under the figure

Rev viii. 1.   of "silence in heaven (for) about the space of half an hour."* During this silence the absence of the full Intercession must affect the universal Church; for the Body of Christ is one, and we are members one of another. Yea, it must affect not only Christendom, but all the nations of the earth. Surely, if the significance of full apostolic intercession on the earth were rightly apprehended, every spiritually minded person would pray to the Lord to bring this time of silence to a speedy termination, and to crown the faith and hope of His people, in order that the whole Church may be perfected, and

---

* It is remarkable that Mede, Daubuz, and Bishop Newton, as quoted by Mr. Elliot (*Horæ Apocalypticæ*, Vol. I. page 323), interpret the half hour's silence as "the cessation of prayer in the Church."

made ready as a bride for her heavenly Bridegroom in His glorious and everlasting kingdom.

Our testimony is that God has indeed visited His people, and has sent to them His apostles to make ready the way of the Lord   We cannot but speak the things which we have seen and heard.   Let every one who reads these pages ask the Divine help, that he may prove, according to the measure of his discernment, whether these things be so, and let him sigh for the resurrection of the faithful departed, and for the change into immortality of the living saints, as well as for the deliverance of the groaning creation; crying — " Come, Lord Jesus, come quickly."

"Lord of the bounteous harvest!
    Thou sendest forth again,
  With gracious showers of blessing,
    The latter rain.

The summer-tide hath ended;
    The seed hath taken root;
  And now Thy Soul desireth
    The first-ripe fruit.

Now through the field Thou treadest,
    O merciful High Priest!
  The first-ripe ears to gather:
    Bless Thou the feast!

So shall Thy twofold witness
    Be gathered from the field,
  And all the golden harvest
    Its treasures yield.

And soon shall " he that soweth
    And he that reapeth," come,
  To bring Thy sheaves together,
    Rejoicing home."

E. W. Eddis, 1863.

NOTE.

The following note, from the pen of a late highly respected American divine,* has it value and interest as a testimony from a foreign land to the reality of this divine work of restoration in the Church of Christ, in these last days.

"This spiritual movement, which had its beginning in Great Britain more than sixty years ago in the restoration of the supernatural gifts of the Holy Ghost, we believe to be a divine work for the recovery of the original constitution of the Church, in preparation for the now imminent coming of our Lord Jesus Christ. What the primitive ministries were St. Paul plainly tells us in Ephesians iv. 8-16, where, in speaking of Christ's gifts to His Church on His ascension into heaven, he says that "He gave some, apostles; and "some, prophets; and some, evangelists; and some, "pastors and teachers," (these last two being joined by one article, showing that they express different functions of the same office), "for the perfecting of the "saints, for the work of the ministry, for the edifying "of the body of Christ," not for temporary ends, but till the perfection of stature is reached.

"In another enumeration of spiritual ministries and gifts (1 Corinthians xii. 28), he places apostles first, because they are called and commissioned immediately by Christ, and are invested with universal spiritual jurisdiction; and second, prophets, because they are the special organs of the Holy Ghost for supernatural revelation of the mind of God, to be ministered by apostles.

* Rev. W. W. Andrews, Hartford, Connecticut, U.S.A.
From the *Hartford Times*, April 15th, 1896.

"Of the four classes of ministers thus given in the beginning, evangelists and pastors are all that have remained through the ages. Without them the Church could not have lived, for existence requires that the gospel be preached to bring men to Christ, and the Christian flocks be nourished and cared for. The names of apostle and prophet have disappeared. Bishops are chief pastors. The Bishop of Rome claims to be *Pastor Pastorum*. The great preachers like Savonarola, Luther and Wesley have been evangelists. The Church, by means of these defective ministries, has struggled through the revolutions of the centuries, for she has had the promise that the gates of hell should not prevail against her. But unity of faith and action, and fulness of spiritual life and light and power, have been wanting. The one Body has been torn asunder, and evils of all sorts affecting doctrine, morals and worship have abounded.

"A divine interposition to recover the Church, so far as may be possible, out of these evils and to prepare her for the next great stage in the progress of Christ's redemptive work would be according to the analogies of the past. Every great step forward hitherto has been by means of a special ministry, as the bringing in of the new world after the flood by Noah, the transition out of the bondage of Egypt by Moses, and the first advent of our Lord by John the Baptist. The restoration of apostles and prophets to prepare for the second coming of the Lord would be in perfect harmony with His methods in other ages. It would be a fulfilment of the promise, 'I will restore thy judges as at Isa. i. 26. the first, and thy counsellors as at the beginning.'"

CHAPTER XI.

The Mimicry of Satan.

ONE of the characteristics of the evils of the last days which has been too much overlooked (whilst attention is concentrated on external troubles, such as wars, earthquakes, pestilences, democratic lawlessness, and such like), is "*spiritual wickedness*" (*wicked spirits*, margin), or the evil which is wrought through the agency of evil spirits. There has been a great development of what is called spiritualism or spiritism, a kind of pseudo-religion which is condemned by the orthodox Church as dangerous, illicit, and is expressly forbidden by the LORD in Holy Scripture; and there is also in these last days a recrudescence of many forms of spiritual evil which were rampant in the early days of the Christian dispensation, when the Church was surrounded by the entanglements and corruptions of heathenism.

Even in these days of progress and of great physical discoveries, there are many mysteries both in the natural and in the spiritual world, such as those of matter, life, and force, which cannot be solved even by the most profound scientists: but Holy Scripture emphasizes two great spiritual mysteries; the one is called "the mystery of godliness," the other "the mystery of iniquity." The latter seems to be a parody or perversion of the former, and its

Marginal references:
Eph. vi. 12.
Lev. xix. 31. Deut. xviii. 10-12. Isa. viii. 19, 20.
1 Tim. iii. 16.
2 Thess. ii. 7.

central personality is the devil.   The first name
given to him in Holy Scripture is "the serpent"—a   Gen. iii. 1.
name suggestive of subtilty—and other names are
applied to him in the Book of the Revelation. Whilst   Rev. xii. 9, 10.
in the New Testament thousands of demons are
mentioned (δαίμονες, translated "devils" in the Authorised Version), there is only one personality called
the devil, or Satan.   In the original Greek, the word
used to denote *the* devil, or Satan, occurs only in
the singular, viz., ὁ διάβολος, and these two Greek
words have always the same meaning in Holy Writ.
It is supposed that Satan was once an archangel, and
ranked among the highest of created intelligences.   Isa. xiv. 11-14.
He fell through pride; wishing, it may be, to be
equal to the Most High.   Some have imagined that
the cause of his fall was a foreknowledge of the
Incarnation of the Son of God, a resentful forecasting
of the dignity to which the human race should thus
be exalted, even over the angels and archangels,
and over all the works of God's hands.   Psa. viii. 5, 6.

Not only is great subtilty characteristic of the
devil, but great power also, and these are two fearful
qualities in combination.   Diabolic traits may be
found even in man, if he stand in his own strength,
failing to abide in the grace of God, and thereby
falling into that pride which is the condemnation   1 Tim. iii. 6.
of the devil, whom God will destroy in righteousness
and wisdom, when the time for so doing arrives.
The devilish malice of Satan shall then be turned
into shame, and he shall be righteously condemned
and cast into the lake of fire.

Ever since his fall, the devil has been the enemy

T

of God, even as men hate those whom they have
injured; as the insubordinate adversary of Christ,
he meets his doom; and, as he has no Redeemer,
and will neither repent nor efface his sin of pride,
rebellion, and ingratitude, he must abide in the same
condition of impenitence and revolt for ever. Having
brought sin, ruin, and misery into the terrestrial
paradise of God, he may have thought that he had
triumphed over God in marring His work, and in
causing the revolt and banishment from His presence
of His chief creature *man*. Thus he "brought death
into the world, and all our woe."*

The object of this chapter is not so much to consider the subtilty and power of the devil, as his
imitation or mimicry of the work and plans of God.
If he cannot by force thwart the divine purpose, he
would if possible resist and defeat it by guile and
deceit; and with this object, he would counterfeit
the work of God by every available means. In all
imposture, there will be found an element of perverted
truth, and some apparent resemblance and mimicking
homage to the truth, else would the counterfeit be
self-condemned; and, having little chance of acceptance, its object of deception would be frustrated.
The closer the counterfeit is to the real thing, the
more dangerous it becomes; for, while the one is the
truth, the other is the lie, whatever the resemblance.

2 Cor. ii. 11.   St. Paul writes concerning Satan, "We are not
"ignorant of his devices"; and the apostle often
speaks of hindrances to the Gospel, which must
have been of a spiritual character; as when he says

* Milton's *Paradise Lost*, Book I.

that we wrestle with wicked spirits in heavenly places, i.e., with the emissaries of the devil. Satan's antagonism to God was most marked in his prompting Herod to slay the infant child Jesus; in his subtle temptation of the Lord; and in his inspiring the Jews to impute the Lords miracles, wrought by the Spirit of God, to Satanic power (Matt. xii. 22-32; Mark iii. 22-30; Luke xi. 14-22).

Eph. vi. 12. (margin.)

In the early history of the Church the same diabolic opposition and mimicry are found. Simon Magus is an instance of one who received baptism without having apprehended the truth of the Gospel; for, having exercised an evil power over the people of Samaria, he judged the miracles done by Philip in the name of Jesus Christ from the same standpoint; and so impressed was he by the visible results of the reception of the gift of the Holy Ghost, through the laying on of the apostles' hands, that he sought to purchase with money this same power for himself, hoping thereby to augment his magic influence over the Samaritans. It was this motive, no doubt, which drew forth the scathing rebuke from the apostle Peter, when he told him that he was still "in the " bond of iniquity."

Acts viii. 9, 10.

Acts viii. 18-23.

Acts viii. 16-24.

The case of the sons of Sceva, as recorded in the Acts of the Apostles, is also a striking one. They wished to discredit the special miracles that God had wrought by the hands of Paul, and they blasphemously attempted to work similar miracles in the name of the Lord Jesus—the result being that they were overcome by the evil spirit which they had sought to exorcise.

Acts xix. 13-16.

See Jer. v. 2.

Turning to the Old Testament, we see something of the power and of the mimicry of Satan in connection with the miracles of Moses. When the rod of Moses was thrown down and became a serpent, the sorcerers and magicians of Egypt apparently did the same with their enchantments, their rods, it is said, becoming serpents. This seems to be a case of simulated creative power, for that they could do more than produce serpents by sleight of hand is not to be supposed. Likewise, when the river Nile was turned into blood, the magicians of Egypt wrought some similar wonder with their enchantments; and in the second plague, when the frogs came up and covered the land, the magicians with their enchantments also brought up frogs. But the miracle of the lice, or sand flies, they were unable to imitate.

Exod. vii. 8-12.

Exod. vii. 19-22.

Exod. viii. 5-7.

The vision of the prophet Micaiah concerning the lying spirit in the prophets of king Ahab affords a glimpse into the working of the spiritual world, in so far as it is controlled by Satan. So also does the narrative in the Book of Job, where Satan seeks to prejudice God against His servant Job. The going to and fro in the earth, and walking up and down in it by Satan, there mentioned, gives peculiar force to St. Peter's warning against the devil, who "as a roaring lion, walketh about, seeking whom he may devour."

1 Kings xxii. 15-23.

Job i. 6-12.

1 Peter v. 8-9.

One phase of the mimicry of Satan consists in his endeavouring to anticipate, or plagiarize any revealed work of God. It must not, however, be thought that Satan can foreknow any *secret* counsel or future work

of the Most High, but when it is revealed, or has actually taken place, he may by imitating or simulating it, discredit it, and turn men from its acceptance.*
Whence does he obtain his knowledge? Either from the light he received in his unfallen state, when, perhaps, the scheme of Incarnation was foreshadowed, or from the revelations of God to His Church. The devil doubtless is a student of Holy Scripture. That he knows its text is evident from his quotations (or misquotations) when tempting our Lord; and he may still have some power of interpreting the prophecies of Scripture, vainly hoping that he may arrest their fulfilment, and frustrate the counsels of the Most High.

The devil and his angels must know well enough from the Scriptures, that it is the Lord's purpose to effect the deliverance of His saints on earth by translation, and that he will use every means in his power to intercept the rapture of the saints, and to prevent their escape, may be seen in his attempt to devour the man child, as predicted in the apocalyptic vision.

Rev. xii. 3, 4.

If God's great acts cannot be known beforehand save as He may have been pleased to reveal them,

* Satan has often been described by the Fathers as the executioner of God's wrath on those who have despised and forfeited the blessings and shelter of His Church. But he is no less the ape of every work of God. Though he still retains his now perverted place and power, he is neither omniscient nor omnipotent. See *Door of Hope for Christendom*, pp. 41, 42.

" There is a path which no fowl (no evil spirit) knoweth, and which the vulture's (the devil's) eye hath not seen " (Job xxviii. 7).

nevertheless they may, when they have been revealed, be denied or misrepresented; and we are warned by our Lord and by His apostles of the wonderful and lying miracles that the enemy will be permitted to do in the last days (Matt. xxiv. 24; 2 Thess. ii. 8-11; Rev. xiii. 14).

John x. 38.
John xii. 37-38; xv. 24.

Although miracles are not necessarily a proof of the truth of any doctrine, yet our Lord's miracles were so numerous and so benevolent in their character, that He could confidently appeal to them as a distinct confirmation of the truth of His mission. But our Lord gives a clear warning as to the signs and miracles which the Evil One may have power

Matt. xxiv. 24.

to do, and which He said might, if it were possible, deceive the very elect. St. Paul warns the Thessa-

2 Thess. ii. 9, 10.
cf. Rev. xiii. 14.

lonian Church against "him whose coming is after the working of Satan, with all power and signs and lying wonders, and with all deceivableness of unrighteousness." From this it is evident that evil spirits will work miracles in support of false doctrines which will perplex Christian men. Miracles, therefore, are not necessarily any test of truth, though they may from their character confirm the truth, while they may also be used to advertise and confirm a lie. Thus, although a miracle may really take place and cause men to wonder, it may, nevertheless, be wrought by an evil power to confirm unrighteousness.

In considering some of the false ways of Satan, in which he endeavours to discredit the words and actions of God, his power to transform himself

2 Cor. xi. 14.

into an angel of light must not be ignored; for,

in counterfeiting some of the gracious acts of God,
he will beguile the minds of Christian men from
the simplicity that is in Christ.   In this manner
he would mimic the central act of the Incarnation.
From what the Scriptures say, it is evident that
Antichrist—the incarnation, and masterpiece of Satan
—will be the enemy, the substitute, the parody,
of the Christ of God; and, being endowed with
extraordinary power, will bring about the apotheosis
of fallen humanity.   Satan's action in endeavouring
to forestall the kingdom of God will be seen in
Antichrist, in whose manifestation St. Paul's words
will be verified:—"Who opposeth and exalteth 2 Thess. ii. 4.
"himself above all that is called God, or that is
"worshipped; so that he as God sitteth in the
"temple of God, shewing himself that he is God."
This will be nothing less than the deification of
man, who, having changed the truth of God into Rom. i. 25.
a lie, will then be worshipped and served more
than the Creator.   Moreover, in power, in apparent
benevolence, and perhaps through simulated resurrection, Satan will employ all his powers to counterfeit
the Christ of God.   Antichrist will also institute
something analogous to the sealing of the saints by
setting his mark in the right hand or on the foreheads
of his votaries.   Our Lord, when on earth, warned
His disciples against false Christs and false Messiahs Matt. xxiv. 23,
who would shew signs and wonders.   Many examples 24.
of this could be found in history; for even in our
own day we have heard of "Messiahs" in Russia,
in Africa, in Arabia, in the United States of
America, and even recently (1903) in England.   A

remarkable case of a pretended Jewish Messiah occurred in the seventeenth century. His name was Zwi Sabbathais (A.D. 1641-1677). The excitement he created was wonderful, and though he did nothing to warrant it, some 80,000 persons were believers in his claims. To save his life, he became a Moslem, and ultimately was put to death.

Further, in the case of individual men, the devil encroaches on the work of the Holy Ghost, by invading His domain in the spirits of the Baptized. For, man having been created in the image of God, his spirit was formed to be a dwelling place for his Creator; but, when Satan tempted Adam, he began his obsession or influence over man's spirit, in order to take tyrannical possession of it and to make it his abode—thereby usurping the prerogative of God, to make man his own dwelling place. Thus, urging man on in the path of revolt, he held him in the bondage of sin, until "the Son of God was "manifested, that he might destroy the works of "the devil," and thus liberate the enslaved spirit of man, that it might become a habitation of God, through the Holy Ghost. It is important to note that the Spirit of God, who dwells in man, respects his freewill and the integrity of his manhood, and that *He does not possess the man*, nor make a slave of him. The devil cannot take possession of a baptized man, without that man's first yielding his will— which may have been weakened by deadly sin— to be controlled and enslaved; and, even if those who have allowed themselves to be taken captive

1 John iii. 8.

2 Tim. ii. 26.

by the devil at his will become conscious of their grievous sin, God may give them repentance to the acknowledgment of their sin, and His free forgiveness. Then will their souls escape as a bird out of the snare of the fowler, and be delivered from the power of the evil one. So wonderful and mysterious is the spirit of man, that it is possible for many evil spirits to take up their abode in him; even as our Lord cast seven devils out of one repentant woman, and many devils out of a demoniac, whose name was "*legion*, because many devils were entered into him." Nor can it be denied that there is much evil spiritual power abroad in Christendom in the present day; hence the importance of the admonitions of Holy Scripture: "Neither give place to the devil"; and again, "Resist the devil, and he will flee from you."

2 Tim. ii. 25.
Psa. cxxiv. 7.

Mark xvi. 9.

Luke viii. 2, 30.

Eph. iv. 27.
James iv. 7.

"In every crisis, and at every closing period of the dispensations, unclean spirits, or demons, have been active, seeking to influence, teach, or take possession of children, and women, and men. In fact it has been the irruption of unclean spirits, and daring wickedness of men departing from the faith, and giving heed to deceiving spirits and teachings of demons, which have on all such occasions contributed to the hastening of judgment. It has been this which has filled up the cup of iniquity to the full; and the closing period of the Christian dispensation promises to be no exception. The modern phase of this delusion, called 'Spiritualism,' although only dating from March, 1848, has spread so rapidly, that it now numbers its

supporters in America by millions. And it has
gained no inconsiderable footing in England, on
the Continent, and in the Colonies of the British
Empire." *

Another characteristic of Satan, is his obstruction
as well as his mimicry of the Gospel. Our Lord

Matt. xiii. revealed this by His parables of the sower and
of the tares of the field.   In the first parable,
when the word of the kingdom is heard but not
understood, the wicked one catches it away from
the heart of the hearer.   In the second parable,
the sowing of the tares by an enemy, points to
Satan's emissaries preaching another gospel, it may
be one with some semblance of truth,† which,
whether by adding to or taking away from the
Gospel of Jesus Christ, subverts His doctrine; or
it may be one with the pretensions of a new religion
of man's own devising, such as the so-called " gospel
of humanity."   To some such gospel St. Paul may
allude when he pronounces an anathema on those

---

* *The Restoration of Apostles and Prophets*, p. 177, footnote.
Glasgow, Hobbs & Co.

† Wheat (Heb. *Chittah* : Gk. πυρός *Triticum compositum*);
Tares (Gk. ζιζάνιον, *Lolium temulentum*). " The Arabic,
zawân, the bearded darnel, a kind of rye-grass, which is
found as a weed among corn crops in Britain, as well as
in the countries bordering the Mediterranean.   It is a
larger plant than the common rye-grass, closely resembling
it until its ear appears. When the seed is ground with
the corn, and made into bread, it produces poisonous
symptoms. The proper rendering would be 'darnel' (as
in R.V. margin)." This may help to explain our Lord's
command about not rooting up the tares prematurely, lest
the wheat were rooted up also (Matt. xiii. 29).

who, be they men or angels, shall preach any other
gospel than the Gospel of Christ. The new or false
gospel which is already being preached in modern
days, is briefly this: that there is good news for
man apart from God; while they who assert that
man is sufficient to be his own saviour, deny the
existence of the devil, or of sin, or of the need
of atonement and sacrifice. If man, in any true
sense, were really sufficient unto himself, he might
regard himself practically as God; and they who
aim at perfection in man apart from God, necessarily
use every endeavour to banish God altogether from
the earth. The new gospel of humanity, combining
a false altruism on the one hand, with self-deification
on the other, has thousands of intelligent and
zealous votaries. But God declares that man's
fallen nature cannot be improved; it must be crucified; it must die; thus only can the new life of
the second Adam be imparted to man, "the gift of   Rom. vi. 23.
"God (which) is eternal life through Jesus Christ our
"Lord." Fallen man has no desire for the kingdom
of God; he seeks rather to bring in that condition
of things which may be designated as the kingdom
of man. But his efforts will end in failure; for,
though Satan may mimic the kingdom, Ithuriel's*
spear will expose the imposture. The promise of
God stands firm—"When the enemy shall come   Isa. lix. 19.
"in like a flood, the Spirit of the LORD shall lift
"up a standard against him."

* The disguise of the devil is supposed to be instantly
unmasked by the touch of Ithuriel's spear. See Milton's
Paradise Lost, conclusion of Book IV.

An example of what the reign of Satan will be
may be seen in the extraordinary history of the
Anabaptists in Munster, in Germany, in the sixteenth
century. It is difficult to conceive the existence
of such a state of things, where thousands were
absolutely enslaved by the selfishness, tyranny,
caprice, and lust of one man who was nothing but an
arch-deceiver and hypocrite. Again, the condition
of things in France, before and during the Reign
of Terror, was a fearful demonstration of Satanic
energy; no one knowing whether, before the end
of the day, he might not be in prison, or on the
scaffold; and when rank, learning, virtue, fortune,
might mark a victim for the bloodthirsty mob—
the many headed *demos*, symbolized by the miry
clay of the ten toes of the great image which
Dan. ii. 31-45.   king Nebuchadnezzar saw in his dream.

The subtilty of Satan may be seen further in
his mimicry of the office of apostle in the Christian
2 Cor. xi. 13-15.   Church; for in the New Testament *false apostles*
(ψευδαπόστολοι) are mentioned, of whom St. Paul
gives an account. "For such are false apostles,
"deceitful workers, transforming themselves into the
"apostles of Christ. And no marvel; for Satan
"himself is transformed into an angel of light.
"Therefore it is no great thing if his ministers also
"be transformed as the ministers of righteousness;
"whose end shall be according to their works."
And in the Book of the Revelation, our Lord
Rev. ii. 2.   commends the Church in Ephesus for having tried
them which said they were apostles, and were not,
being found liars, i.e., false apostles.

Again, Satan has from time to time imitated the working of the Lord, by inspiring *false prophets*. In the Old Testament there are frequent allusions to these lying prophecies, with certain converse cases, such as when the prophet Balaam was compelled by God to speak truly concerning future events; and the old prophet of Samaria who misled and then rebuked the prophet who came out of Judah. In some cases it seems as if a false prophet might have a prevision of the truth, so as to reveal something which would, or did take place. The law of Moses, the history of the Jews, and the books of the prophets are full of allusions to false prophets. During the reign of Ahab, there were at least four hundred prophets of Baal; Jeremiah was encompassed by false prophets, of whom Hananiah was one; and Ezekiel denounces "the foolish prophets" of Israel. The same thing is mentioned in the New Testament as existing in the Christian Church; for that there should be false prophets was foretold by Christ and by His apostles Paul, Peter, and John. St. John writes thus—"Beloved, "believe not every spirit, but try the spirits whether "they are of God: because many false prophets "are gone out into the world. Hereby know ye "the Spirit of God: Every spirit that confesseth "that Jesus Christ is come in the flesh is of God: "and every spirit that confesseth not that Jesus "Christ is come in the flesh is not of God: and "this is that spirit of antichrist."

Our Lord specially warned His disciples saying: "Beware of false prophets, which come to you in

1 Kings xiii. 18.

Deut. xiii. 1-5.

1 Kings xxii. 15-28.
Jer. xxviii.

Ezek. xiii. 1-16.

1 John iv. 1-3.

Matt. vii. 15.

"sheep's clothing, but inwardly they are ravening "wolves;" these wolves putting on the sheepskin, so that, by their disguise they might the more easily deceive the sheep of Christ's pasture, and compass their destruction.

Further, that there will be some simulation or imitation of the *resurrection* may be inferred from the Book of the Revelation, in connexion with the career of the last Antichrist. The first beast mentioned in Rev. xiii. represents Antichrist, who receives power from the dragon, or Satan. One of his heads was seen to be wounded to death (*slain*, margin), but his deadly wound was healed; and all the world wondered after the beast. In the same chapter we are told of the wonderful miracles performed by the second or lamb-horned beast, who apparently heads up the apostate ecclesiastical authority, for he regulates public worship; and "causeth the earth and them which dwell "therein to worship the first beast." These have been seduced by this beast, who is called the false prophet, and who comes up out of the *earth*, not out of the *sea*, as does the first beast. The false prophet is seen in the vision to make an image to the first beast, or Antichrist, by which may be signified the devising of a system of worship, an εἰκών of earthly things, just as the Church's worship is the εἰκών or very image of the heavenly things. This, however, may include an actual image; and, after working many signs and lying wonders, the false prophet claims "to give life (*breath*, margin) unto the image " of the (first) beast, that the image of the beast " should both speak, and cause that as many as would

Rev. xiii. 3.

Rev. xiii. 12, 13, 14.

Heb. x. 1.

Rev. xiii. 15.

" not worship the image of the beast should be killed."
This appears to be the crowning act of many lying
wonders which the lamb-horned beast performs, when,
by apparently infusing life into the image of the
beast, he will cause all the world to worship this
quasi-resurrection image.

Satan will no doubt do his utmost to discredit the
great facts of the resurrection and translation, as
wrought by God; and, judging from analogy and
past history, it is most probable that when these acts
have taken place he will simulate both, so as to
cause men to reject the witness which will be borne
to the divine reality.

It has been an old tradition, that Antichrist, or
that individual "man of sin" who shall be the head
of the Antichristian power, and "king over all the   Job xli. 34.
" children of pride," is to be a man raised from the
dead by the power of Satan. It is certain that in
that "coming man" will be seen the putting forth
of all the power of Satan; that through his means
Satan will make his final effort at least to defeat God's
purpose in His Church, as he cannot scale heaven
and resume his own former place among the sons of
God. This he will seek to do by making the man
whom he will use as his instrument to be, to the
utmost of his power, a successful counterfeit of the
God-Man Christ Jesus, the risen Saviour. It is,
therefore, not incredible that Satan will seek to
persuade men that Antichrist is one raised from the
dead. But that God would for such a purpose raise
anyone is incredible; nor is it easier to understand
that Satan should be permitted, to bring back a

departed spirit, and to raise and really restore to life any one who had died.

Satan's effort is to prevent men from obtaining life from God, the only source of life and immortality, and it is an error and a delusion to think that in any sense Satan can be a *source* of life, which is the prerogative of God the Father who only hath life in Himself.

John v. 26.

There is a wonderful parallelism in Holy Scripture between Christ and Antichrist; and, as the rival and caricature of the Christ of God, Antichrist will be the devil's climax in his final effort to seize the kingdom for himself, and to thwart the purpose of God in His incarnate Son. Innumerable blasphemous delusions shall then overspread the world, and men shall be deceived and caught in the snares of Antichrist, "because they received not the love of the truth, that they might be saved." *

1 Tim. iv. 1, 2.

2 Thess. ii. 10.

Turning to contemporary history, we cannot but notice an evil work which appears to be a Satanic counterfeit of the work of God described in the last chapter.

A seemingly religious movement began in America some seventy years ago, almost simultaneously with the Apostolic work of restoration, originating in alleged visions, and in a professed new revelation from God. Now looking at the true work of God in the Church Catholic, there is a striking parody or mimicry of it in that pseudo-spiritual work known

---

* It is a curious tradition, dating from very early times, (Hippolytus, A.D. 220), that Antichrist will be a Jew, of the tribe of Dan, the only tribe that is omitted in the sealing mentioned in the seventh chapter of the Book of the Revelation (see Gen. xlix. 17).

by the name of "Mormonism," or, as its votaries
call themselves, "The Church of Jesus Christ of
Latter Day Saints." The following are some of its
leading features:—They have twelve apostles; they
have prophets, evangelists, and pastors, imitating
the fourfold ministry; they have laying on of hands,
or sealing, for bestowing the gift of the Holy Ghost;
they have prophecy, spiritual gifts, the gift of tongues,
healings and professed miracles; and they insist on
the payment of tithes by every member. * These
things when given and accredited by God are in
themselves true and good, they all existed in the
early days of the Christian Church, and they are
embodied in the present apostolic work of the Lord.
It may be asked — If these good things be found
among the Mormons, why should their system be
branded as false? The answer may be given in the
language of St. Paul: They "hold the truth in   Rom. 1. 18.
"unrighteousness." Despite their nominal adhesion
to the Scriptural truths catalogued above, there is
nothing in Mormonism beyond the most barefaced
simulation of the marks of apostolic Christianity as
seen in the first days of the Church, and as displayed
in these last days through the restoration to her of her
original endowment –the fourfold ministry of Christ,
and the exercise of the gifts of the Holy Ghost.
Mormonism has simply parodied the organization
of apostolic Christianity, and grafted its caricature
upon a corrupt fleshly imposture. Moreover, it

* The Mormons' organization also includes a quasi-
Sanhedrin or "Council of the Seventies," borrowed from
the time of Moses, and in imitation, no doubt, of our Lord's
mission of the Seventy sent out after the Twelve.

U

stands condemned by features which place it outside
the pale of any form of orthodox Christianity.   Its
tyranny on the one hand, and license on the other,
as evidenced by the "institution" of polygamy,
suffice to stamp its origin as not of God, and to
show its unchristian character: but this is not
all.   In the first place it claims to have received a
new revelation, as given in the Book of Mormon;
secondly, it claims for its so-called "prophet,"
supremacy over those whom they call "apostles"; *
while, thirdly, the institution of polygamy betrays
the utter fleshliness of this wicked system by which
Satan has sought to entrap the Baptized in his
parody of the special work of the Lord in the
Church in these last days.

The plague spot of Mormonism is to be found in
its denial of the existence of the Church of Christ
between the death of the Lord's apostles and the
appearance of Joseph Smith.   This is true also of
Swedenborgianism, Christian Science, and some
other great religious and philanthrophic institutions
devised by the ingenuity, caprice, and will of man.
All these act *apart from the Church of Christ*, which
alone received the life of Christ, His ministries, His
faith, His hope, His love, and all spiritual gifts, in

---

* "God hath set some in the Church, *first* apostles,
secondarily prophets" (1 Cor. xii. 28).   This precedence
of the apostolic ministry has failed to be recognized in
spiritual or prophetic movements during the history of
Christianity.   The Didaché affords the earliest example of
this, and another prominent instance appears in Montanism,
which arose at the end of the second century.

the gift of the Spirit on the day of Pentecost. These precious treasures abide in the Church of Christ for ever, and all who desire them *must come to the Church of Christ* for them as to a mother, for she is "the mother of us all."

Gal. iv. 26.

It is impossible not to shrink from contrasting so evil a thing as Mormonism with the Lord's blessed work in these last days, of which the former is Satan's device for the purpose of discrediting the latter. But this chapter has to do with the great adversary's mimicry of the working out of the divine purpose; and this is so marked in Mormonism, that it has not been possible to draw the veil over a form of apostasy which, while outraging every feeling of Christian propriety, has blasphemously parodied the divine constitution of the Church, just when, by the outpouring of His Spirit and the revival of His heavenly ordinances, God has sought to recall her to her true position, viz.:—to "earnestly contend for the faith which was once delivered unto the saints," and to embrace afresh the blessed hope of her Lord's appearing and kingdom. This work of divine revival rests upon no new revelation, but is an appeal to the Baptized to seek the old paths; the instruments employed are Christ's four ministries headed up by His apostles, given again to the Church for her perfecting, while her surviving ordinances are fully recognized and thankfully accepted by the faithful. This work of God is marked by its purity, its sobriety, its jealousy for the Catholic faith, its spirituality, its spirit of worship and of devotion to God, its jealousy for the honour of Christ—ever upholding Him as the

Jude 3.

Eph. iv. 11.

only Saviour of mankind and the one Head of His Church ; its reverence for the authority and sufficiency of the Holy Scriptures as handed down in the Church ; its dislike of proselytism, and of fanatical or hysterical excitement: such is the work of God, presenting a marked contrast to all previous religious movements, not to say to all spurious imitations of Satan. It is also noted for its strict conservative spirit, for the morality of its adherents, for its Christian freedom combined with its law-abiding principles, for its respect for authority, whether in Church or State, in the family or in other relationships of life, and for its large-hearted charity towards all sections of the Church of Christ.

Another remarkable movement, and which can only be defined as a religious imposture, has arisen in America. The originator of it has founded a city near Chicago, which he calls Zion, and apparently has amassed great wealth by his pretensions. Some time back he announced himself as the prophet Elijah who had returned to earth, and now he has appointed himself as chief apostle to the Lord, and states that he will shortly select eleven other men as fellow-apostles (Sept. 12, 1904). In support of his position and action, he quotes 1 Corinthians xii. 28, stating that God hath set some in the Church, *first* apostles, secondarily prophets. After what has been already said in the preceding chapter, it is almost superfluous to remark that the very name and function of apostle implies *one sent from God*, so that self-election and the choosing of fellow-apostles is not according to Scriptural precedent, and condemns such proceedings as clearly not the work of the Holy Spirit, but rather what must be an evil spiritual work devised by Satan.

The next point for consideration is that of *the signs of the times* in which we live, concerning which St. Paul gives clear warning in his second Epistle to Timothy, to whom he writes :—" This know also,   2 Tim. iii. 1-5. " that in the last days perilous times shall come. " For men shall be lovers of their own selves, covetous, " boasters, proud, blasphemers, disobedient to parents, " unthankful, unholy, without natural affection, truce- " breakers, false accusers, incontinent, fierce, despisers " of those that are good, traitors, heady, highminded, " lovers of pleasures more than lovers of God ; having " a form of godliness, but denying the power thereof." " For the time will come when they will not endure   2 Tim. iv. 3, 4. " sound doctrine ; but after their own lusts shall they " heap to themselves teachers, having itching ears ; " and they shall turn away their ears from the truth, " and shall be turned unto fables." A remarkable sign is that, though spiritual falsities have been simmering for ages, and now and then have burst forth into overt action, it is only within the last fifty years (since about 1847) that they have assumed enormous proportions in what is called Spiritism, Theosophy, Occultism, and other kindred Satanic inventions ; it is supposed, indeed, that there are some twelve million persons in the United States of America who are professed Spiritists, and make this delusion their cult and occupation.

"As Mormonism, which originally assumed a highly spiritual and prophetic character, arose simultaneously

with the outpouring of the spirit of prophecy in 1830,
so that other Satanic mockery, "Spiritualism," arose
in 1848; its most remarkable and chief feature
hitherto having been the appearance and touch of a
hand, as though in some mysterious counterfeit
correspondence with apostleship, of which the laying
on of hands is the chief symbol." *

"The Apostles' Creed is the confession of the
fundamental Christian truths; it acknowledges God
the Father, who created heaven and earth: God
the Son, who has redeemed mankind; God the
Holy Ghost, who sanctifies the elect of God.
Against these three acknowledgments of truth the
godlessness of our days rises up in three chief
forms:

"*Materialism* denies that God the Father has
created the world or matter in general, saying
that it is self-existent.

"*Socialism* denies that God has redeemed mankind.
Men must by their own efforts redeem or deliver
themselves from all their miseries.

"*Spiritualism or Spiritism* denies that God en-
lightens the elect; professed mediums claiming to
receive light through intercourse with the dead." †

Many have been the extraordinary spiritual manifestations in Europe during the last two hundred
years, which it would be difficult to describe.

The following is an analysis of supernatural

* *The Restoration of Apostles and Prophets*, p. 177.
Glasgow: Hobbs & Co.

† From *Die drei Artikel der Gottlosichkeit.* (The Three
Articles of Godlessness.) Berlin, 1895.

phenomena recorded in the Gospels, which are simulated by Satan and his evil spirits :

   (1) Appearance and sudden disappearance.
   (2) Transport from place to place.
   (3) Resurrection.

   (1) As regards appearance and sudden disappearance. This occurred in the case of our Lord before His death, and also after His resurrection. St. Luke narrates His marvellous disappearance from His fellow citizens at Nazareth, who in their anger had risen up "and thrust him out of the "city, and led him unto the brow of the hill "whereon their city was built, that they might "cast him down headlong. But he passing through "the midst of them went his way." On another occasion, as St. John writes : "Then took they up "stones to cast at him : but Jesus hid himself, "and went out of the temple, going through the "midst of them, and so passed by."

Luke iv. 29, 30.

John viii. 59.

Many similar phenomena have been professedly wrought in these last days by occult agency; which, if real, can be due only to evil spiritual power.

   (2) Transport from place to place. This is said to be practised by adepts in Occultism. The soul, or what is called the astral body, they say, is projected out of the literal body, and becomes capable of transporting itself to a distance. Now, is there anything wrong *per se* in these surprising phenomena? Will not powers such as these be inherent in our bodies when we are raised and changed? The answer is plain, that in the resur-

rection (or change) the spirit or the soul will not
be projected out of the body, but will thenceforward
reside, not in a natural (psychical) body, but in a
spiritual body, bearing no longer the image of the
earthy, but bearing the image of the heavenly,
becoming thus capable of putting forth the powers
of the world to come in wondrous phenomena, and
among others in those of instantaneous movement
from place to place.   But we who have been
1 Cor. xv. 47-49. baptized into Christ dare not anticipate that day
by unhallowed means, nor seek by evil power and
sorcery (so severely condemned in Holy Scripture)
for manifestations of power from the spiritual world,
these being *now* both unlawful and defiling; but
we are to wait in faith and patience for our
manifestation as the sons of God, which in the
Lord's good time, shall be our glorious privilege in
His kingdom, about to be revealed.

(3) The third point is that of *resurrection*. Most
of these modern Sadducees do not believe in the
incarnation of Jesus Christ, the eternal Son of
God, and totally deny the resurrection of the
body, so that by them this phenomenon may not
have been attempted. But the possibility of resurrection or resuscitation by the unseen powers has
none the less been ventilated; and it has thus
received a currency which may tend to throw
discredit on the truth of the resurrection of the
dead, a miracle to be effected in God's own time
and manner; and it is probable that the so-called
"materialization of spirits" was introduced by Satan
in anticipation of the resurrection, which, when

it shall have taken place, he may attempt to
imitate; as, for instance, through the agency of
the false prophet in apparently giving life to the
image of the beast, and making it an object of
worship. — Rev. xiii. 15.

The mystery of godliness and the mystery of
iniquity present striking contrasts as well as striking
parallelisms, even as light is opposed to darkness,
and truth to error. It is clear from the Scriptures
that certain Christians will be changed into the
immortal condition and pass into the presence
of the Lord without seeing death; but it is no less
clear that there will be those who are described
under the typical names of "the beast" and "the
false prophet," who with their followers will, *without
dying*, be swept from the earth to their final
doom. In these, the words of the Psalmist will
find their fulfilment: "He (God) shall take them — Psa. lviii. 9.
"away as with a whirlwind, both living, and in
"his wrath."

Alas, what a moral cataclysm will ensue when man
has done his worst, and the earth has practically
become a hell under Antichrist! Wherefore, it should
be our prayer in these perilous times, that the promise
to Philadelphia may be fulfilled to us, that we may be
kept from "the hour of temptation which shall come — Rev. iii. 10.
"upon all the world, to try them that dwell upon the
"earth," and thus may not be subjected to this fearful
trial of faith, either through persecution or through the
seductions of wicked spirits. That dire persecution,
stimulated by the dragon, will revive seems certain
from Holy Scripture; and it may occur again within

the visible Church herself; for the advance of civilization, and the scientific discoveries of modern times
have not altered the natural hatred of the human
heart of that which is good, since it is alienated from
God by wicked works. Then, how wonderful will
God's power and goodness appear in ushering in that
glorious Day of the Lord, which shall lead to the
bringing in of "new heavens and a new earth, wherein
dwelleth righteousness"; when Creation, purged from
sin, shall have learned its great lesson of the safety,
liberty, and glory of obedience, as well as the further
lesson, that "there is none good but one, that is, God."

2 Pet. iii. 13.

Matt. xix. 17.

Well may we all pray in these well-known words :—
"O God, merciful Father . . . . graciously
" hear us, that those evils, which the craft and subtilty
" of the devil or man worketh against us, be brought
" to nought . . . through Jesus Christ our Lord."

But these fearful spiritual evils, however Satanic in
their origin, pale before their climax, the worship of
the devil himself.* In the city of Paris there are two
sects of devil-worshippers, "The Luciferians" and the
"Satanists." The former worship Satan as a spirit of
light, misrepresented in the Scriptures. The latter
worship him as the enemy of God, their argument
being that he is more powerful than God, as events
past and present seem to indicate. Alas! that St.
Paul's warning to the Corinthians should have its
application in these days of an advanced Christian
civilization. "Ye cannot drink the cup of the Lord,
" and the cup of devils; ye cannot be partakers of
"the Lord's table, and of the table of devils." Such

1 Cor. x. 21.

* See Appendix XI.

things seem to point beforehand to the apocalyptic vision under the sixth trumpet, where we read that " the rest of the men which were not killed by these " plagues yet repented not . . . . that they " should not worship devils." Alas! Babylon (apostate Christendom) will become, as Holy Scripture prophesies, "the habitation of devils, and the hold " of every foul spirit, and a cage of every unclean " and hateful bird."

Rev. ix. 20.

Rev. xviii. 2.

Startling as the above statement may appear, and openly as the diabolic cult may be avowed in these last days, it is not a new thing even in France. After the murder of King Henry IV. in A.D. 1610, we read concerning the state of things in that country:

"No wonder that the devil-worship of the Middle Ages, with all its horrors of witchcraft and sorcery, became once more rampant in the country; no wonder that midnight revels, in which Satan was adored with every horrible and immodest rite which could denote hatred and contempt of the lords and priests of the land, were for many years to come of frequent occurrence throughout all the districts of France. And thus, with the hatred born of a misery so great that it sought for relief in the hell of Satan from the hell of living, was handed on from father to son that hope of revenge some day against the nobles and the priesthood which was realized in the revolution of 1789, and in the Reign of Terror of 1793."*

We have been startled lately (April 14, 1904), by

---

* *Sidelights on the Court of France*, chap. xxi. p. 200, by Lieut.-Colonel Andrew C. P. Haggard, D.S.O.—1903.

the order of the French Government for the removal
of all the religious emblems from the Courts of Law,
a proceeding which has excited consternation in
religious circles in France.   It would appear as if
an increased hostility has arisen in France, not
merely against Romanism, but against God and His
Christ.   On April 15, 1905, a Bill for the separation of Church and State was passed by a majority
of a hundred in the French Chamber, declaring that
"The Republic neither recognizes nor subsidizes any
form of worship."

The great meeting of Freethinkers, to the number
of five thousand delegates, which took place in
September, 1904, in the city of Rome, may afford
another pregnant sign of the last days of anarchy
and unbelief, and a characteristic speech was much
applauded by a crowd of fifty thousand persons.   But
it were vain to multiply statements, for every day
brings fresh signs of the approaching end of the
age, which become more significant when taken,
not separately, but in their cumulative power.

In a pastoral letter on the occasion of the Jubilee,
which commenced October 8, 1904, and terminated
on December 8, Cardinal Richard, Archbishop of
Paris, wrote thus:

"It is no longer possible to have any illusion.
The anti-Christian sects are seeking to efface the
name of Jesus Christ from the world.   Wherever
the name of God and of our Saviour Jesus Christ is
written in the Institutions or in Books, it has to
disappear.   Christians are called upon to renounce
their faith in order to be considered worthy and

capable of filling any function in society. In speaking thus we exaggerate nothing. We only note facts."

Signs are increasing with startling rapidity, both in the Church—with its prevailing superstition, will-worship, and infidelity—and in the world, with its numerous catastrophes, earthquakes, and fearful volcanic eruptions, to assure us of the truth of the Lord's predictions concerning the end of the age, and to warn us that the close of this dispensation is at hand.

It has been said by one of the English bishops that we seem drifting "into a condition of refined Paganism"; but it is feared that it would be more correct to say, "into one of avowed infidelity or Paganism." It will cause wonder, no doubt, if the Christian nations in the coming apostasy (which we are assured from Scripture will really take place) should throw off all Christianity, and revert to Paganism pure and simple. But signs of this may already be discerned in the revival of æsthetic Pagan cults and of the ancient Grecian games.

A few years ago, to have spoken of Christendom throwing off Christianity and relapsing into Paganism, would have been thought too absurd to contemplate, but there are many indications that this fearful apostasy will, before long, become an accomplished fact.

May the Lord deliver His saints, by translating them and hiding them in His pavilion before that appalling evil day, when the blast of the terrible ones shall be as a storm against the wall.* Isa. xxv. 4.

* See Appendix XI.

CHAPTER XII.

The Duty of Watching and Praying for the Attainment of the Hope of Translation.

ALAS! in our review of the past we must be aware that we, the Baptized, have sinned and come short of the glory of God, and that the Church has become entangled with the world, and has been unmindful of the hope of her calling. With humble confession the best of us must acknowledge that we have forgotten it, and do forget it daily; and, even if a few devout persons here and there remember, or struggle to remember, this catholic and God-given hope, there are millions of the Baptized who shew indifference, and even antagonism to the same. Wherefore we are all under condemnation, and share the common sin; for, as members of Christ, we are members one of another, and, hence we have to confess both our corporate and our individual sins. We have in this regard been guilty of a spiritual sin which has led on to all those forms of fleshly sin that exist everywhere, and are rampant in every large town in Christendom. We must acknowledge our general unfaithfulness in having turned aside, like Israel, as a deceitful bow.

Psa. lxxviii. 57.

Forgetfulness of a hope so clearly revealed in the word of God is a grave spiritual sin on the

part of the visible Church.   Men think little of
spiritual sin, no matter how much they may
condemn fleshly sins which affect society and injure
their interests; and yet, of the two, spiritual sin
may be the more grievous in the sight of God,
as being more insidious, pervasive, and diabolic.

The Church is heavenly in her nature and destiny;
therefore spiritual sin not only wounds her in all
her memberships, but delays the Lord in carrying
out His purpose of grace and full salvation, thus
entailing injury on the whole spiritual and intelligent creation of God.   Neglect of these special
hopes of resurrection, change, and translation must
be a sin of no ordinary magnitude; because, if we
believe not the promises of God, and make no
effort to further their accomplishment, it is equivalent
to disbelieving them and to making God a liar.   1 John v. 10.
But "if we confess our sins, He is faithful and   1 John i. 9.
just to forgive us our sins," through Jesus our Lord;
and, after confession, our plain duty is to stir up
ourselves to lay hold earnestly upon the hope set
before us, and to watch and pray for its attainment.

To the reasons already given for the forgetfulness
of these hopes set before the Church, two others
may be added:

(1) The incorrect popular belief and teaching
on the condition of the saints after death.   The
opinion has been held for centuries, and is still
held by the great majority of Christians, that the
spirit of a believer dying in a state of grace is
instantaneously glorified with Christ, and, being
thus admitted into the presence of God, enters

on a condition of happiness and perfection independently of the resurrection of the body.   The
Roman Church, however, interposes Purgatory
between death and the beatific vision, while some
Protestants assume that Christian perfection can
be arrived at only in this life. These ideas seem
to dispense with any need for the resurrection of
the just, and the *first* resurrection must necessarily
lapse out of memory, and cease to be a living
hope.   It is the special office of the Holy Ghost
to remind the Church of forgotten truths, and
in these last days He has prevailed to bring them
to the remembrance of a remnant.   But if the voice
of the Comforter be silenced in the Church, and
there be no audible reminder of these truths and
hopes, they must needs slip from memory, as
experience proves has been the case.

(2) The other reason for the Church's forgetfulness of the hope, is the holding of incorrect
views as to the conversion of the world before
the end of this dispensation.

"The most commonly received view of the Second
Advent, i.e., of the Parousia, is that it occurs at
the close of human history, introducing a final
judgment upon all men and a general and
simultaneous resurrection of all mankind.   This
view is common to the Roman Catholic Church
and to the greater number of the members of the
Anglican communion, as well as to other Protestants
who have not cast aside all belief of a personal
coming of Christ."* The majority of professing

* *Parousia*, page 4. Hobbs & Co., Glasgow.

Christians entertain the thought that the world will be converted before the Lord's coming, so that they put off the coming of the Lord to an indefinite period. This view rests on an erroneous interpretation of the parable in the leaven,* Matt. xiii. 23. for that parable — rightly interpreted — indicates the reverse, and confirms the other teachings of our Lord and of His apostles concerning the end of this age, and of the intense evils which shall signalize the last days. Many things afford evidence that this dispensation will end, as the two previous ones have ended, in failure, apostasy, tribulation, and judgment; in short, the great majority of students of the prophetic Scriptures are persuaded that we are approaching the time of the manifestation of the personal Antichrist, the time of sorrow and temptation which our Lord foretold, the like of which has not been since the beginning of the world.

The apostle Paul was not only the most definite teacher concerning the truth of the change of the living saints and of their translation, but he was a most earnest expounder of the Christian behaviour which the hope should inspire, as his Epistles to the Thessalonians bear witness. In visiting Salonica (the ancient Thessalonica), it is mournful to note the present depressed condition of the Greek Church

---

* In Holy Scripture, leaven never signifies anything good, and in the parable of the leaven it points to the working of the old leaven in the three great divisions of Christendom—Greek, Roman, and Protestant, through the worldliness of the Church, which is typified by the "woman."

x

in the crushing moral atmosphere of the lethargic Turk. The fact that these truths of the first resurrection, including the change and joint translation of the raised and changed, were first committed to this ancient Church, gives a special interest to its ecclesiastical relics; whilst it is melancholy to recall the troubles and persecutions which have taken place during the generations that have passed away since the Apostle's inspired words of comfort were addressed to that Church. In that city of some hundred and thirty thousand inhabitants, probably not one single soul is looking for the change and the translation! There as elsewhere, it has been forgotten for centuries; although, thank God, the original hope, as enshrined in Holy Scripture, has lingered on in the Church Catholic, and has not been quite extinguished under the *débris* of ages.

The admonition of our Lord and Master to His disciples is urgent. "Watch ye therefore, and pray "always, that ye may be accounted worthy to escape "all these things that shall come to pass, and to "stand before the Son of man." In these words the Lord commanded His apostles, and in them the whole Church, to *watch*; and this He enforces by many parables, and endorses with many promises. This command has been disregarded by the Church, which, being sunk in worldliness and indifference, has been forgetful of her Lord's return, and of the need of watchfulness and preparedness for the same. "While the bridegroom tarried, *they all* (all the ten virgins) slumbered and slept"; nevertheless, five of them were watchers in heart and spirit, and had provided them-

Luke xxi. 36.

Matt. xxv. 1-5.

selves with sufficient oil for their lamps. To WATCH is
a difficult thing, as the Lord implies when, to St.
Peter's question, "Speakest thou this parable unto   Luke xii. 42-44
" us, or even to all?" He answered, "Who then is that
" faithful and wise steward, whom his lord shall
" make ruler over his household? . . . . Of a
" truth I say unto you, that he will make him ruler
" over all that he hath." To watch implies that we
do not slumber, that we do not bend our eyes downwards, but look up—before us, beyond us, around us,
above us; this was the attitude of the faithful Israelite
when he ate the Passover with his shoes on his feet
and his staff in his hand, ready to leave Egypt at a
moment's notice. Watchfulness is a virtue essential
to the soldier. It was death for a Roman soldier to
sleep at his post, and the same law applies now to
those on picket duty in the face of the enemy. The
sentinel on duty, the man at the helm on board ship,
or those who keep the city watch against fire during
the silent hours of the night—as in certain Swiss
villages, when the scorching *Foehn* wind blows, which
would speedily fan a tiny spark into a raging confla-
gration—afford apt illustrations of the reality and
meaning of watchfulness.

There is one feature about the translation of the
saints which enforces the necessity of vigilance, viz.,
its suddenness. The coming of the Lord will take
place in a moment, in the twinkling of an eye; for,
though He has warned us concerning it in His holy
word, and through living men from time to time; yet
He tells us that His actual appearing will come "as a   Luke xxi. 35.
" snare on all them that dwell on the face of the

"whole earth." Men are immersed now, as they have ever been, in their worldly pursuits, not necessarily sinful, nay, probably lawful and imperative; but they are liable to be absorbed in them, and to forget the sudden appearing of the Lord. They build, they plant, they marry wives, they are full of the cares and pleasures of this life, and so that day will come upon them unawares.

In what way our readiness will be tested is unknown; but, as a colossal magnet driven and piercing through a mountain of sawdust would instantly gather out any hidden steel particles, so will it be at the coming of the Son of man. His coming will have this instant effect on the honest and good hearts of those who are abiding in the attitude of prayer, of faith, of hope, and of purity, and who, moreover, love 2 Tim. iv. 8. their Lord's appearing (Greek, ἐπιφάνεια).* The Lord's second advent shall come in an hour when we think not; but the holy watchers will not be in darkness 1 Thess. v. 3, 4. that that day should overtake them as a thief. It will be like a flash of lightning. Hence for this sudden appearing of the Lord, it is the duty of the faithful to *watch*, that they may not miss its blessing.

* The three words used in the Greek with reference to the Lord's coming have their shades of meaning, though it is sometimes difficult to distinguish them. "Apocalypse" seems to take in the general idea of unveiling, the lifting up a veil (*revelare* in the Latin); "Epiphany," a sudden shining forth in glory; and "Parousia," a personal presence which shall be the glory of the next dispensation. St. Paul, 2 Thess. ii. 8. in 2 Thess ii., unites two of the above ideas when he speaks of the Lord destroying the man of sin by the epiphany of His parousia ("the brightness of His coming," A.V.; "the manifestation of His coming," or presence, R.V.).

It would seem as if every future event depends in the first instance on the absolute will of God the Father. At His will, Christ will cease His intercession; at His will, Christ will leave His throne in heaven; at His will, Christ will descend into the air, and dependent on this event, the dead in Christ shall be raised first, and may like the Lord, remain on the earth for a season; after this (ἔπειτα) the living saints shall be changed; and, possibly after an interval, they will both be caught up together to meet the Lord in the air. Will the living know at once when the dead have been raised? Will they immediately see them, and converse with them; or, as in the case of the disciples with whom the Lord talked on the way to Emmaus, will their eyes be holden, so that they fail to recognize them at first? Should there be an interval between the raising of the dead and the change of the living, and should the latter see their risen brethren, will they not be stimulated to increased desire and preparation for that sudden moment when they themselves shall be changed from mortality into immortality?

What a high standard is that of so abiding in faith, hope, love, and holiness in the Holy Ghost, as to be ready *at any moment* to welcome with joy the instant appearing of the Lord! Is any higher standard of preparation for it, and for His likeness conceivable?

We are not only to watch, but also to pray; for the second command is to *pray* : "pray always." Where would the suffering Church be if she were voiceless? Where would each one of us be without prayer? Who can estimate the irreparable loss suffered by the

Col. iv. 2.   soul that neglects prayer?   We are bidden to "con-
"tinue in prayer and watch in the same"; the
morning and evening sacrifices of prayer and praise
should ascend like the daily burnt offering from our
hearts, from our hearths, and from all the Churches.
We should pray always, at all times, in every place,
under all circumstances; for prayer, as the poet has
it, is "the Christian's vital breath." *

          The parable of the importunate widow in the
Luke xviii. 1-8.   eighteenth chapter of St. Luke's gospel, appears to
be connected with the subject of the translation of
the saints, alluded to in the context of the preceding
chapter, although by the artificial arrangement of
chapters it is separated from its preface.   The Lord
spake this parable with one object—to enforce the
command, "that men ought *always* to pray and not
"to faint," and the parable points to the state of
the world at the period of the translation; for the
saints, like the importunate widow, keep crying—
Luke xviii. 3.   "Avenge me of mine adversary," i.e., of him who
Rev. xii. 10.   is their great adversary, the accuser of the brethren,
Heb. ii. 14.   even "him that had the power of death."   They
must give the Lord no rest until He come and deliver
them from the malice and power of the devil.

Matt. vii. 7-11.   It is a law of God, that we must ask if we would
receive.   We are exhorted not only to believe the
Ezek. xxxvi.37   promise, but to plead for its fulfilment.   "I will yet
"for this be enquired of by the house of Israel, to do
"it for them," saith the Lord to Israel by His prophet
Ezekiel, and the same injunction holds good for the
spiritual Israel.   In Psalm xxi. we read of the king's

                    * Montgomery.

request; "He asked *life* of thee, and thou gavest it him, even length of days for ever and ever." Why should not the Church, why should not each individual Christian ask for preparedness to meet the Lord when He returns, for the change into immortality without seeing death and for translation to the throne of God? The Lord has set before His people these blessed hopes; they are not begotten of man's imagination; therefore let us obey the command and plead for their fulfilment. Psa. xxi. 4.

Those who have entertained these hopes have been called *visionary*, but these hopes are nevertheless founded on the revelation and promise of God; they are Scriptural, rational, and practical, and if God has promised that the translation shall take place (and the word of prophecy and the immutable types of the Law declare the same), surely, according to the analogy of His dealings with men, the approaching fulfilment of the promise will be witnessed to by the faithful ones who not only believe it, but plead for its speedy accomplishment.

That the hope of the first resurrection is forgotten is shewn by the fact that the Church does not pray for it in her recognized formularies. But after the silence of centuries the cry once more ascends from the saints on earth to the Lord, that He would come and set them free, and change them into His likeness without death. And the presumption that the time—"the set time"—is at hand is therefore well founded. How often—or how seldom—in the day do we individually pray for it, or ask for translation? Do we follow the Psalmist's example Psa. cii. 13.

in all sincerity and in spirit: "Evening, and morning,

Psa. lv. 17.
Psa. cxix. 164.

"and at noon will I pray, and cry aloud: and he shall "hear my voice." "Seven times a day do I praise "thee because of thy righteous judgments." Do we not often allow a day to pass without praying for the change and translation?

"What man is he that liveth, and shall not see

Psa. lxxxix.48.

"death? shall he deliver his soul from the hand of "the grave?" Although no one may say, "I shall "not die; I will not die," yet, looking for the Lord's appearing, we should all cherish the *hope* that we may not die. By no efforts of our own can we attain to it; but only by the grace and power of the Holy

Eph. iii. 20.

Spirit of God, "according to the power that worketh in us." We must remember that there is only one possible way of escaping death, and that is by the coming of the Lord, and our being caught up to meet Him in the air. And, moreover, while we should be individually watching and praying for the fulfilment of this hope, we should not forget that a wider application must be given to the words of our Lord, and that they are addressed to the whole Church. For it is the Church as a whole, the chosen Bride of the Lamb, which should watch and pray for the attainment of the blessed hope of translation at her Lord's return.*

The Lord gives two reasons to enforce the necessity for watchfulness and prayer, viz., that we may

Luke xxi. 36.

"escape all these things that shall come to pass, and that we may "stand before the Son of man." But these two points, having been fully considered in Chapter III., need not be enlarged upon again.

* See Appendix XII.

We are to watch and pray that we may "be ac- Luke xxi. 36. counted worthy." What a wonderful thought, that any sinner should, by the grace of God, be *accounted worthy* of so great a reward! But all intrinsic merit must be ascribed to the Lamb; our worthiness is due only to His grace, to the indwelling of His Spirit, and to the abounding mercy of God. When creation was challenged as to who was worthy to open the sealed book and to loose its seven seals, "No man in heaven, nor in earth, neither under Rev. v. 1-10. "the earth, was able to open the book, neither to "look thereon"; and the apostle wept much because no man was worthy to do this. But he was comforted when he was told that the Lion of the tribe of Judah had prevailed to open the book and to loose the seven seals thereof; and, in the sequel, the four living creatures and the twenty-four elders fell down before the Lamb, and sang a new song saying, "Thou are worthy to take the book, and "to open the seals thereof: for thou wast slain, Rev. v. 9-14. "and hast redeemed us to God by thy blood"; and then the chorus widens; and not only myriads of angels join in the song, saying, "Worthy is the "Lamb that was slain"; but "every creature which "is in heaven, and on the earth, and under the "earth, and such as are in the sea," add their tribute of praise, saying, "Blessing, and honour, and glory, "and power, be unto him that sitteth upon the "throne, and unto the Lamb for ever and ever."

The *character* of the firstfruits is given in Rev. xiv., and at this high standard of spiritual perfection, Matt. v. 48. the whole Church, and every individual member,

should aim, according to the axiom laid down by
1 John iii. 3. St. John—"And every man that hath this hope
"in him purifieth himself, even as he is pure." We
must all strive to be pure and guileless, to discharge
our duty to God and man in faith and obedience,
in love and righteousness, and to owe no man anything but to love one another. No debts must bind
us with chains to earth, and hinder our being caught
up to meet the Lord in the air. We must so walk
that we can be *righteously* translated, and that no one
shall suffer loss in any way by our removal. Death
is due to a moral cause, which is sin, and thus
resurrection may, in one aspect, embrace a moral
and spiritual cause, which is holiness. Christ's flesh,
Acts ii. 24. saw no corruption, "because it was not possible
that he should be holden" of death, and He burst
its bonds, not only because He was the Son of God,
but because of His perfect holiness in flesh; and
He teaches us the practical lesson that all those
who are looking for resurrection, or rather for the
change without death and the translation, should
seek to be full of the Spirit of God, the spirit of life
and holiness, so that, having no fellowship with sin
or death, they may be ready for the instantaneous
change into everlasting life.

The idea of a prize, or special reward, set forth in
Phil. iii. 14. Holy Scripture, has a practical connection with the
subject of the translation of the saints. St. Paul
speaks of pressing "toward the mark for the prize of
the high calling of God in Christ Jesus," and there is
special glory attached to what is set before us under
the figure of a prize. This does not impugn the

doctrine of the antecedent "*gift* of God," which "is eternal life through Jesus Christ our Lord." Rom. vi. 23.

The idea of a prize, involving labour and effort in the contest, is twice brought before us by St. Paul in his epistles. The great prize of which he writes in his Epistle to the Philippians is nothing less than the first resurrection. He counted all things but loss for Christ, if by any means he might attain unto the resurrection *from the dead* (that *out from among the dead*, Greek, see Chap. I, p. 10). He felt that he was called to something higher than to attain to the general resurrection. The first resurrection was the prize which he sought, and for this he felt that every sacrifice was true wisdom. The apostle's aim was to forget those things which were behind, and to reach forward unto those things which were before, pressing toward the mark for the prize of the high calling of God in Christ Jesus. Here is an illustration taken from the earnest runner, who might be seen in the Olympian games contending for the Panathenaic prize. In writing to Greek converts in the Church at Corinth, the apostle says, " Know " ye not that they which run in a race run all, " but one receiveth the prize? So run, that ye " may obtain." He draws a pointed illustration from the adjoining Isthmian games, adding that every man that striveth for the mastery is temperate in all things. Even so must we also strive lawfully; and by yielding ourselves to God, as those who are alive from the dead, and our members as instruments of righteousness unto God, we shall prevail to obtain the necessary training for the attainment of our high

Phil. iii. 11-14.

1 Cor. ix. 24.

1 Cor. ix. 25.

Rom. vi. 13.

calling. Let us not confound *life* with the *crown of life*. We are given life, eternal life, freely in Holy Baptism and in response to our faith; but the crown of life will be given as the reward for patient and faithful service. "If any man's work "abide, ... he shall receive a reward," and those whose works stand the fiery test will receive a crown. The Lord Himself tells us that the first resurrection with its special glory, and the escape from the great tribulation, are not necessarily a part of the gift of eternal life to simple faith, but are, by the grace of God, rewards for diligent and faithful service; and He bids the Church in Philadelphia— "Hold that fast which thou hast, that no man take *thy crown*." A millennium, a thousand years of special honour and bliss, may seem little when compared with eternity, but it is not so when compared with the duration of the history of man; for a thousand years are one seventh of this whole period, and those who attain to the millennial honour shall be known as God's kings and priests for ever and ever. This kingship will be the immortal crown to which, by the grace of God, they shall have attained, and which they shall possess and enjoy for ever.

While the Scriptures shew that we cannot be justified or accepted before God on account of our own merits or good works, they teach further that individual effort is requisite; for we are instructed by St. Peter to give all diligence to add to our faith seven other graces, and to give diligence to make our calling and election sure. The parable of the pounds and that of the talents teach the same truth:

1 Cor. iii. 13,14.

Rev. iii. 11.

2 Peter i. 5-7, 10

that rewards will be granted in proportion to the faithfulness and diligence manifested by us, even though we have been justified freely by the grace of God, through the blood of the Lamb. The Holy Scriptures are full of the doctrine that every man shall be judged according to his works.

But effort is intensified when we seek to gain a *prize*, and the prize of the first resurrection will be attained by an exceptionally limited number, and that of the change without death will be attained by a much smaller number. What a prize must this be, when, on looking down the ages, we see the roll of names, beginning with the first apostles, saints and martyrs, who have not attained to the fulfilment of the hope! Nevertheless, we, the living, should desire and watch and pray for the realization of this practical and special hope, which has been brought before us personally and collectively.

What is our practical duty? To watch for the Lord's instant and sudden appearing; to pray for sudden change and rapture; to intercede for the whole Catholic Church, for the completion of the number of the firstfruits, for the accomplishment of God's gracious purpose in Christ, and for the bringing in of His kingdom and glory. While we are com-manded by our Lord, through the prophet, to ask   Zech. x. 1. for rain in the time of the latter rain, we may also ask for bright clouds, for showers of rain, that every one may have " grass in the field."

That the counsel of God shall stand, even though all men should be indifferent, nay, even antagonistic to the fulfilment of the same, is shewn from the prophetic visions given to St. John. Therefore, though the hope be delayed, yet let us cling to it, being assured of its ultimate realization, since it is a distinct and faithful promise of God to His Church. It is not a hope that has been held out to us by man; on the contrary, man has been slow to grasp it since it was revealed by God. But it has been revived in these last days, not so much as a doctrine as in the form of *a living hope.* There is a great difference between a doctrine and a hope; a doctrine may be coldly received by the intellect, and, though true, may not incite to action; but *a hope* fires the soul and becomes a spring of action. This, then, is the question before us:—Is the hope of escape from the coming storm with its avalanche of trouble and sorrow, and of the prize of the first resurrection, or that of the translation of the living, cherished with lively desire by the Church, or is it almost ignored and forgotten? The sorrowful answer has been given in these pages.

The Church Catholic, by her lethargy, has kept the Lord waiting for nearly two thousand years, because she did not cherish His promise to come and take her to Himself: but this is no proof of the falsity of His promise, nor of the uncertainty of the event set before her as her hope; it only proves her indifference thereto. Nay, more, she has even resisted the doctrine of the Lord's second advent, fulfilling St. Peter's prophecy, "that there 2 Pet. iii. 3, 4. "shall come in the last days scoffers . . . . "saying, Where is the promise of his coming?" No external signs in the world—such as earthquakes, wars, pestilences, revolutions (although predicted in the word of God), will cause men to believe, or to watch and pray. Those only will do so who have the grace and light of the Holy Ghost, who have "understanding of the times," like the men of Issachar, being able to discern the *signs* of the times. It should be observed that these signs are not merely on the earth in the form of physical phenomena or historical occurrences among the nations; they are also in the heavens or spiritual region, in the Church and in her experiences of the Lord's dealings with her in these last times. To such signs attention has been directed in these pages. *1 Chron. xii. 32.*

But what of those who, having failed to watch and wait for the Lord's appearing, will be overtaken by the dawning of the day of the Lord, as by a thief in the night? Having put off that day in their hearts and said, "My Lord delayeth his coming," He shall find them unprepared when He comes. They are not necessarily only the wicked; there may be multitudes of devout persons among them; only they are *unprepared* for the Lord's appearing, and will have to pass through the fires of judgment in that time, when "many shall be purified, and "made white, and tried." *Matt. xxiv. 28.* *Dan. xii. 10.*

What should be our attitude towards God at this crisis of the history of the Church? It should be one of confession of our unfaithfulness, in that we have let slip the things which God has revealed, in that the professing Church, as a whole, has ceased to love the appearing of the Lord Jesus, and has forgotten the hope of the change and the translation which is bound up therewith. Nevertheless our confession should be mingled with thankfulness, that at the eventide of this age there are those who cry—"Hasten, O God, the time when Thou shalt send from Thy right hand Him whom Thou wilt send; at whose appearing the saints departed shall be raised, and we which are alive shall be caught up to meet Him, and so shall we ever be with the Lord." "Shew us Thy MERCY, O Lord, and grant us THY SALVATION."

Psa. lxxxv. 7.

It shall be seen at length that the whole of the dealings of God with man for his salvation have, from first to last, been dealings of PURE MERCY AND FREE GRACE.

Come Lord Jesus, come quickly, and set us free. Change us without death into Thy likeness, that we may be like Thee, and be with Thee for ever, through Thy merits and through Thy grace, for Thou only art the God of our salvation. "O LORD, "thou hast brought up my soul from the grave: "thou hast kept me alive, that I should not go "down to the pit. O LORD my God, I will give "thanks unto thee for ever."

Psa. xxx. 3, 12.

> " Hasten, Lord, the blissful morning
> When the sleepers shall awake,
> Cast their burial garments from them,
> And immortal bodies take;
> Then may we, transfigured, rise
> To be with Thee in the skies."　　E. W.

Psa. lxxii. 18.

"Blessed be the LORD God, the God of Israel, "who only doeth wondrous things"; and to Him be praise for ever!

APPENDIX I.   Page 33.

The Case of Mr. John Asgill, A.D. 1703.

THERE are many truths that lie on the surface of Holy Scripture, and yet, though they may be called open secrets, they are secrets still; for it needs the grace and illumination of the Holy Ghost to lay hold of them by a living faith, and to turn them into principles of action. This holds good of the revealed truths which have been considered in this treatise.

A remarkable testimony was given to the Christian hope of translation without seeing death, about the year A.D. 1703, by Mr. John Asgill. Before quoting from Mr. Asgill's treatise, the following brief biographical sketch of his life may be given.

Asgill was born in the middle of the seventeenth century, and bred to the law in Lincoln's Inn Fields, under Mr. Eyre. The whole strength of his mind was devoted to his profession, so that he acquired a habit of looking at everything from a legal point of view. He searched the Old and New Testaments to find "something more than was considered his share." As the result of these studies, he published in 1700, "An argument proving that, according to the Covenant of Eternal Life revealed in the Scriptures, man may be translated from hence into that Eternal Life without passing through death, although the human nature of Christ Himself could not thus be translated, till He had passed through death." Many a book has originated in the misfortunes of its author. Asgill's harmless heresy began in a confinement to which he was reduced in consequence of an unsuccessful speculation, for he had incurred so great a loss, that he was compelled to keep his chambers in the Temple for some years. Then he began to study "the book of Law and Gospel," commonly called the Bible. He desired that his pamphlet should not be published until after he had left Middlesex; but the book was eventually published in Ireland, giving rise to a rumour that he had gone mad. He was told that his practice was ruined, but this was not the case, for people crowded to the Courts to see him and

Y

hear him speak, and he soon earned enough to purchase a large estate, which previously belonged to Lord Kenmare.

From the *Biographia Britannica* we learn that "he received his seat in the Irish House of Parliament in consequence of his position as a land-owner in Ireland. He was in Munster at the time, and set out for Dublin, but learned on the way that his book had been examined and pronounced blasphemous," and had been burnt by order of the House, without his having been heard in its defence. Nothing more was considered necessary than to prove him to be the author and expel him forthwith, which was done in the course of four days in the year 1703. He returned to England in 1705 and obtained a seat for Bramber, apparently with the object of securing himself from his creditors. He represented this borough for two years; but, in the first parliament after the Union, some Scotch members took exception to a man being allowed his liberty under privilege, and, instead of attempting straightforward means, they took the easier course of getting a committee appointed to examine his book. It was reported to be profane; but, although he was allowed to make his defence, he was expelled from the House. The remainder of his life was passed within the walls of the King's Bench Prison, where he died in 1738, at an advanced age. It is said that "he nearly attained the age of one hundred."—From *The Doctor* by Southey, part ii., p. 446.

The following notice of his book is taken from *Biographia Britannica*, S.V. :—

"Asgill's argument proving that, according to the Covenant of Eternal Life revealed in the Scriptures, man may be translated from hence into that eternal life without passing through death, although the human nature of Christ Himself could not be thus translated till He had passed through death."

"For writing this book, Asgill was expelled from the House of Commons, and committed to the Fleet, where he died after thirty years' imprisonment, at the age of nearly one hundred years."

"The pamphlet was ordered to be burnt by the common hangman; and, for writing it, the author was expelled from both the Irish and the English Houses of Parliament."

"This tract is scarce, but it may be seen in the British Museum and in the Bodleian Library at Oxford. Mr. Asgill was expelled the House of Commons in Ireland, 1703, and the House of Commons in England in 1707. It is to the latter expulsion that reference is made in the ' Defence,' N. & Q., vol. vi., pp. 3, 300."

We here append the vote of the House of Commons in the Kingdom of Ireland, with reference to Mr. Asgill's expulsion ; *Lunæ 11 die Octobris, 1703 :—*

> "RESOLVED, *Nemine Contradicente*, that it appears to this House, That John Asgill, Esqre., a member of this House, is the author of a book, entitled : An Argument proving that, according to the Covenant of Eternal Life revealed in the Scriptures, man may be translated from hence into that Eternal Life without passing through death, altho' the human nature of Christ Himself could not be thus translated till He had passed through death.

> "RESOLVED, *Nemine Contradicente*, That John Asgill, Esqre., a member of this House, be expeld this House, and be for ever hereafter incapable of being chosen, returned, or sitting a member in any succeeding Parliament in this Kingdom."

There are various notices of his books in the catalogues of booksellers, which it is not necessary to subjoin, as they are merely repetitions of what has been mentioned above.

Southey suggests that his expulsion from Parliament and his subsequent imprisonment was due to his insolvency, and not to his religious eccentricities.

Extracts from the Preface to Mr. Asgill's Tracts :—

"To them that knew not the reason, it looked like a whym for the man in the Gospel to walk about the streets with his bed on his back on the sabbath day, while the rest of the people were at their devotions.

"And perhaps it may seem more odd in me to bolt out an argument in Divinity (as a bone of contention) into the world, at a time when the rest of mankind are so deeply engaged in secular affairs.

*   *   *   *   *   *   *   *   *   *

"And having thus delivered my part of the message, I

look upon myself as having no more to do with it after-wards than you have.

"But hereby I shall know whether this doctrine be mine or no.

"If it be mine, it will sink and fall and die; but if it be His—I think 'tis—it will kindle itself like a firebrand from one to another, till it hath set the world in arms against death. And having thus lost the decision of the truth of its success, I begin to feel myself more easy under it.

"And as the four leprous men said to one another in the gate of Samaria: If we sit here, we are sure to die with famine, and if we go into the camp of the Syrians, we can but die by the sword; so I have said to myself: If I submit to death, I am sure to die; and, if I oppose it, I can but be killed and die.

"And, should I be baffled in this essay, I can lose nothing by it, but that little credit with the world which I value not in comparison with this attempt.

"And as those four desperate men, venturing themselves upon this resolution, did thereupon find that they had been before more afraid than hurt:

"So, in making this sally against death, methinks I have discovered it to be rather a bugbear than an enemy.

"So, if my news be true in itself, why should it fare the worse for being told by the greatest of sinners?

"Tho' it be in contradiction to the most received truth in the world, *That all men must die.*"

Extracts from the Pamphlet itself:—

"I defy the logicians to deny my argument, of which this is the abstract:—

"That the law delivered to Adam before the fall is the original cause of death in the world. That this law is taken away by the death of Christ. That therefore the legal power of death is gone. And I am so far from thinking this Covenant of Eternal Life to be an allusion to the forms of title amongst men that I rather adore it, as a precedent for them all, from which our imperfect forms are taken; believing with the great Apostle, that the things on earth are but the patterns of things in the heavens, where the originals are kept."

"But why then doth death remain in the world ? Why, because man knows not the way of life—'the way of life, they have not known.' Or (as I said at the beginning) that death maintains its dominion over us by our fear of it; having no other right to remain with us; but because our faith is not yet come to us. 'When the Son of Man comes, shall He find faith upon the earth ?' Man is a beast of burden that knows not his own strength in the virtue of the death and the power of the resurrection of Christ; which ignorance does not proceed from want of revelation of the truth, but from our neglect to study and inaptitude to believe it."

"The motto of the religion of the world is, as I have said, *Mors janua vitae*—death is the gate of life. Now I say, if we do by this mean the death of Christ, then we are in the right. But if by this we mean our own death, then we are in the wrong. The death of Christ was necessary for Him and us both, because the Covenant of Life would not take effect but by His death, which in the Covenant hath two capacities."

"Now, I say this, that as Christ did thus change His state upon earth, without change of His person or place, so man may do too, with this difference, that the Christ passed this change by His own death and resurrection, yet we can't do it by our own death and resurrection, but must do it by passing through the death and resurrection of Christ in that legal form prescribed by the Covenant of Eternal Life; because His death, and not ours, is made the seal of that Covenant."

"And yet far be it from me to say that man may not attain to Eternal Life though he should die; for the text runs double—'I am the resurrection and the life: he that liveth and believeth on Me, shall never die; and though he were dead, he shall live.' But this I say, by this very text, there is a nearer way of entering into Life Eternal than by the way of death and resurrection. Whatever circumstances a man is under at the time of his death, God is bound upon His fidelity to make good this text to him, according to which part he builds his faith upon. If he be dead, then there is a necessity for resurrection; but if he be alive, there is no occasion for death or resurrection either."

"We must all be changed, but we need not all die in order to be changed, for 'tis not death that works the change, but the death and resurrection of Christ, which we may pass through without death. Paul was of this religion, that we may be changed without death. 'We shall not all die, but we shall all be changed.' And yet, though he had delivered this to be his faith in general, he did not attain to such a particular knowledge of the way and manner of it so as to prevent his own death. And his confession tells us the reason of his failure. That he had not yet attained to the resurrection of the dead, but was pressing after it."

' Though God hath formed this covenant of Eternal Life against death, man still maintains a covenant with it. They have made an agreement with death and hell."

"And, tho' now I am single, yet I believe that this translation by faith without death will be general before the general change (Paul speaks of) shall come."

"And that then, and not before, shall be the resurrection of the just (which is called the first resurrection).

"And after that the dead so arisen, with the living then alive, shall have learnt this faith (which shall qualify them to be caught up together in the air), then shall the general resurrection of the dead be."

Of course, Mr. Asgill's book provoked many satirical and antagonistic replies; but, on the other hand, it also elicited some that were favourable to his views. Thus we have: "A vindication of Mr. Asgill's book: 'Thro' the manifesting how man may arrive at perfection, and that the same things that were transacted in the beginning of the world, will be transacted before the end thereof, for translation and trans- figuration of souls and bodies.'"

In 1705, there was a pamphlet printed, called, "A letter to a friend, in vindication of Mr. Asgill's book concerning walking with God, as did Enoch, and for translation of the body and soul, as was both Enoch and Elias, by a person of honour." London: Printed and sold by Anne Baldwin, in Warwick Lane, 1705.

The author concludes in the following words: "I do verily believe that some men will be fitted for translation and transfiguration before the day of judgment. For before that time there will be the most miraculous things transacted

in doing miracles for the conversion of the Jews, and for
the bringing all nations into one religion as must be effected
before the end of the world.   Even so come Lord Jesus;
come quickly.   Amen."

It seems clear that Mr. Asgill, from his study of the
Bible, was led to discern what is a cardinal hope of the
Gospel.   But he did not hold the truth in its relation to
other truths.   He was looking for an *individual* translation,
on which he expressed himself somewhat strongly, and to
which he did not attain; for he failed to understand that
the promised change or translation of the saints is not to
be that of solitary individuals, but of a corporate body.

Nevertheless, let us thank God for Mr. Asgill's witness
to the forgotten truth of the translation of the living, and
hope that some of the seed he scattered has germinated,
and that his "labour has not been in vain in the Lord"

APPENDIX II.   Page 38.

Extract from "The Coming of Messiah in glory and majesty," by Ben-Ezra, A.D. 1812.

THE following is the quotation from "Ben-Ezra" referred to in Chap. II., p. 38.

Extract from *The coming of the Messiah in glory and majesty*, by Juan Josafat, "Ben-Ezra," translated by the Rev. Edward Irving, vol. I., chap. VI., p. 101 :—

"Christ comes from heaven to earth in the glory of His Father with His angels: at the first sound of His voice forthwith arise those who hear it; that is, all His saints, the dead in Christ shall rise first. These being risen, shall immediately ascend through the air to receive the Lord, and enjoy His bodily presence : together with them shall likewise arise, or be caught up, the living saints who are upon the earth. These living saints who have not passed through death, shall in a moment die, there, in the air, before arriving in the presence of the Lord ; or according to the opinions of others, they may perhaps die and revive in a moment, before being caught up."

That the learned father is incorrect in his suggestion of the changed saints having momentarily to taste of death before their change into immortality is shewn in chap. II., p. 38. When that passage was written the author was in ignorance that this idea had been broached by "Ben Ezra," and the theory is unscriptural and unreasonable. Nevertheless from the following extract it appears as if he accepted the teaching of St. Paul as given in the passages which he quotes.

In reference to the petition in the Lord's Prayer, "Thy kingdom come," and to Christ's millennial reign on earth, and the blessings fraught with it to all nations and all mankind, "Ben-Ezra" writes as follows :—

"Therefore be it far from me to fear the coming of the Lord in glory and majesty, for I yearn for it with the greatest longing, and pray for it with all the earnestness of which I am capable; for it will bring full salvation to the unhappy Jews, as well as to the heathen. . . . . The glorious advent of the Lord Jesus is a divine truth, which is as essential and fundamental to Christianity, as His first advent to suffer in the flesh. . . . . When that great day has come which heaven and earth await with earnest desire, then will 'the Lord Himself descend from heaven with a shout, with the voice of the archangel, and with the trump of God.' Then, in that moment (as I conceive it), at the Lord's contact with the atmosphere of our earth, this will occur first, the resurrection of all the saints who are accounted worthy of the resurrection *from* the dead, of whom Paul says, 'And the *dead in Christ* shall rise *first*.' In a moment, when this *first* resurrection of the saints of the first order has taken place, then will those few among the living who will be counted worthy of this designation of *saints*, on account of their wonderful faith and of their righteousness, be caught up, together with the sleeping saints who have been resuscitated, and will ascend with them to meet the Lord in the air. All this is very clear, and very comprehensible."

1 Thess. iv. 16.

Luke xx. 35.

1 Cor. xv. 51.
1 Thess. iv. 17.

APPENDIX III.   Page 95.

On the Book of Enoch.

THE Apocryphal "Book of Enoch" from which St. Jude
may have taken his quotation, is remarkable. The book was
widely circulated in the second century, and was known to
Justin, Irenæus, Clement of Alexandria, and Origen. It
is an Ethiopic Manuscript and is divided into five parts. It
was not admitted into the category of the Canonical
Scriptures, but it was familiar to scholars until the eighth
century of the Christian era, after which it seems to have
sunk into oblivion; and it was only at the end of the
eighteenth century that the traveller Bruce discovered its
existence and brought back three copies from Abyssinia.
He deposited a copy in the Bodleian Library at Oxford,
which remained there undisturbed until it was unearthed
about 1838, and translated into English by Dr. Richard
Laurence, afterwards Archbishop of Cashel, but then Pro-
fessor of Hebrew in the University of Oxford. The passage
quoted by St. Jude is taken from Chapter 2, Part 1.

APPENDIX IV.   Page 151.

Remarks on the "Man-child," by the Rev. G. S. Faber, B.D.

THE symbol of the man child in its relation to the firstfruits of the Church and their translation has been fully considered in this treatise. The Lord in His good Providence has taught the Church practically what the symbol sets forth, though it has not yet been realized in the actual translation of the saints; but the accompanying extract from the writings of the Rev. G. S. Faber, a pious and learned student of prophecy, is instructive, showing as it does his anticipations of the meaning of the symbol, and the difficulties he discerned in the way of its interpretation before it should be expounded by actual facts. The following was written in 1828, before the first word of prophetic utterance was heard in England.

Extract from Faber's *Sacred Calendar of Prophecy* * (first published in 1828).

" The hieroglyphic of the man child still remains to be interpreted, and it is by far the most difficult symbol in the prophetic picture, for if the woman denote the whole collective body of faithful worshippers within the visible Church of the West, and if the dragon in his borrowed members and the stars which he draws into apostasy denote the whole collective body of unfaithful worshippers within the same visible Church, no additional character within that Church seems left for the man child to typify.
Rev. xii. 4.

" In the symbolic language of the ancient prophets, the birth of a male denotes the setting apart of a community from the great general mass with which it was previously commingled, while the gestation and labour throes, which precede it, refer to the difficulties and the trials and the troubles, of whatsoever description they may be, which precede the setting apart of the community in question.

" Such is the abstract import of the birth of a man child, but in the present vision this allegorical phraseology has

*Vol. III. pp. 117-119.

a special and particular relation to Christ, for the man child is described like Christ Himself (compare Rev. xii. 5 with Chap. ii. 26, 27, and Psa. ii. 8), as one who should rule all nations with a rod of iron.

"Hence, according to a very just observation by W. Mede, the man child of the Apocalypse must denote Christ in some sense. But he cannot denote the literal Christ, because such an application is not consistent with the established language of Scripture, which invariably represents our Lord as the Husband, not as the Son, of His Church.

"This being the case, the birth of a man child denotes generally the setting apart of a community, whether civil or ecclesiastical, from the mass with which it was hitherto mingled; and if the man child of the Apocalypse denotes a faithful Christian ecclesiastical community distinct from the great mass of God's true worshippers, henceforth, safe under the care of an Almighty superintending providence, it might bear witness to the Gospel in its *corporate or collegiate capacity*, while the remaining mass out of which it was taken should do so only *individually and unconnectedly*. It presents therefore a problem of no very easy solution—a problem in fact, which, as far as application is concerned, can only be resolved by history."

We have sought to shew that the figure of the man child must have its application to the Christian Church and to a body separated therein for a certain purpose, for change and translation, and we now testify that this is practically carried out into action in the company of firstfruits gathered under apostles in these last days, who are looking for the second coming of the Lord and for the translation or rapture of the raised and living saints, which may the Lord graciously hasten to His glory and to our salvation.

APPENDIX V.   Page 197.

On the Didaché or Teaching of the Twelve Apostles.

THE *Didaché or Teaching of the Twelve Apostles*, is an ancient MS. which has lately come to light. Its origin as to locality is uncertain, but as to its date there is no reason against assigning it to the last quarter of the first, or more probably to the first quarter of the second century. It may indeed, from its internal evidence, well be one of the oldest Christian writings after the books of the New Testament, if not older than most of them in their present form.

Some years ago Philotheus Bryennius, then Metropolitan of Serre, in Macedonia, afterwards transferred to Nicomedia, discovered in the Library of the Most Holy Sepulchre belonging to the Patriarchate of Jerusalem at Constantinople, a MS. written at Jerusalem A.D. 1056. The volume bears the Library mark No. 456 and is of parchment, small 8vo., about eight inches by seven; and it was completed, according to an inscription at the end, on June 11, A.D. 1056, by a notary named Leo.

The following is an extract from the last chapter (XVI.) of the Didaché referring to the coming of the Lord and the first resurrection.

Extracts from *The Teaching of the Twelve Apostles* (Chap. XVI., pp. 87, 88), edited by H. de Romestin in 1884:—

3. "For in the last days shall the false prophets and destroyers be multiplied, and the sheep shall be turned to wolves, and love shall be turned to hate.

4. "For when lawlessness increaseth, they shall hate and persecute, and deliver up one another; and then shall appear the deceiver of the world as God's son, and shall do signs and wonders, and the earth shall be delivered into his hands, and he shall commit iniquities which have never yet been from the beginning of the world.

5. "And then shall the race of men come into the fire of testing, and many shall be offended and perish, but they who endure in their faith, shall be saved under the curse itself.

6. "And then shall appear the signs of the truth, first the sign of opening in heaven, then the sign of the voice of the trumpet, and the third, the resurrection of the dead.

7. "Not, however, of all, but as was said, 'The Lord shall come, and all the saints with him.'

8. "Then shall the world see the Lord coming upon the clouds of heaven."

The following is the critical note on the last part of Chap. XVI. by the editor, who refers the Didaché to a later date in the second century than that above suggested.

"These last lines speaking of the resurrection 'but not of all,' coupled with the quotation from Zechariah, *may* denote a tendency to Montanism, as Millennarianism was strongly held by that party. But Christ Himself says, that the angels will be sent to 'gather together the elect'" Matt. xxiv. 31. Cf. 1 Cor. xv. 23; Rev. xx. 4, 5.

The Didaché, however, contains no very conclusive teaching as to the first resurrection and the change and translation, perhaps because at the time it was written these scriptural truths were the accepted doctrine of the whole Church.

APPENDIX VI. Page 199.

The Mosaic over Bishop Alexander's grave at Tipasa, near Algiers—Date about A.D. 390.

IN the year 1899 the author was travelling in Algeria and visited the old Roman city of Tipasa, where he found an ancient Christian mosaic of great interest. The following is a memorandum from his diary with reference to this subject.

"About the third, fourth, and fifth centuries, the Christian Church flourished in North Africa, and in the time of Augustine a synod of 300 or 400 bishops could be convened.

"These churches have long been swept away, and before A. D. 1830, North Africa was Mohammedan from the Nile to the Straits of Gibraltar.

"A few weeks ago, I stood amid the ruins of an old Roman city overlooking the sea. On the eastern side there was an ancient Roman cemetery, and there were hundreds of empty coffins, or sarcophagi, indenting the ground for nearly a rood; whilst at the other or western end of this city was the Christian cemetery, also full of empty stone tombs lying thickly together, and here there is an ancient ruined Christian church, called the Basilica of Bishop Alexander, in which there is a mosaic of black and white stones, dating from the end of the fourth century, about A.D. 390, and now, alas! in danger of perishing.

"In this mosaic are these words, which are still legible, expressing the hope of that bishop:—

"'*Corpus in pace quiescit resurrectionem expectans futuram de mortuis primam*'; which may be rendered:—'His body rests in peace, awaiting in the future the *first* resurrection from the dead.'

"This is a blessed testimony to the hope of the first resurrection before the year 400 A.D., and a confirmation of the faith and hope once delivered to the saints, and universally held up to that time.

"Although the hope of the first resurrection is comparatively

rarely preached even in England, and is unknown to millions
of professing Christians, it is no new doctrine.

" God be praised for this testimony in that neglected corner
of the earth. Efforts have been made that this uncared-for,
yet precious relic of Christian antiquity may not perish."

The following letter was received from the Governor General
of Algiers; but, though the subject has been brought before
the Government at Paris through one of the French deputies,
the author fears that no steps have been taken for the preservation of this precious relic, and that it will eventually
perish :—

"Alger, le 12 Juin, 1899.

REPUBLIQUE FRANCAISE.

Monsieur,

Vous avez bien voulu m'adresser une lettre relative
à la basilique de St. Salsa, à celle de l'Evêque Alexandre, à
Tipaza, ainsi qu'aux mosaiques chrétiennes que vous y avez
vues et aux mesures qu'il conviendrait, selon vous, de prendre
en vue de la conservation de ces monuments historiques.

J'ai l'honneur de vous accuser réception et de vous remercier
de votre interessante communication.

Veuillez agréer, Monsieur, l'assurance de ma considération
très distinguée.

Le Gouverneur Général,
Le Secrétaire Général du Gouvernement,
M. LAUNAY."

APPENDIX VII.   Page 209.

Extracts from Sermons by Martin Luther.

ALTHOUGH Luther is revered as a zealous protester against errors and abuses in the Roman Catholic Church, which he endeavoured to reform, and, hence, is regarded as the greatest of the Reformers, yet, in following him, his adherents and admirers stop short at the first principles of the doctrine of Christ, at the work of Jesus Christ on earth and at the Father's right hand for us, which, after deep study of the Scriptures, he brought very fully to light out of the darkness of prevailing superstition. But, grand as these truths are in their complex simplicity, Luther sought further to learn the mind and purpose of God towards His redeemed, both individually and collectively as the Church of Christ, and he longed for the time when the Lord would come again for His own. He believed that so many of the predicted signs previous to the second coming of the Lord were then being fulfilled, that in preaching "On the Coming of Christ" (from Luke xxi. 25-33), on the second Sunday in Advent, A.D. 1532, he addressed his hearers thus:

. . . . "Therefore we should deem it a joyful sight when we see such signs beginning to take place, for therewith God comforts us and shows us that He will at last deliver us from all distress and misery; also that we should not only await this blessed day with joy, but that with longing and sighing, we should cry to our Lord Christ for it, saying. 'Thou hast promised the day when Thou wilt 'deliver us from all evil, so let it come, even this very hour, 'and make an end of all misery' . . . . Accustom yourselves therefore to regard the signs aright as I set them before you. For you have no cause to be troubled or to mourn, but on the contrary you have every reason to rejoice as those to whom they—the signs—show nothing less than that your deliverance is at the door. Therefore, with courage and

z

hope, pray, 'THY KINGDOM COME. . . . .' Whosoever is not so prepared and ready as to *desire* that day, does not yet apprehend the Lord's Prayer, much less can he, from his heart, pray it. Wherefore, if thou dost not desire this day, thou wilt never be able to pray the Lord's Prayer, nor rightly to repeat the Creed. For how canst thou say, *I believe in the resurrection of the body, and in the life ever- lasting*, when thou dost not desire it? But if thou believest, thou shouldst heartily wish for that day and love it, other- wise thou art not yet a Christian, and canst not boast of thy faith. . . . .

"From the beginning of the world, the dear dead saints whose blood is still unavenged, cry with great desire and longing for *this* day, that they may return to life and honour, and be avenged on the world. . . . . Hence, both the living and the departed saints desire that we help them by crying to God for deliverance. . . . .

Rev. vi. 11.

Tit. ii. 13. "St. Paul describes it as 'that blessed hope, and the glorious 'appearing of the great God and our Saviour Jesus Christ.' Therefore should we be of good courage. And when He shall suddenly come and rend all things in pieces, yet be not afraid that He will strike thee, causing thee to sink or to be destroyed; but *thou shalt either be caught up to heaven from the grave and dust, or else be changed in a moment to everlasting glory*, where there will be no sin, no terror, danger or sorrow, but only righteousness, joy and life. *For this we wait, and this we preach to the few who will accept it.* And for this we endure, that we may live unto and see the glory of this day; even as we hope and desire with our whole heart (since so many signs are being fulfilled) that He may be at the door and will not long delay. . . . . Behold, this is the comfort, the like of which no man on earth can give or conceive, except by the Holy Spirit through the word of Christ. . . . ."

From two sermons preached by Luther on 1 Thess. iv. 13-18, the following extracts are taken :—

" 'For this we say unto you by the word of the Lord, 'that we which are alive and remain unto the coming of 'the Lord, shall not prevent them which are asleep.' "

"St. Paul has already said that 'them also which sleep 'in Jesus, will God bring with Him' Here it might be

asked—since he says this only of those who sleep in Christ,
that is, who died in the faith of Christ—where then will
those be left who are alive at the coming of Christ? What?
Will these have the advantage of first seeing and being
taken to Christ, before those who died? To this he (the
Apostle) replies—I will tell you a secret, that you have
heard from no one before, and will find nowhere so clearly
written, but it has been revealed to me from Heaven;
therefore I tell it to you as *the word of the Lord*, which is
certain and true; the which you should accept and believe
as if you yourselves heard it from the Lord's mouth, viz.:
'that we which are alive and remain unto the coming of
the Lord, shall not prevent them which are asleep." That
is, we who live to see the coming of Christ, shall neither
see Christ, nor come to Him before those who sleep; but
this is how it will happen. In that moment when Christ
shall come, and the last trump shall sound, the dead in
Christ shall arise immortal and incorruptible, and with a
transformed body. Meanwhile, we who are alive at that
time shall be changed, *i.e.*, we shall neither die, nor be
buried, like all men from the beginning, who, through old
age or other causes, have died and been buried, or been
burnt to powder, or torn by beasts, etc., but we shall be
simply changed, so that our body will be transformed—
formed differently to what it is now, viz: it will no longer
be a mortal, corruptible body, but it will be spiritual, immortal,
and glorified, much brighter and more beautiful than the
sun. Therefore shall we—both those who have died and
been buried, or in whatever manner they have been destroyed,
and we who are found alive at that time—be suddenly and
in a moment, changed from the corruptible state of being,
into that which is incorruptible, and together we shall be
caught up into the clouds to meet the Lord in the air.
He (St. Paul) speaks of this in 1 Cor. xv. 51-53," (which
Luther quotes in full).

"THIS IS THE MYSTERY OF WHICH THE WORLD KNOWS
NOTHING, NOR DOES ANYONE, EXCEPT WE HAVE THE
HOLY SPIRIT. IT IS A GREAT THING TO BELIEVE THAT
THIS IS INDEED TRUTH.

"But whoso taketh counsel with the natural reason will
never believe; nevertheless, God will manifest His Godlike

power and majesty; like as when He created the heavens and the earth from nothing, when He spake the word and it was done; so also will it take place in this instance. . . ."

"Many have troubled themselves as to what the shout, the voice of the archangel, and the trump of God will be. He speaks of the matter in the ordinary way and in such words as men are in the habit of using, when speaking of a great and splendid progress of a mighty king or emperor. How they will sound I know not, but I imagine it will be as the Fathers have interpreted it, that they will sound forth, 'Arise, ye dead!' I do not trouble myself as to how it should be that such a voice should sound and be heard throughout the whole world, but I take heed to St. Paul's words: 'The Lord Himself shall descend with a shout, and with the trump of God. . . . '"

(1 Thess. iv. 17 is here quoted in full.)

"What then shall take place when the voice of the archangel, and the sounds of the trump go forth, and Christ shall come at the same time? In an instant, the dead in Christ shall arise; but we who are alive and remain shall, in the same moment, be changed, and with them be caught up into the clouds, to meet the Lord in the air: and so shall we ever be with the Lord.

"These are short and plain words; but who can express what lies behind them: let everyone think earnestly over them, and find comfort in them in all kinds of temptation, especially in the perils of death."*

---

* These quotations have been translated from the extracts of Luther's sermons given in *Stimmen aus der Kirche*, by K. von Mickwitz, 1902.

APPENDIX VIII.   Page 216.

The Prophetic Anticipations of Jane Lead, A.D. 1697.

THE following is a notice of Mrs. Jane Lead which Herr von Mickwitz gives in his book on the testimonies to the hope of the Lord's return during the Christian dispensation, and which is translated from his work "Ein Zeitbild in wichtigen Zeugnissen," 1902.

"In the British Museum we find the old books of *Jane Lead*, née Ward. They contain testimonies to the more esoteric truths of the gospel of extraordinary precision and clearness. Jane Lead was born A.D., 1623, in Norfolk, and was married at the age of twenty-one. Becoming a widow in 1670, she desired to follow in the path of Anna, and to serve in the temple of God, day and night. She, with Prodage and his wife, with Bromley and others, formed a "Philadelphian Society." She would give rise to no sect, no schism . . . but rather bear all things in patience, with her heart set upon the *Magnalia Dei*, the great wonders of God in creation, in the new creation, regeneration or completion (perfection) upon the revelation of the Messianic kingdom, upon the glorious and blessed issues (events) of the future world. She maintained an active correspondence with Spener, Francke and Petersen. She died in 1704 in the fear of God, in firm faith of His help to the Church, for which she longed so intensely. She knew that she would not live to see that period about which she had received so much light, but she felt assured it was reserved for a glorious time, in which a new generation would spring up, who would receive the heavenly blessings in preparation for the coming of the Lord.

"There is a rustle (whisper) in her writings like a breath of true prophecy. We stand amazed when we note how this woman, filled with a burning love for the appearing of her Lord and the completion of the Church, saw two hundred years ago, the particulars—identically—of what God has done in our days, viz.: that the Lord would bring a work to pass in England for the help of the whole Church; in London He would find His instruments; the gifts of the Holy Ghost would be revived; the Lord would send His apostles to cleanse the Church and to rebuild her ruins; the true worship, the old ministries and ordinances of the Body of Christ would again be established; the 144,000 would be sealed. Then would the Lord present the firstfruits to the Father. From the Mount Zion the twenty-four and seventy mighty ones would gather the harvest, and so prepare the Church to enter upon the kingdom with the Lord."

In one of Jane Lead's pamphlets, entitled: *Ascent to the Mount of Vision* (part II., p. 39), printed in A.D., 1699, she writes thus:

"(LI) Then it was further shewed to me concerning this Nation, that as light and knowledge was breaking forth as a mighty Stream upon it, so it should still go on further to increase and multiply, and many should now run to and fro here, for the opening of the Fountains and Deeps of such Blessings, as therewithal the whole earth should be covered: and this Land become as a Springing Paradise. And no devouring Beast, or Hurtful thing shall abide in it: but the Holy People shall be for Bulwarks, and a flaming Wall of defence to it. Which blessed Day is near at hand: for which upon our Watch Tower we are all charged to stand and to be found in readiness to entertain this Joyful Message with all the Precious and weighty things that therein are prophesied of. But here caution is given, that all do stand in a ready posture, yielding to Wisdom's Divine Discipline, who will instruct her children to be obedient to the Law of Love, whereby they will be able to stop that Flying Roll of the Curse which is going forth: and to open the Heavens, out of which may descend Flying Angels, who will proclaim to this Island and to all Nations, and Tribes of the Earth, the everlasting Gospel of Love, Goodwill, and Peace; whereby all Internal and External Wars may cease Which will open a torrent of boundless Blessings upon the World. . . ."

From another pamphlet of Jane Lead's the following quotation is drawn:

" O England, England, know the Day of thy Visitation, for a wonderful morning light is springing. Therefore open the

windows of thy Mind and let it in, for then it will usher in
the LORD of Glory: who hath said, Behold, I come to reign
in Love's kingdom."

Again, in another book entitled *The Wars oj David* (A.D.,
1697, reprinted 1816), she writes concerning this country :
"Hear and hearken: O England's Inhabitants, for unto you
a Great Light is shined! O let it not cloud and pass over
you, but be ye wise in this your day to follow the Spirit's
bright guiding star which is arising amongst you. O London,
there is hid in thee them that have a true and right mission
from the Munition Rock, to give out the waters of the Spirit
plenteously. For a cry is gone forth for persons to be prepared
and sanctified by this Water of life, that so they may receive
the Holy Ghost and be witnesses of His power—Hear and
hearken in the Spirit; O hearken, you will hear the 7th
Trumpet sound from the seven spirits that are before the
Throne; that do tell that the mystery of Time is now finishing,
and that the everlasting Gospel of Love is opening, and that
the Heavens are ready to roll down to open their glory upon
the earth, that the inhabitants thereof may no longer be
buried in the dark shade of an earthly life.

"Over thee, O city of London! a mighty angel doth fly,
with this thundering cry, saying—do not despise prophesy,
neither decry down the Ark of the living Testimony, from
which the Spirit as a flowing stream would renew Paradise
upon the Earth. This warning is given to all of what rank
or degree soever; whether high or low, whether in the outward
grandeur or in the private and inferior means of this world.
Even to you all, and every one this call doth reach."

In this book—"The Wars of David"—will be found "Sixty
Propositions" extracted from a book entitled "A Message
to the Philadelphian Society whithersoever dispersed over
the whole earth, by Jane Lead, 1697." They were thus rendered
by a member of the Society, and as they contain some remarkable prophetic prognostications relative to a revival in the
Church, and in preparation for the Lord's second advent at
the close of this dispensation, a few of these Propositions
are here given :

* *A Third Message to the Philadelphian Society*, p. 37, by
Jane Lead.—British Museum.

"Proposition 11. There shall be an authoritative decision given forth immediately from Christ, to the putting an end to all controversies concerning the *true* Church.

"Proposition 12. The decision will be by the actual sealing of the members of this Church with the name of God . . . This new name will distinguish them from the seven thousand names of Babylon.

"Proposition 13. The election and preparation of this Church is to be after a hidden and secret manner. . . .

"Proposition 16. The birth of this Virgin Church was visionally typified to St. John, by the great wonder in heaven bringing forth her firstborn, *that was caught up to the throne of God.*

"Proposition 17. For, as a virgin woman brought forth Christ after the flesh, so, likewise, a virgin woman is designed by God to bring forth the Firstborn after the Spirit, who shall be filled with the Holy Ghost and with power.

"Proposition 24. Until there be such a church made ready upon the earth, so holy, so catholic, and so anointed, and *that is without all spot or wrinkle*, and that is adorned as a bride to meet her bridegroom, Christ will not personally descend and solemnize this marriage, and present the same to His Father.

"Proposition 26. There is not this day visible upon the earth any holy, catholic, anointed, and bridal church; all the churches and professions being found light when weighed in the balance, therefore they are rejected by the Supreme Judge.

"Proposition 27. Which rejection and condemnation will be for this end, that out of them a new and glorious church may rise up, in whom there shall be no fault found, like as He findeth none with the Philadelphian Church (Rev. iii.)

"Proposition 29. Though this Philadelphian Church is not known in visibility, yet it may lie hid at this present time, as in the womb of the morning.

"Proposition 30. Notwithstanding it will be brought forth, as coming out of the wilderness, into visibility within a short period.

"Proposition 31. Then it will go on and multiply . . . not only to the number of the firstborn, (which is one hundred and forty-four thousand), but also to the remnant of the seed: against which the Dragon shall make continual war.

"Proposition 36. Christ, before His own distinct and personal appearance, will first appear and represent Himself in some chosen vessel, or vessels anointed to be leaders unto the rest, and to bring them into the promised land—the new creation state.

"Proposition 37. Thus Moses, Joshua, and Aaron may be considered as types of some upon whom the same Spirit may come, yet to rest in a greater proportion ; whereby they shall make way for the ransomed of the Lord to return to Mount Zion.

"Proposition 45. Wherefore it is required on our part to suffer the spirit of burning to do upon us the refining work . . . searching every part within us till all be pure and clean, and we thereby arrive to this Fixed Body from whence the Wonders are to flow out.

"Proposition 46. This body will bear the sealing character of the Philadelphian Church.

"Proposition 47. Upon this Body will be the fixation of the URIM and THUMMIM . . .

"Proposition 53. There must be a manifestation of the Spirit wherewith to edify and raise up this Church suitable to the resurrection of Christ.

"Proposition 54. This manifestation must be in the absoluteness of power, as well as in the beauty of holiness; so—bringing down Heaven upon earth, and representing here—the New Jerusalem State.

"Proposition 57. Now He that is ascended and glorified has made himself as it were our debtor; consequently He will not be wanting in qualifying and furnishing certain high and principal instruments, who shall be most humble and as little regarded as David was, whom He will dignify with great honour and Priestly sovereignty, for the drawing to them the scattered flocks and gathering them into one fold out of all nations and languages and kindreds."

APPENDIX IX.

A Short Notice about Count von Zinzendorf.

"NICOLAUS LUDWIG, Count von Zinzendorf and Pottendorf, was born at Dresden, on the 26th May, 1700. He studied law and theology at Wittenberg, and after a short residence abroad gave himself up to evangelical labours.

"The account of the conversion of Count Zinzendorf is remarkable. He was a gay young nobleman, bright, intelligent, and rich. Passing through Düsseldorf, while his horses were baiting, he went into its famous gallery and saw Stenburgh's picture of the Crucifixion, with the words written beneath :—

'All this I did for thee ;
What hast thou done for me ?'

"The Count was fascinated. He read and re-read the legend on the frame ; he could not tear himself away. The love of Christ laid its powerful grasp upon his spirit. Hours passed, the light faded, the curator touched the weeping nobleman, and told him it was time to close the gallery. He re-entered his carriage and returned home, throwing his life, fortune, fame, at the feet of Him who had spoken to his heart in the above lines.

"He became the father of the Moravian missions, and his devoted life became the answer to the above question.

"Stenburgh's picture no longer hangs in the gallery at Düsseldorf, for it perished when the gallery was destroyed by fire some years ago, but though destroyed it yet speaketh.

"He founded on his estate at Berthelsdorf, a religious community, chiefly consisting of men who had been driven out of Bohemia and Moravia on account of their religious opinions in 1723. This community was called "Herrnhut" (protected of God), and it soon attracted great attention in Germany, from the zeal of its members, the high position of Zinzendorf, and the constant intermeddling of Church and State with its affairs. Zinzendorf qualified himself for the Pastoral Office in 1737, at Berlin, and was consecrated as Bishop with the sanction of the Government. . . . . He died May 9th, 1760, at Herrnhut.

"Zinzendorf held the usual orthodox Protestant views with but little modification, but he held them with the fullest concession of the right of free opinion to others.

"He was an earnest, sincere, and noble man. His writings, among which are several collections of hymns, were entirely of a religious character." *

That Count von Zinzendorf did not consider that all things would continue as they were, but that with the advance of the Christian dispensation there would be special signs denoting the appearing of the kingdom of Christ, and of a further unfolding of the purpose and work of God, is evident from the following extract from his *Discourses on the Four Evangelists* (Vol. IV., p. 47), where he writes as follows:—
"This dispensation, I say, must also come to its appointed end. When shall our time come to its end? When our understanding and our courage no longer suffice; when things shall come to pass in the kingdom of Christ, to which we have to submit, things which are beyond our power to help; when *the signs of the kingdom of Christ* appear in an unknown manner to us, which we feel, and yet cannot grasp, *then will another work of God appear.* . . . . If then we be wise, we shall join it forthwith, and yield ourselves to that new thing which the Saviour shall bring to pass; but not in a thoughtless manner, for we must be able to discern it as a remedy, and as a means of help in time of need.† Thus let us lay hold of it in single-mindedness. . . . . I see no appearance of this taking place shortly, for we are not yet disenthralled, ‡ and consequently we might turn away again from it. My brothers and sisters, I pray you to stir up the gift that is in you. An economy of God must not only have ministers and

---

* From the *Oracle Encyclopædia*, p. 218.

† The German word "Nothnagel" here used is difficult to translate. It means a nail or staple to which we may cling in the time of need, and thus escape destruction.

‡ The German word "durchgebrochen" means breaking through and breaking loose from bonds in which we have been held.

labourers to work, but also prophets and seers to whom it seemeth good (Acts xv. 28). . .   . who act in the Spirit, and do a blessed work We, and all the children of God, must be on the watch for the signs of the kingdom of Christ, and for the manifestation of power revealing the glory of the Gospel."

Count von Zinzendorf, in one of his works, has written as follows about the last days before the coming of the Lord : —" The time will come when God will send messengers, who can lay their hands upon the children of God, and the Holy Ghost will be communicated to them as in the beginning. The Lord also will give prophets, and the gift of prophesying, as it is foretold in Joel. And, along with it, the gift of healing in the blessed name of the Lord Jesus. Such a work of the Spirit of God will come."

APPENDIX X.

On the Biblical use of the word "Apostle."

IN regard to the full meaning of the word ἀπόστολος, it would seem in classical Greek to have denoted an ambassador; one not only sent forth and carrying a message (ἀγγελός), but one who is the personal representative of him who sent him (cf. Herodotus I. 21 and V. 38). In Hastings' *Dictionary of the Bible*, it is remarked (Art. "Apostle"), that "for Apostles a direct call was needed, because no human authority could choose an Apostle. He was an ambassador on behalf of Christ, the whole world was his mission-field. The Apostle belonged to the Church in general, and had no local ties. There is no sign that he took any share in the ordinary administration of the churches. St. Paul interferes with it only where the churches have gone seriously wrong. In general, the Apostle is not a regular ruler in the same sense as a modern bishop" (cf. Lightfoot on Galatians *in loco*). In Acts xx. 24, Gal. i. 1. etc., St. Paul insists strongly on the direct nature of his call to be an apostle; so that clearly he does not consider the events of Acts xiii. 1, 2, but those following upon his conversion as having to do with his call and appointment to the apostolate.

The word ἀπόστολος occurs eighty one times in the Greek text of the New Testament, and in seventy eight instances it has reference to the apostolic ministry proper, as exercised by apostles to the circumcision and to the uncircumcision. The three exceptions are in Heb. iii. 1, where the reference is to the Lord Himself, and in 2 Cor. viii. 23, and Phil. ii. 25, where the word is translated "messenger," it being used in a modified sense. But in five instances, out of the seventy-eight of the normal use of the word, it may be remarked that two refer to the claim of false apostles, ψευδαπόστολοι (2 Cor. xi. 13, Rev. ii. 2), while the remaining three instances call for further remark.

(1) St. John xiii. 16, ". . . . neither is he that is sent

"greater than he that sent him." In the Greek of this
passage we find the word ἀπόστολος; and that the allusion
is to the eleven apostles present with the Lord seems clear
from the context, for the Lord had *named* them apostles.

(2) Romans xvi. 7, ". . . . Salute Andronicus and Junia
". . . . who are of note among the apostles" (ἐν τοῖς
ἀποστόλοις). Here the text of the Revised Version gives
Junias, a man's name, with *Junia* in the margin—implying,
as some would contend, that the two persons named were
themselves apostles. But this seems, to say the least, to
be a very strained rendering of the passage, when it is considered that these persons are nowhere else mentioned in
the New Testament, much less as having been notable in
the highest ministry of the Christian Church (cf. 1 Cor. xii.
28). It seems therefore much more natural and probable
that they were a man and his wife, relatives of St. Paul,
whose Christian love and zeal had brought them under the
notice of the Apostles, and that the text of the Authorised
Version rightly renders the second name *Junia*, the expression ἐν τοῖς ἀποστόλοις not necessarily implying that the
persons named were themselves apostles. This is Bishop
Ellicott's view in his commentary on the Epistle to the
Galatians, where he quotes the Latin translation of Fritzch
—*quippe qui in Apostolorum Collegio bene audiant*—as the
probably correct rendering of the sense of the Greek text.

(3) Gal. i. 19, "Other of the apostles saw I none save
James the Lord's brother." This passage has given rise to
controversy, partly as to the meaning of the expression εἰ μή
and partly as to which James is referred to. As to the first
point, the use of εἰ μή elsewhere, as in verse seven of the
same chapter, shews that it may be translated "but only"
(see R.V., margin), in which case the second point need not
be considered, viz.: as to whether this James was one of
the apostles. It is, however, supposed by some that he was
the surviving James of the apostles to the circumcision,
viz.: James the less, so-called, the son of Alphæus (Cleopas),
whilst others say that he was that other James who presided
over the Church in Jerusalem (see Alford *in loco*). Bishop
Ellicott, however favours the former view, thinking that, as
James the son of Alphæus (Cleopas) was our Lord's cousin,
the word ἀδελφὸν (brother) in the text may be equivalent to

ἀνεψιόν (first cousin). This would accord with the Hier-onymian hypothesis as to the Lord's brethren ; but, whether this view be adopted or the passage be read—"Other of the apostles saw I *none*, but only [I saw] James the Lord's brother," the argument as to the normal New Testament use of the word ἀπόστολος would remain unimpaired.

It must, however, be admitted that St. Paul, who so care-fully defines the characteristics of the *ministry of apostleship*, uses the *word* ἀπόστολος with less definitive intention in a few passages—e.g. 1 Thess. ii. 6, cf. i. 1; but this is unimportant, looking at the general context.

APPENDIX XI.

The Sect of the Luciferians and their Work.

THE motto of the Satanists is, "Voluptas Peccati"—enjoyment of sin. They have "pleasure in unrighteousness" (2 Thess. ii. 12).

The French religious organ LA SEMAINE wrote in 1896 of the gigantic plot which has been made by the sect of the *Luciferians* against the religion of Christ, and in favour of the substitution of that of Lucifer, as the future belief to be followed by mankind. After describing the worship of Lucifer as nothing new, and as professing to embody a doctrine more befitting the developed mental and physical strength which distinguishes the present race of men—as they think—than Christianity, which must be removed to give it place, *La Semaine* says: "The doctrine has been accepted, and holds a place in the category of religious beliefs." It also says that the heads of the Roman Catholic Church have given warning "of the efforts about to be made to dethrone Christianity at the end of the present nineteenth century, and of the advent of THE REIGN OF LUCIFER, according to the Apocalypse."

The names of persons, places, and facts connected with the organization of this system are given.

A town in America, designated "the Jerusalem of the Messiah Lucifer," is the headquarters of the new religion, which is styled *Palladism*, its aim being not merely the conquest of all political power, but the possession of the entire world : and this end, in the estimation of its followers, can only be obtained by the ABOLITION OF CHRISTIANITY.

The ramifications of this system are stated to be widespread, and its executive committee to have its seat at Rome, the direction of the whole administration being at Berlin.

La Semaine further says: "The work of the Luciferians is all marked out; they are to rally round the anarchists, the nihilists, and all sects devoted to destruction; for all is to be destroyed, and another order of things set up."

What a lurid light the above throws upon the fearful trials and persecutions that the followers of Jesus Christ will have to endure during the Great Tribulation!

Like the long shadows cast by the setting sun ere the day closes, so also does this aim of the Luciferians to obtain possession of the whole world, and to abolish Christianity, shadow forth the time of darkness foretold in the Book of the Revelation, when the dragon and the beast will be   Rev. xiii. 4, 7. worshipped; when, after the beast has received power from the dragon, it will be "given to him to make war with the " saints, and to overcome them: and power was given him " over all kindreds, and tongues, and nations."

Well may we give heed to the Lord's command: "Watch   Luke xxi. 36. " ye therefore, and pray always, that ye may be accounted " worthy to escape all these things that shall come to pass, " and to stand before the Son of man."

2 A

APPENDIX XII.

Ancient Collects, and Prayers from "The Liturgy and other Divine Offices of the Church."

"We beseech Thee, Almighty God, let our souls enjoy this their desire, to be enkindled by Thy Spirit; that being filled, as lamps, by the Divine gift, we may shine like blazing lights before the presence of Thy Son Christ at His coming; through the same Jesus Christ our Lord."—*Gelasian Liturgy.*

"We beseech Thee, O Lord our God, let us all rejoice with upright hearts, being gathered together in the unity of the faith; that at the coming of Thy Son our Saviour, we may go forth undefiled to meet Him in the company of His saints; through the same Jesus Christ our Lord."—*Gelasian Liturgy.*

"O Christ, our God, who wilt come to judge the world in the manhood which Thou hast assumed, we pray Thee to sanctify us wholly, that in the day of Thy coming, our whole spirit, soul, and body may so revive to a fresh life in Thee, that we may live and reign with Thee for ever."—*Mozarabic Liturgy.*

"Hear us, O merciful God, and grant our minds to be lifted up, whither our Redeemer hath ascended; that at the second coming of the Mediator, we may receive from Thy manifested bounty what we now venture to hope for as a promised gift; through the same Jesus Christ our Lord."—*Leonine Liturgy.*

"O Lord Jesu Christ, who at Thy first coming didst send Thy messenger to prepare Thy way before Thee; Grant that the ministers and stewards of Thy mysteries may likewise so prepare and make ready Thy way, by turning the hearts of the disobedient to the wisdom of the just, that at Thy second coming to judge the world we may be found an acceptable people in Thy sight, who livest and reignest with the Father and the Holy Spirit ever one God, world without end."—*Book of Common Prayer—Collect for third Sunday in Advent.*

" O Almighty God, who hast builded Thy Church upon the foundation of the apostles and prophets, Jesus Christ Himself being the chief corner-stone; Grant that, being illuminated through the words of Thy prophets, and joined together in unity of spirit through the doctrine, precepts, and ministry of Thine apostles, we may grow unto a holy temple in the Lord, and may be builded together for Thy habitation through the Spirit; for the merits of Jesus Christ our Lord and Saviour; to whom, with Thee and the Holy Ghost, One God, be glory for ever and ever.—Amen."

" O Almighty God, who abhorrest the deeds of unrighteousness, and the words from lying lips; Grant unto thy people, we humbly beseech Thee, such purity of heart, that of Thy mercy they may ever be defended from false apostles and deceitful workers, and may also be enabled joyfully to obey Thee in those whom Thou choosest and sendest forth unto the blessing of Thy Church: through Jesus Christ our Lord—Amen."

"O Lord Jesu Christ, who art the Resurrection and the Life, we acknowledge Thy goodness in restoring the ministry of Thine apostles, in gathering and sealing Thy firstfruits, and in warning us through Thy prophets of the nearness of the day of Thine appearing. Hasten that day, that we may see Thee as Thou art, and be changed into Thy likeness. Bring back Thine apostles, and all those our brethren, who have rejoiced with us in Thy returning grace unto Thy Church, and have fallen asleep, and all who sleep in Thee. Restore to them their bodies raised in glory and immortality; and vouchsafe to us who are alive and remain to be sanctified wholly; and may our whole spirit and soul and body be preserved blameless unto Thy coming. We pray that the time may speedily come when we, and all Thy saints in all generations who have been elected to this glory, may stand with the Lamb upon Mount Zion, a holy firstfruits redeemed from among men, without fault before the throne of God: and unto Thee, with the Father and the Holy Ghost be all honour and glory, now and for ever.—Amen."

" O Almighty God, who has sent down the Holy Ghost upon Thine elect, endowing them with His manifold gifts, and knitting them together in one communion and fellowship in

the mystical Body of Thy Son; Grant unto us grace to use
all those Thy gifts alway to Thine honour and glory, and
to abound in faith, hope and charity, waiting for Thy Son
from heaven: that, when He shall appear, we with all Thy
saints may be found of Him in peace, and by Him may be
presented before Thy glorious presence with exceeding joy;
through the same Jesus Christ our Lord, who liveth and
reigneth with Thee, O Father, in the unity of the same Holy
Ghost, One God, world without end.—Amen."

"Hasten, O God, the time when Thou shalt send from Thy
right hand Him whom Thou wilt send; at whose appearing
the saints departed shall be raised, and we, which are alive,
shall be caught up to meet Him, and so shall ever be with
Him. Under the veil of earthly things we have now communion with Him; but with unveiled face we shall then
behold Him, rejoicing in His glory, made like unto Him in
His glory; and by Him we, with all Thy Church, holy and
unspotted, shall be presented with exceeding joy before the
presence of Thy glory. Hear us, O heavenly Father, for
His sake, to whom, with Thee, and the Holy Ghost, One
living and true God, be glory for ever and ever.—Amen."

"We come unto Thee, O Lord our God, to plead before
Thee for the fulfilment of Thy gracious promises. We do
not presume to come trusting in our own righteousness, but
in Thy manifold and great goodness; we ask, not for our
sakes, but for Thy holy Name's sake, for the accomplishment
of the things Thou hast spoken of old. We pray Thee now
to accomplish Thine ancient promise, that the seed of the
woman shall bruise the serpent's head. We pray Thee to
give David Thine anointed to rule in Thy holy city for
ever. We pray Thee to send Jesus Christ, whom the heavens
have received and do hold until the times of the restitution
of all things. We pray Thee, that we, Thy Church and
people upon earth, may not see death, but be caught up
to meet the Lord in the air, and so be ever with Him;
that we may not be unclothed, but clothed upon with
light and immortality, receiving spiritual bodies. We pray
that Jesus Christ, who is the only King of kings, and
Lord of lords, may now take unto Himself His kingdom,
and set up His throne upon the earth.—Amen."

"O Most merciful Father, who hast so wonderfully constituted Thy Church, that the whole body doth participate in the honour and strength, or in the suffering and weakness, of every member; Grant, we beseech Thee, that through the partaking of these holy mysteries, Thy whole Church may receive increase of life, renewed health, and abundant energy of Thy Holy Spirit, to the glory of Thy holy Name, through Jesus Christ our Lord; Who liveth and reigneth with Thee, O Father, in the unity of the Holy Ghost, One God, world without end.—Amen."

"We pray Thee to look down in mercy upon Thy desolate heritage, upon Thy scattered and divided people; heal the schisms of the churches, put away all heresies from among them; bring back all who have wandered; cleanse Thy sanctuary from all defilement of superstition, will-worship, and infidelity; and grant unto Thy Church unity and peace.—Amen."

". . . . We bless Thee for the sure hope of the speedy appearing and kingdom of Thy Son, who shall come again in the brightness of Thy Majesty, and gather unto Himself His saints, both living and departed, and reign with them in the glory of the resurrection in the age to come.—Amen."

"O Almighty God, grant that those necessary works wherein we are engaged, whether in the affairs of Thy Church or of this world, may not prevail to hinder us, but that at the appearing and advent of Thy Son we may hasten with joy to meet Him; for the merits of the same Jesus Christ our Lord, Who liveth and reigneth with Thee, O Father, in the unity of the Holy Ghost, One God, world without end.—Amen."

"Lord, hear our prayer; and let our cry come unto Thee."

"O God, make speed to save us: O Lord, make haste to help us."

"Show us Thy MERCY, O Lord; and grant us Thy SALVATION."

Laus Deo.

Printed by
HOBBS AND CO.,
GLASGOW.

Printed in the USA
CPSIA information can be obtained
at www.ICGtesting.com
LVHW020907121024
793646LV00009B/502